T0291319

The Fundamentals of Developing Operational Solutions for the Government

The Fundamentals of Developing Operational Solutions for the Government

Chiang H. Ren, Ph.D.

A PRODUCTIVITY PRESS BOOK

Routledge
Taylor & Francis Group
711 Third Avenue, New York, NY 10017

© 2019 by Taylor & Francis Group, LLC
Productivity Press is an imprint of Taylor & Francis Group, an Informa business

No claim to original U.S. Government works

Printed on acid-free paper

International Standard Book Number-13: 978-1-138-03922-3 (hardback)

Library of Congress Cataloging-in-Publication Data

Names: Ren, Chiang H., author.
Title: The fundamentals of developing operational solutions for the government / Chiang H. Ren.
Description: New York, NY : Routledge, 2018. | Includes bibliographical references and index.
Identifiers: LCCN 2018006795 (print) | LCCN 2018008036 (ebook) | ISBN 9781135176068 (eBook) | ISBN 9781138039223 (hardback : alk. paper)
Subjects: LCSH: Public contracts--United States. | Government contractors--United States.
Classification: LCC HD3861.U6 (ebook) | LCC HD3861.U6 R46 2018 (print) | DDC 352.5/30973--dc23
LC record available at https://lccn.loc.gov/2018006795

Visit the Taylor & Francis Web site at
http://www.taylorandfrancis.com

and the Productivity Press site at
http://www.ProductivityPress.com

To Kelly, Heather, and Gloria

Contents

Acknowledgment

Select graphics in this book include free Creative Commons CC0 public-use images from Pixabay.com.

Author

Dr. Chiang H. Ren is an entrepreneur, C-level executive, and operations research expert who is currently the Chief Solutions Architect for Planned Systems International, Inc. Prior to this appointment, he served as chief technology officer for two other companies. In these positions and as a senior analyst for multiple U.S. government agencies, Dr. Ren has published numerous peer-reviewed journal articles in operations research, disaster preparedness, information technology management, systems engineering, theoretical biology, and particle physics. His book *How Systems Form and How Systems Break: A Beginner's Guide for Studying the World* (Springer, 2017).

Dr. Ren holds a BSE degree, magna cum laude, in mechanical engineering and applied mechanics from the University of Pennsylvania; an SM degree in aeronautics and astronautics from the Massachusetts Institute of Technology; and a PhD degree in systems analysis from the University of Bolton. He has received multiple presentation awards from the Military Operations Research Society, a letter of recognition from the U.S. Secretary of the Air Force, and additional recognitions from senior government leaders. Dr. Ren is a certified Six Sigma Black Belt, a member of the Tau Beta Pi engineering honor society, and an associate fellow of the American Institute of Aeronautics and Astronautics.

Chapter 1

Introduction

In the United States today, there are approximately 22 million people employed in some capacity through federal government funding [1]. This is almost double the number of people who are still left in U.S. manufacturing jobs. Of those working under government funds, 2.7 million people are direct civilian employees of the U.S. government and approximately 1.3 million people are active-duty military service personnel [2]. The rest are federal contractors who provide systems and services through close working relationships with federal agencies, vendors who provide commercial products to federal buyers, researchers at federally funded research and development centers (FFRDCs), analysts at some not-for-profit companies, universities with federal grants, and even individual consultants. Some politicians and social activists have argued that the U.S. federal government has become too big and with too much waste of resources. However, governments of modern democratic nations have a responsibility to manage large, complex societal operations that offer social services, national defense, infrastructure sustainment, law enforcement, monetary control, and other benefits for their citizens.

To fulfill its responsibilities, the government of the United States spends approximately $3.7 trillion each year. Over two-thirds of the money go towards nondiscretionary obligations (mandatory spending) such as Social Security, Medicare, and interest payments on the national debt. However, the United States also spends more than $1 trillion per year on discretionary activities involving the purchase of systems and services [3]. Maintaining national security alone requires more than $500 billion in spending. These facts make the U.S. government one of the largest buyers in the world. Its buying process has evolved over the years to reflect the needs of government agencies and advancing national priorities, and a massive federal workforce has grown to execute this process for each government agency.

Contractors wishing to receive money through the federal systems and services acquisition process must therefore gain a deep understanding of federal statutes and regulations; policies within the departments, agencies, and organizations; and approaches adopted by different acquisition communities. Despite all the layers of constraints on how acquisition must be done, the government still needs solutions. This is because the functioning of the government generates performance issues, new operational needs, and new performance-enhancement opportunities. Complying with the federal acquisition process will reduce the likelihood of one's proposal being disqualified. However, it is having the right solution that will help one to win contracts. The right solution is not just about formulating the best idea and having good technical writing. It includes knowing the federal customer, having the correct team members, selecting low-risk technologies, getting clear and complete business intelligence, designing the most optimal processes, having the right price, and presenting the end-to-end plan for supporting the user community. *This book is designed to help readers find the right solutions and win federal contracts with the right solutions.*

We start the discussion with the topic of knowing the customer, those people working directly for the government with influence over the procurement and management of the systems or services that we wish to provide. When the acquisition is substantial, a government program management office (PMO) is sometimes established to execute the entire procurement and management process. Alternatively, the acquisition can be managed as a project with more process flexibility. Either way, the management philosophy of most government leaders tends to focus on identifying risks and maintaining control. Government staff tasked with acquiring capabilities often wants to be a part of the solutioning process. This is reflected in PMOs and their support contractors developing detailed requirements, formulating initial concepts of operations (CONOPS), analyzing technology alternatives, and even creating in-house prototypes. This underlying government desire for participation amplified by established processes can sometimes be interpreted or misinterpreted as the government not calling for solutions but instead calling for compliance. Thus, there are many books written about how to create winning proposals to the federal government through compliance and presentation style. Techniques upon techniques have been developed on how to read request for proposals (RFPs) and figure out how the government will evaluate them. Armies of government business development (BD) professionals have worked over the decades on building relationships so that they can gain competitive insights. Countless teams of proposal managers, technical writers, and subject matter experts (SMEs) have labored repeatedly on proposal after proposal based on business intelligence, identified win themes, and projected probability of win.

All the endeavors of the BD and RFP winning strategy analysis are very important. However, the need to develop coherent solutions cannot be lost in the endeavor or else the immediate proposal wins will face difficulties in contract execution and long-range prospects of winning more proposals will diminish as the lack of solutions become apparent. Proposals without coherent solutions will, in many cases, become eloquent words that (1) mirror government language in the performance work statements (PWS) or statement of work (SOW), (2) state in detail what occurred in past contract endeavors as qualification for the future work, or (3) describe in detail the current state of technologies and processes as validation of technical know-how. Unfortunately, none of these proposal elements are actual solutions. Government source selection evaluation teams (SSET) may nevertheless score such proposals highly through checklist evaluation processes. When contract performance has declined, we then see the government either being more specific about communicating what they perceive as solutions or being more analytical about the solutions content of future proposals.

Government direct involvement in formulating solutions can be a problem; because internal quests have also garnered a spotty record in the age of information technology (IT). For example, we have seen the U.S. government ambitiously trying and failing to build mass enterprise IT systems, and we have seen the government shifting toward building smaller, more compartmentalized systems as a reaction to major program failures. We have seen mandates to use commercial technologies, and we have seen failures in adapting commercial technologies to government requirements during blind attempts at following mandates. In solutions for providing IT services, we have seen years where some government organizations only want to rely upon contractor expertise. Then, we have seen years where the government tried to build up capabilities within the federal civilian workforce. *So, the best path is still for contractors to have complete solutions from the start and then inspire government confidence through successful implementation of solutions.* The alternatives of no one developing solutions and everyone (government and contractor) developing solutions each has its challenges.

The government's attentiveness to commercial trends has attracted the attention of many contractors. So, we will periodically hear a call for transformation. The term *transformation* can have significant meaning, but this too is not a substitute for having solutions. Solutions can transform and solutions can stably maintain the current state. When a transformation does not have a specific solution, however, people tend to end up repackaging standard operations research and business process improvement techniques into branded general solutions. When these general solutions are applied, old processes are sometimes torn down with an unclear understanding of how to reach objective states. Thus, transformations detached from specific solutions are risky in terms of process stability, continuity of operations, preservation of key information and functionalities, and user adoption. *The philosophy of this text is to focus on the specific solutions and let others determine whether such can be considered transformations.*

In the current environment of federal contracting, there are great financial opportunities, complex processes, and competing forces. Thus, there is a great need for a book dedicated to the fundamentals of developing operational solutions. This book seeks to guide you in winning proposals by innovatively solving the government's problems. In this context, BD is a part of the solutioning process and the idea of tactically gaming the government acquisition process is superseded by the idea of strategically gaining the trust of government leaders. This book adopts two paths in achieving this objective. One path is to create a framework for thinking about government problems and opportunities so that innovations can be promoted and solutions can be formulated. The other path is to establish a deep understanding of government activities through the discipline of operations research. This understanding enables the endeavor of formulating solutions to be placed in precise context for government implementation. There are massive tomes dedicated to the theories and mathematical models of operations research. This book is devoted to making operations research techniques simple enough for professionals to apply in the course of developing proposals and delivering systems and services. Introducing methods and techniques for quickly developing solutions that are implementable within the constraints of government statutes/regulations/policies and government requirements is thus the central focus of this book. The timing for this book is appropriate given highly publicized contract performance failures such as with the healthcare.gov portal. The government turning away from traditional federal contractors to seek help from Silicon Valley experts should have been a wake-up call. Now, the words *innovation* and *solution* are starting to become more prominent in RFP language.

The following chapters on developing solutions assume a basic knowledge of acquisition history and processes within the U.S. government. For those newly acquainted with systems and services acquisition by the United States, this book offers three useful appendices. The reader may wish to first review these appendices before proceeding.

Appendix A presents the history of the U.S. Department of Defense's (DoD) systems and services acquisition activities. Through this history, we see changes in acquisition policies, organizations, and capabilities over the decades, and we see great successes as well as some major failures that remind us of the challenges in being a government contractor. This history takes us to today's DoD acquisition process, and we can, through lessons learned from history, create solutions for future RFPs that are free from the mistakes of the past.

Appendix B presents a summary of the federal government's basic requirements formulation and source selection processes. This summary is comprehensive and written for contractors planning to bid on government RFPs. The objective is to bridge the knowledge divide between contractors and government acquisition career field professionals who have received formal training in Federal Acquisition Regulations (FAR) and agency-specific acquisition policies. The limited and controlled interactions between these two communities, as required by regulations, has only served to emphasize the knowledge divide. Even when federal acquisition professionals have decided to join contractor organizations, their roles are often stovepiped within the BD communities to further hinder knowledge dissemination. When those involved in BD and developing proposals gain an understanding of how the government source selection teams will evaluate proposals, the probability of winning will be dramatically enhanced. At the very least, those responsible for the formulation of solutions must understand how their solutions will be received by government evaluators.

Appendix C presents government expectations on how contractors will manage and report on their work after being awarded contracts. Developing and delivering solutions is still the objective for supporting the government. However, this appendix explains the equally important day-to-day tasks and process of doing business with the U.S. government. It explains how the government wants to see the contractor's program management organization, established development methodologies for solutions involving new systems, and quality control and risk management mechanisms.

Based on the understanding of the government established in the appendices, the chapters of this book then take the reader from understanding how to work within the government processes to how to innovative and develop solutions for the government processes. It may appear strange that we cannot jump straight into developing solutions. The reality is that the complexity of interacting with the government should be mastered in a way that enables us to gradually step into developing solutions. Solutions architects have tried to bend the government to their solutions, to no avail. This is because only those companies that have a monopolistic hold in key product areas, such as Microsoft, have ever succeeded in such endeavors. If you are one of those commercial industry-dominant companies, then do not bother reading this book and go straight to imposing your solutions on the customer. All you then need is a good number of lawyers to handle the government contracts. For the rest of us who do not dominate a commercial technology sector, we need to bend our solutions to the government, and that is how this book must begin.

Regarding who should read this book, we presented the idea of dedicated solutions development teams for proposals and other BD activities with the government. The members of this team need to have subject matter expertise in relevant technical areas, and they must also have the ability to think broadly about the systems and processes within the overall government operational environment. If we call these people solutions architects, they must be more than those solutions architects who specialize in one collection of technologies and products. Instead, they must be able to learn quickly about all new technologies, conduct comparative analysis, and conceptually explore new paths of utilization. This is why we cannot just pull experts from narrowly defined programs and ask them to write pieces of a proposal. Such experts can write about what they know, but may struggle with the totality of the government problem. In a solutioning endeavor, it is perhaps better to have a solutions development team reach back into the company workforce to gather expert knowledge and then let the team integrate the knowledge within the context of the required solution.

For members of the solutions development team, the abilities to decompose problems and integrate technologies, processes, human skills, and system architectures are far more important than subject matter knowledge. Thus, those in the field of systems analysis and operations research will have an advantage in solutioning endeavors. Business leaders who are skilled at strategically solving current customer problems could also be contributors in the solutions development team. As solutions are ineffective if people cannot understand them, communications is an equally valued capability. Team members must be able to write and effectively express ideas. They must be able to develop diagrams using common tools to express concepts, workflows, and architectures. And, they must be able to read and work with financial spreadsheets on labor categories and rates because price is a component of all solutions.

Last, before we proceed to the next chapter, success in solutions development is a matter of attitude. The understanding of customers, technology opportunities, and best practices is a lifelong pursuit for those who want to develop solutions. Arrogance about one's solution is the surest way to fail because all solutions need to be challenged and refined. Through the crucible of rework and more rework, the solutions architect finds the best way forward. Once an actual proposal process starts, the solutions development team is on the field with the clock ticking. Schedules must be met and long hours of work deep into the night may be required. The proposal process is a contact sport and sometimes it is a battlefield. Members of the proposal team cannot work in silos even though they may have individual areas of responsibility. A solutions architect might take ownership of the technical volume, but he or she must communicate the direction of solutions development to others helping with technical writing and those writing sections on staffing, pricing, management approach, and past performance exhibits. The most elegant solution that is not supported by the rest of the proposal will not win.

Returning to the difference between this book and so many others on winning proposals, our objective is to succeed in selling solutions and succeed in implementing solutions so that the operational state of the government is advanced through the government's investment in our company. The next chapter starts this endeavor on creating solutions by asking the question, "What is a real operational solution?"

References

1. Jeffrey, T. P. 2015. Government Employees Outnumber Manufacturing Employees 1.8 to 1. CNS News.com (published September 8).
2. Jennings, J. 2016. Federal Workforce Statistics Sources: OPM and OMB. Congressional Research Service (published December 7).
3. Budget of the United States Government, Fiscal Year 2017. Office of Management and Budget.

Chapter 2

What Is and Is Not an Operational Solution

The first step in understanding how to invest in achieving operational solutions for the federal government is to explore the definition of what an *operational solution* is. Incorrect or inconsistent understanding can lead to mistakes in the proposal development process. We have noted that the government is often involved in the solutions development process. So, a PWS or SOW may contain descriptions of the desired solution or constraints on what the solution cannot be. Only the statement of objectives (SOO) places the burden of solutions development completely on the proposal development team. Despite the details provided in many RFPs, proposals that merely affirm delivery of what the government wants may be compliant but do not present solutions. In fact, RFP instructions will sometimes stipulate that the PWS or SOW should not be merely reiterated as a proposal response. Even the most detailed PWS or SOW must therefore be treated as guidance on how to develop the winning solution.

Assertions to the government that PWS or SOW tasks can be done and that there are examples of past contract performance for similar work also do not constitute solutions. If there are technologies, architectures, processes, or staff capabilities from past work that can be applied to the current PWS or SOW, then the application of those elements to current PWS or SOW tasks must be explained in the form of a new or adapted solution. Referencing past experience in a proposal's technical volume will strengthen a solution by reducing perceptions of risk. However, merely referencing past experience causes the technical proposal to be essentially an extension of the proposal's past performance volume.

Finally, detailed expressions of subject matter knowledge are not solutions. Understanding of current architectures, technologies, and processes demonstrate our capability to development a solution. However, unless we show how this knowledge is applied to alter the current operational state to resolve problems or capture opportunities, a solution has not been presented. Even when new processes and techniques are introduced through our knowledge, the complete solution is still missing if the processes and techniques are not connected to achieving a planned outcome.

A solution must take a government organization from an initial operational state to an operational state that is better than the state resulting from the organization continuing on its original path without the solution. So, if an organization's operations are starting to decline due to internal or external problems, a new way to sustain operations at initial levels is considered a solution. Alternatively, if an organization is operating at a steady level, a valid solution should increase the efficiency, reliability, capacity, velocity, scope, affordability, or user satisfaction of such operations. As Figure 2.1 shows, the context in which a government solution can be established has four elements. First, the government organization must have a definable current operational state for which a solution is needed. Second, the organization's operational state must have definable relations with the greater external environment. If this environment is evolving, then our solutions development team must further project the path of changing external drivers and how these drivers will impact the operational state as our solution is being applied. Third, we must

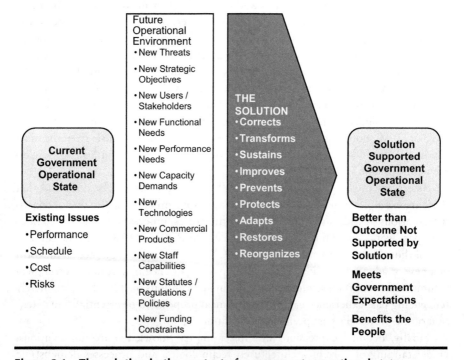

Figure 2.1   The solution in the context of government operational states.

be able to apply our solution as the organization moves toward a future operational state. Finally, the effect of applying the solution must take the operational state of the government organization to an outcome that is measurably better than if the solution had not been implemented. Any proposal that meets this criterion has an operational solution. However, the best solution must demonstrate how it benefits people, such as government users of new systems, and the tax payers funding the contract. The best solutions will exceed government expectations on systems and services performance, contract cost, delivery schedule, and risk management.

The term *operational solution* is used to show that the scope of this book does not cover the many other types of solutions that may receive government funds but are not associated with the operations of government organizations. For example, multiple government agencies fund scientific research without requiring such research to be directly usable by the government. So, while finding the cure for cancer under a government grant will be an awesome solution, it is not an operational solution. Likewise, some government agencies fund artistic endeavors that also can be considered solutions. Unfortunately, this book cannot help with solutions development for basic research grants and artistic endeavors grants. The solutions that we will develop might not save the world or reflect the height of human achievement, but they will meet and exceed government requirements, resolve pain points, transform organizations, and grow the business.

Since the solution changes the current government operational state, the first determination is that the current operational state needs to be changed or that the operational state going into the future needs to be changed. We will discuss the definition of government needs in Chapter 3. For now, we can ask the question of what would indicate that the current operational state can benefit from a solution for change. The basic metrics in program management can give us this answer.

- ■ **Performance Metrics:** A solution might be needed if any aspect of current performance is falling below levels for optimal operations, and a solution might be needed if there are ways to elevate performance to achieve operational states that have not been realized in the past. The rates might be too slow, the functionalities might be incomplete, the tools might be too hard to use, the technologies might be obsolete, the capacity might be too low, and the processes might be too cumbersome.
- ■ **Schedule Metrics:** A solution might be needed if any part of operational activities is not meeting schedule. The processes might have crept up in complexity, the systems and tools might have degraded, the staff capabilities might have shifted, and the tasks might have become more challenging. While most organizations try to operate at steady and stable states, few government organizations are simple enough that they can operate by continuously repeating activities. Operational states shift, and proactive management as well as self-adaptation by the government staff can sometimes bring schedules back on track. Other times, a solution is needed.

- **Cost Metrics:** A solution might be needed if operational cost starts to creep up beyond projected annual escalation rates due to schedule delays, additional resources required to complete tasks, market price of products, or expansion in scope of work. A solution might also be beneficial if there are new tools and techniques that can lower cost. If so, then current cost projections can be viewed as excessive even though they had been reasonable prior to the availability of new tools and techniques.
- **Risk Metrics:** A solution might be needed if there are potential events that could seriously harm the current operational state. These events are unique to the nature of each operations. Like all risks, we can describe an event based on level of risk impact and probability of risk occurrence. All operations live with risks because even the idea of being destroyed by an asteroid is a risk. However, some risks will require mitigations while others are merely a reality of operations. When required mitigations are not available, new solutions will be required.

Even if the current operational state of a government organization has no issues, the environment of operations can change as the organization heads into the future. These changes can drive down operational performance in different ways. Performance issues can emerge, instabilities can grow, and delays can increase. If additional resources are blindly applied to deal with these issues, such a brute-force solution might work for a while at great cost. The best solution requires formulation and planning. A part of this formulation is determining when during the degradation of operations should the solution be applied. If applied too early, the environmental effects might not have emerged enough to be accurately countered. If applied too late, the damages to operations might be very difficult to fix. The following are some of the potential environmental effects on the operations of government organizations.

- **New Threats:** Changes in the path of a hurricane can threaten government facilities. Increased earthquake activities can threaten the national power grid. A pandemic can cripple the number of federal workers showing up to work. Other natural and man-made disasters can disrupt operations in individually unique ways. Cyberattacks on government systems, for example, are continuously increasing and evolving. New adversaries, new systems, and new government missions can all yield unique vulnerabilities and outcomes. Thus, solutions development needs to start with threat assessment, modeling of impact, and development of countermeasures such as expanded or restructured redundancies, recovery capabilities, passive defensive measures, and offensive means.
- **New Strategic Objectives:** Changes in objectives by the White House, Congress, specific government agencies, cognizant organizations, or other governing authorities could create a misalignment between current operational

states and new operational states required to meet objectives. Sometimes, the implications of new strategic objects must filter down from language in statutes and presidential directives to interpretations of new process requirements by agency policymakers, and to identification of new procedures by operational units. The focus of solutions development is then on how to satisfy the new operational processes and procedures.

▪ **New Users/Stakeholders:** The users of current operational capabilities provided by government organizations can grow in number and in their needs. Those affected by current government operations can also grow in number and in their discontent with the effects. This shift might not initially require any changes to the current operational state, but the increasing effects could eventually lead to several mechanisms of system, process, and support staff failures. Delays in operations due to system inability to handle the capacity of use can disrupt workflows. Breaks in the workflow when old systems lack needed functionalities can block the delivery of federal services. And, people negatively affected by current operations could protest against government processes as frustrations grow and voices can be heard. These changes might not be initially noticeable as operations press forward. As situations intensify, however, solutions may be required to halt further operational degradation, more drops in performance, or prevent yet unrealized failure modes. The solution focus should be on how to increase capacity, add or expand functionalities, and correct the user experience.

▪ **New Functional Needs:** Changes in the user and stakeholder business processes can introduce the need for new functional capabilities in the systems supporting current government operations. The solution development focus should first be on whether the new functional needs can be satisfied through new ways to reconfigure and use existing systems. If not, then new system requirements must be established. These requirements can then be satisfied through modifications of the current systems, modular additions to the current systems, new systems integrated with current systems, or replacements for the current systems.

▪ **New Performance Needs:** The current level of operational performance may no longer meet the needs of the users and stakeholders. For example, federal users might compare how they are supported by current operations with how commercial world users are being supported by similar operations. The solutions development focus should be on differences in human performance, system capabilities, processes and procedures, and overall operational architectures. When the adoption of commercial technologies and processes is still merited after considering all the differences, the solutions must include ways to increase performance without force fitting the uniqueness of government processes into commercial frameworks.

▪ **New Capacity Demands:** Beyond the increase of users and user activities, the need for greater capacity could be caused by changes in external technologies, more demanding operational schedules, loss or degradation of current capacity, or evolution of architectures. For example, the advent of smartphones created a huge capacity demand on wireless networks, new deadlines could create a demand for more staff, higher rates of staff retirement could create additional demand, and the self-organization and proliferation of information flow paths could increase capacity requirements in unprojected ways. The solutions development focus in addressing capacity issues is to understand the total demand on current capacity and segments of the operational process where local capacity increases will yield higher total capacity.

■ **New Technologies:** New technical breakthroughs offer the promise of upgrading or replacing the systems in the current operational environment. If these breakthroughs are not in the form of commercial off-the-shelf (COTS) products that can fit into the federal architecture, then new systems development requirements may have to be established. The solutions development focus is then on the compatibility of the new technology with legacy (current) system technologies. This compatibility determination is on whether the current system functions can be used in part or as a whole in the development effort. If the entirety of current systems can be left operational as new technologies are integrated, then the development can be considered an upgrade. Otherwise, they are replacements with or without the leveraging of legacy components.

■ **New Commercial Products:** One of the greatest impact on federal users is the availability of commercial products/devices that they do not have. Because of the unique processes, systems architecture, and security requirements needed for federal operational environments, commercial products cannot always be immediately inserted into the current operational state. Therefore, the solutions development focus must be on what modifications to the federal environment and what modifications to commercial products must be completed in order to achieve effective and security-compliant integration. The modifications can be simple configuration changes, but they may also involve developmental changes to software, application program interfaces (APIs), and databases.

■ **New Staff Capabilities:** The training and experience of employees outside the federal workforce can overtime surpass the capabilities of the existing federal workforce. This is particularly true in the field of information technology. In such a case, the solutions development focus is on whether similar training and practices can be established for the federal workforce, more external employee hires should be conducted to replace the federal workforce, or the federal workforce should be reduced in favor of more contractor-provided workers with better capabilities. The federal debate regarding insourcing and outsourcing talent has gone on for many years.

■ **New Statutes/Regulations/Policies:** Beyond changes in strategic objectives, other changes in statutes, regulations, or policies could also impact current operations. For example, a statute demanding a new congressional report with metrics for approval will change organizational business processes. A regulation that prohibits the use of certain materials due to environmental hazards will require changes in system components. A change in agency policy on staff qualifications will require changes in human resource procedures. The solutions development focus is then on the specific nature of each statute, regulation, and policy. A deep understanding of prior statutes, regulations, and policies superseded by a change and the rationale for the change will help transition operations from the current state to the optimal statutory, regulatory, or policy compliant state.

▪ **New Funding Constraints:** The lack of sufficient funds to maintain the current operational state while the current operational state is still required creates a solutions need. The solutions development focus is then on how to achieve the current operational outcomes while adjusting processes, staff composition and capabilities, and/or means of systems utilization. While it may be impossible to match every aspect of the current operational state when undergoing a consolidation to reduce cost, overcoming current inefficiencies could allow the highest operational priorities to be sustained.

The above descriptions of environmental factors could cause a government organization's operational state to either drop or be lower than its potential. As suggested, these misalignments create opportunities for the application of operational solutions. A solution can be described as a controlled application of state changing forces to achieve results that benefit those who depend on the government organization and meet the expectations of government leaders. Actions that create better outcomes without known causes and effects cannot be categorized as solutions until the forces and mechanisms of change have been identified. Actions that sometimes create better outcomes cannot be categorized as solutions until the probability of success for each action can be estimated in some way. When a solution is understood, it can be explained in proposals and be described through adjectives such as

▪ The Solution Corrects—fixing operational errors.
▪ The Solution Transforms—changing the fundamental operational approach.
▪ The Solution Sustains—keeping adverse forces from affecting operations.
▪ The Solution Improves—taking operations to new levels.
▪ The Solution Prevents—blocking an adverse outcome from occurring.
▪ The Solution Protects—opposing attacks on operations.
▪ The Solution Adapts—shifting operations to integrate, align, or correspond.
▪ The Solution Restores—bringing operations back to former states.
▪ The Solution Reorganizes—creating new operational pathways.

Given our understanding of what constitutes a solution, one can argue that every current effort for the government must have some type of solution or the effort is completely expendable or replaceable. The most challenging solutions development endeavor may be the one that provides the government with the lowest price technically acceptable (LPTA) services. Once a government organization has the mindset that it can live with minimal performance, the performance can drop with each cycle of lowest price winner until the organization becomes completely ineffective. The adverse outcomes of gradual reductions in performance during each new performance period are often very hard to detect. Eventually, the benefits of higher-level performance can be forgotten. A contractor supporting the government in such a situation is therefore vested in showing the government how the lowest price solution is inadequate and what can be gained with proper investments.

Assuming that the government recognizes the true value of current solutions providers, the second problem may be that the contractor themselves have forgotten how to quantify and express their solutions' best value. Their processes might be embedded within the mental knowledge of their top performers, their architectures might have evolved through years of expert adjustments, their technologies might be in place for years with automatic cycles of updates, and their people might be so skilled that there is no longer the need for procedures. Essentially, the contractor is helping the government achieve its desired operational state every day, but the team has been doing it for so long that they cannot explain how they are taking the government from a lower operational state to the current state. This disconnect between providing a solution and explaining a solution is dangerous because the contractor will be challenged in writing an effective proposal to defend their incumbent work. If the government customer recognizes the incumbent's value and manages the source selection so that the incumbent contractor wins despite the lack of a well-expressed solution, then the government is merely perpetuating a disconnect. This disconnect reduces the incumbent's ability to respond to new issues in the government's operational state. When environmental factors shift to present new forces that hinder government operations, the incumbent managers are at the mercy of their staff in their ability to self-adapt. If the incumbent had documented their solution, then that solution could be further innovated to respond to new customer needs.

The lessons learned are that, whether one is an incumbent contractor or a contractor seeking new work with a government organization, having a well-expressed solution is very important. This is not to say that one cannot win proposals by other means. Government buyers and government evaluators are people with individual views on what are acceptable solutions. Unless the process is rigid enough to force people to be completely objective in developing the RFP and evaluating the submitted proposals, people will fold their personal preconceptions of the best path forward into the source selection process. Very few government leaders will give work to a friend regardless of how they will perform. However, if the government leaders have worked with a contractor and is comfortable with a trusted relationship, then the historical performance can significantly influence how the RFP is written and evaluation is conducted. This is a reality of people's inherent desire for risk mitigation at the expense of possibly overlooking better opportunities. The government culture of ascension by avoiding mistakes further pushes for risk-minimized outcomes.

For contractors seeking business with new government customers, the inherent advantage of incumbents is a challenge. The ways to confront this challenge are to (1) find government organizations whose pains are so great that they are willing to abandon the people they know, (2) convince government organizations that their pains are great enough to abandon the people they know, (3) enlist the help of incumbent subcontractors to gain trust by association, and (4) hope that government leaders whom one has relationships with move into target organizations. In all cases, having solutions is the critical factor for success. If a government organization already knows its pain, then the problem is typically very big and the mistakes by incumbents are very grave. The solution for such a big problem can be very complex, but the prize is there to be taken. If a government organization has pain points that one can identify, then a careless incumbent can lose the competition if one presents a solution while the incumbent proposal only reiterates the work statement or their experience. If one wants to court incumbent subcontractors, then having a great solution or the ability to develop that solution goes a long way toward convincing those companies to switch teams. No matter how much workshare on the future contract one offers to court subcontractors, few will want to be on the losing team. Finally, when a new government leader is open to one's support, a first-rate solution will defend that leader's arguments for selecting one's proposal over that of the incumbent and other competitors.

The days when companies accepted the decisions of government have passed. Now, offerors regularly challenge source selection decisions by protesting through the awarding agencies or to the Government Accountability Office (GAO). In many major source selections, we will now see dozens of submitted proposals and so the incumbents are always threatened. From every perspective, solutions matter. How to develop solutions will be the mission of the following chapters.

Chapter 3

Government Solution Needs

During the days of the Cold War, the needs of the DoD dominated the spending of the U.S. government. Technology opportunities drove the investments of the United States and the Soviet Union, and U.S. leaders relied heavily upon the recommendations of analysts to determine solution needs. Most of these analysts worked at FFRDCs, and the RAND (Research and Development) Corporation, formed in 1948 to provide the Air Force with decision support, is one of the first FFRDCs [1]. The Navy sponsored the Center for Naval Analysis (CNA) with more operations focus, and the Office of the Secretary of Defense (OSD) sponsored the Institute for Defense Analysis (IDA) with more strategic focus [2,3]. Over time, more FFRDCs were formed through congressional funding with individual missions to produce objective analysis for the military services and other federal agencies. In addition to RAND, for example, the Air Force formed the Aerospace Corporation, MITRE, and ANSER. These FFRDCs then also became not-for-profit companies, each with a division that managed its FFRDC component and other divisions that allowed the company to grow. As the FFRDCs expanded their roles as trusted advisors to the government, for-profit consulting firms started to provide studies and analysis, decision support, and program management assistance services that were similar to the capabilities of the FFRDCs.

Today, the FFRDCs are still important institutions, and their staff continue to sit in on government staff–only meetings. However, with the end of the Cold War and financial demands of global operations, massive investments in technologies like in the days of the Strategic Defense Initiative (SDI) became a thing of the past [4]. Instead, the few new systems that have been initiated since the Cold War resulted more from political advocacy than analytical recommendations.

Wargames and operational studies still help to establish understanding of needs, but the actual decision that a material solution is needed became more of a judgment call by senior government leaders. With the growing capabilities of IT systems, other federal departments and organizations began to acquire systems like the DoD. These new customers lacked the studies and analysis resources of the DoD. Thus, the decision to invest in IT for many senior government leaders is based upon what they see in commercial enterprises.

Beyond the importance of leadership decisions, the need to periodically update operational IT systems to fix security vulnerabilities, ensure integration with external systems, and incorporate newer commercial components has spawned an automatic requirement for system sustainment solutions providers. As federal contracts are generally limited to ten years with most being four to five years based on procurement strategy, the competition for sustaining an IT system will generally occur in cycles until a decision is made either to satisfy the system's functionalities with a new system or retire the system and functionalities from the organizational workflow. The leadership consideration of trade-offs in deciding whether to acquire a new system/solution includes the following factors:

- The sustainment cost of the operational legacy system facing technical obsolescence compared with the development and operational cost of a new system.
- The point where the legacy system and technology cannot be practically sustained.
- The point where new functional and performance requirements in the evolving government workflow demand additional solutions.
- The ability to upgrade/modify the legacy system to meet new requirements.
- The impact (benefits) of greater functionality and higher performance in a new system for government operations.
- The ability of a new system to fulfill the functionalities of multiple legacy systems.
- The ability of a new system to support a larger or geographically distributed group of users.
- The risks in developing and deploying a new system.
- The challenges in integrating a new system into the operational architecture.

The above factors reveal that even the decision to retain or replace long-operating systems can be supported by operational analysis as in the case of brand-new system concepts. One difference is that there is an incumbent contractor for legacy system sustainment and that the incumbent contractor might have a guarded understanding of the current operational architecture which will be important in presenting a detailed transition plan. The incumbent contractor strategy might be to convince senior government leaders to delay investing in a new system and to craft the sustainment RFP language in favor of the incumbent. Alternatively, the incumbent contractor strategy might be to try to steer the formulation of requirements for a new system to favor its capabilities. The presence of inside track actors/contractors could influence the objectivity of assessments by the government. This does not mean that all RFPs for system sustainment or system replacement are structured to favor the incumbent (wired) in opposition to the policy of fair competition. However, the incumbent will typically enjoy a competitive advantage unless its performance is so poor that the government is intentionally looking for a change or unless the government agency has committed to an LPTA acquisition strategy [5].

The decision process for sustaining or replacing IT systems is emphasized because of the sheer number of IT systems being used by the government and the rate in which IT solutions become obsolete. However, the process is similar for mechanical systems such as planes, ships, and other vehicles. The major differences are that physical components for these systems will have life cycles due to mechanical wear, technologies other than software on these systems tend to advance slower, and the cost of mechanical systems is more driven by number of units eventually purchased. Like software systems, however, there is greater effort in current times to keep deployed systems running longer with refurbishments and repairs.

The harsh reality of the current environment for government needs is presented to properly position our solutions development endeavors and not to discourage anyone from a commitment to solutions development. We just need to recognize that (1) the needs identified by the government may not always be based on well-defended analysis, (2) not all needs are realized by the government, and (3) if one is not influencing government leadership then some other company probably is. Influencing government leaders in most companies falls under the responsibilities of business development, and so much of business development is based on relationships and prior history with a government organization. There is no doubt that relationships with government leaders will help to get solutions and ideas heard. If we believe that the government should invest in a new system or process, that there is a better way to sustain the current system, or that it is time to replace the current system, the starting point is a relationship with the government decision-maker.

Now we have a business development debate. Is the relationship strongest for the business developer who has built a deep friendship with the government leader through social engagements? Alternatively, is the relationship strongest for the business developer who has a track record of delivering successful solutions to the government leader over the years? Some business developers can achieve both levels of relation, but most business developers tend to place priority on one path over the other. Our priority might have to be situational where the importance of delivering solutions depend on the size, visibility, and complexity of the needed solutions. One thing is certain: If we do not have a solution that can influence the decision of government leaders, then the priority of our relationship must be on friendship, and the value of the relationship is to gather intelligence and encourage a favorable evaluation when we respond to their RFP with a proposal.

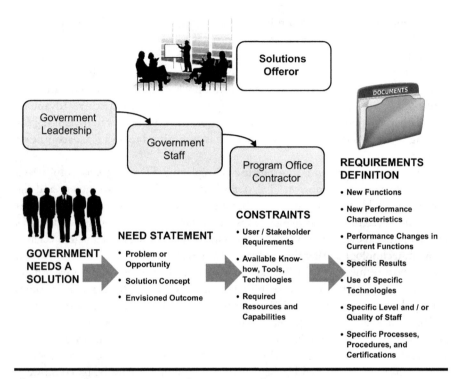

Figure 3.1   The government path to new requirements.

As Figure 3.1 shows, the path from the decision-maker determining that a solution is needed to a fully developed set of requirements to support identification of funding and then to the procurement of a solution is fairly top-down. The leadership will define a broad need based on user/stakeholder community feedback and perceptions of market opportunities. The government staff that receives this direction will try to interpret the need by further determining whether the driver is a problem voiced by the user community or an opportunity presented by the technology community. A user-voiced problem must be matched with technologies and techniques that could fix operational issues. A technology opportunity must be matched with a process for improving the organizational workflow. This leads back to our definition of a solution as bringing the current operational states to better future operational states.

The government staff do not have to create the solution, but they do have to be able to express a concept for the objective government workflow and a definition of desired outcomes. Then, contractors who support the PMO can be tasked with developing the requirements document. While the government staff will generally be able to find an effective way forward, there are cases where the solution need is not realistic and the associated concept cannot be achieved with current technologies and techniques. History will never know the number of times that government staff have questioned and challenged the guidance of their leaders. However, the program failures due to people blindly following orders are more than apparent. In hindsight, we ask questions such as, how could anyone believe that software development will be done at such aggressive pace? What makes one think that such a complex commercial product can be made to fit into this specific set of government requirements? And, how could such a large number of qualified staff be recruited and hired for that remote work location? Miscalculations do occur when leaders are faced with opportunities, and management reviews by higher authorities may not always catch such problems. Thus, the effectiveness of feedback loops within government organizations will impact whether unrealistic requirements are imposed upon the contractor solutions development teams.

When there is minimal feedback, the decisions of government leadership often oscillate between the extremes of exuberance about innovation and risk avoidance. When major IT programs failed, there emerged a desire to address needs through many smaller projects. When government-sponsored software development ran into challenges, there emerged a huge momentum for using COTS products. When acquiring new systems presented risks, there emerged a tendency to keep old systems operating longer. When the government staff was viewed as inefficient, more work was outsourced to contractors. When too much talent was lost within the government workforce, contractor staff were forcibly insourced into the government [6]. When the budget had to be cut regardless of consequences, conducting LPTA procurements was easier than fighting for the funds to maintain quality. If solutions offerors cannot influence such oscillating trends, then we are left in a position of responding and yielding to the currents of change. Not recognizing such patterns has harmed the business endeavors of many solutions providers.

Once the PMO support contractors have been asked to develop the requirements document and conduct acquisition planning in collaboration with government staff, the objective becomes one of placing constraints around the needed solution. Engaging the user community to further identify requirements and priorities in the requirements is a constraint. Agile development principles loosen such constraints with the use of user stories instead of rigid requirements, but the government will tend to add performance, schedule, and cost oversight metrics/constraints on top of Agile processes to limit risks [7]. Defining the technologies that must be used further constrains the solution, and setting required staff qualifications and staffing level further establishes a scope for the solution.

The line between establishing scope and the government staff defining the solution can become very blurred when technically talented professionals support the PMOs. Knowing that they cannot deliver the products or services to address government needs because of the organizational conflict of interest (OCI) boundary, they will still tend to define the solution as much as possible in the requirements document to both limit risks and simplify the source selection process [8]. This in many ways is encouraged through the government preference for PWS over SOO. For how can performance metrics be established unless one has requirements of such fidelity that tasks and criteria for completion of tasks can be established? The acquisition risk in this endeavor is that there is often no check and balance for the PMO team beyond leadership oversight. This PMO team of contractors and government staff will research the market environment, ask for contractor inputs, and allow contractors to review draft acquisition documents to provide comments. However, if mistakes are made in the requirements and in the PWS, such mistakes will sometimes proliferate into the source selection process and even into the resulting contract.

In DoD systems development at the ACAT I, II, and III levels, the Joint Capabilities Integration and Development System (JCIDS) creates a rigorous process which ensures that user-based requirements are fully analyzed, organized, deconflicted, and approved. The DoDI 5000.02 life cycle phases then allow two opportunities to adjust the requirements based on the insights of the technical community [9]. The initial capabilities document (ICD) serves as the starting point for analyzing the solution. The results of the analysis of alternatives (AoA) and other studies are then used to create the capabilities development document (CDD). The CDD reflects an agreement between the government and the development community on what is possible, and the CDD is used to build prototypes for testing, conducting technology demonstrations, and designing the initial system. Such results are used to refine the requirements into the capabilities product document (CPD). The objective system is built, tested, and deployed using the CPD.

If all programs across the federal government can afford the time and resources needed to undergo DoD's official requirements validation process, then the risks of development failures due to unrealistic requirements is minimized. This is not necessarily so for the other federal agencies and even for smaller DoD programs. This is also not so for requirements to provide services such as in maintaining IT systems, building infrastructure, and establishing cybersecurity. As such requirements involve known professional capabilities, commercial standard products, and industry best practice processes, the risks can be viewed as being in staffing level, personnel quality, and cost. What is seldom discussed, however, is the true complexity in human capabilities that cannot be measured by certifications, years of experience, and prior responsibilities. Lacking this understanding, service requirements have at times been overly restrictive on certifications and incumbency experience—to the point where more qualified candidates cannot be brought into the program. Alternatively, service requirements have at other times overlooked unique metrics, such as demonstrated accomplishments, and undervalued staff to the point where performance issues result.

What we can conclude from possible issues in the government requirements process is that solution offerors who are not proactively trying to influence the outcomes of the government processes will very often be caught by the imperfections of the process. This is not to say that companies cannot win government contracts by being merely reactive to officially released RFPs. However, if another company is steering the requirements and PWS toward their core strengths, then one is at a disadvantage. If the requirements are overly demanding on all contractors, then winning a contract could mean a high risk for a company in achieving acceptable Contractor Performance Assessment Reports Systems (CPARS) scores. Historically, companies have faced financial losses in maintaining performance on firm fixed price (FFP) contracts where the requirements are too challenging.

Thus, as Figure 3.2 shows, the time to start solutions development is as soon as the program office is refining requirements and developing the acquisition documents. If one's relationships have been strong enough to influence the definition of need, then this solutions development endeavor should extend from the concepts presented to senior government leaders. Either way, solutions development activities at this point in the process should be focused on helping the PMO team understand requirements and constraints from the perspective of how to get the optimal solution. If the solutions offeror does not have any relationships with the

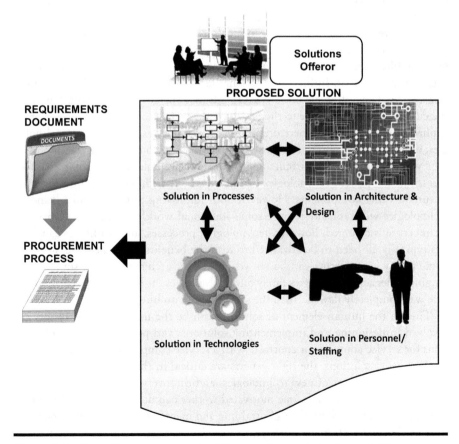

Figure 3.2   Proactive engagement of the requirements and acquisition process by the solutions offeror.

program office, then the offeror must resort to standard mechanisms of communications, such as a request for information (RFI) response, feedback comments on draft PWS, conversations with the program office team at industry day events, and unsolicited presentations. If there is a relationship, then the engagement can be more interactive based on program office interest. The ground rules for the engagement are that the contractor can present any form of documentation and ideas to the government until the final RFP is officially released by the contracting officer. The government can ask questions and hold discussions with contractors about their capabilities and ideas until the final RFP is released. In this engagement, the government can only show contractors elements of draft or final For Official Use Only (FOUO) or Source Selection Sensitive documents that have been approved for release to the public. Many government personnel will simply avoid all unofficial communications with potential offerors even before RFP release for concerns about misperceptions. This preference must be respected, but the alignment between government needs and the best solutions from technology companies must be achieved.

When we think about solutions to satisfy requirements, we are thinking about what enables the current government workflows. A government workflow is enabled by an architecture of systems that allows people and technologies to work together based on processes to fulfill organizational tasks/functions, accomplish core missions, and achieve strategic objectives. To advance the government workflow from the current operational state to the desired future operational state by means of an applied solution, one can therefore improve the processes, architecture, technologies, or human capabilities. For most organizations, the processes can be improved even while leveraging the current architecture and technologies. For some architectures, the component technologies can be advanced without changing the architecture or other components. However, both improving processes and advancing technologies will typically require some additional workforce training. Once the architecture is changed, however, technologies, processes, and workforce capabilities typically all need to be advanced to reap the benefits of the new architecture. Some legacy components can be reused in a better architecture, but simply rearranging all legacy technologies rarely offers advantages, unless the original architecture was completely flawed. Then the solution is an architectural fix.

Finally, the human element of solutions can be the most complex. People are involved in designing and implementing solutions, and people are a part of solutions for service contracts or contracts with a service component. In designing and implementing solutions, the right experts are critical in the creation of new architectures, development of new technologies, and discovery of process innovations. In staffing service contracts, one motivated worker can do the job of multiple discouraged employees. With the right training and mentorship, a younger worker can rival a colleague with many more years' experience. These qualities of the human potential have been exploited by the best of commercial market-oriented companies, and the government has for decades tried to achieve similar levels of success.

New management theories have been applied, and new IT development methodologies, such as Agile development, Spiral development, and rapid prototyping, have been adopted. Yet, the solution for maximizing performance for personnel working on government contracts is still lacking for many government agencies.

Our emphasis on the human element is to argue that practically all government needs and requirements can benefit from innovative solutions. However, innovative solutions may not always be presentable once all the constraints have been established in the final RFP. We will return to discussing how to achieve innovative solutions based on better processes, architectures, technologies, and human capabilities in later chapters. The approaches and techniques to be presented will help us engage the program office and senior government leaders as needs are realized. Before we get to solutions development techniques, however, we must first understand the dynamics of government engagement. The most innovative companies begin solutions development with the end in mind and understand that the mission to advance the operational states of government agencies is a continuous commitment that extends from the understanding of each government agency's strategic vision, plans, programs, and available funding. If solutions are developed with appropriate insight of government funding constraints and organizational limitations, then they will more likely be embraced by government leaders. Many government leaders are indeed very risk-averse. However, good solutions should address the government pain points and not hope to merely attract government interest. Surely when the pain is great due to broken processes and impending crisis, everyone cares about innovative solutions. The challenge in engaging senior government leaders and the program office is to help them understand the potential pain before things get really broken and crisis hits. This engagement can occur in a vast variety of ways based on the talents of business development leads. What matters is that when the opportunity to present to the government emerges, the innovation solution in clear concise language is available.

The collaboration between solutions development and business development is a central theme throughout this book. The ways to achieve this collaboration will become more apparent as we see how solutions can be introduced and how solutions are viewed by the government. Thus, understanding government needs is just the first step.

References

1. Medvetz, T. 2012. *Think Tanks in America*. Chicago: University of Chicago Press.
2. Smith, J.A. 1993. *Idea Brokers: Think Tanks and the Rise of the New Policy Elite*. New York: Simon and Schuster.
3. Independent Advisory Task Force. 1997. *Report of the Defense Science Board Task Force on Federally Funded Research and Development Centers (FFRDC) and University Affiliated Research Centers (UARC)*. Washington: Office of the Under Secretary of Defense for Acquisition and Technology (January).

4. Engel, J.A. 2017. *When the World Seemed New: George H. W. Bush and the End of the Cold War*. Boston: Houghton Mifflin Harcourt.
5. Federal Acquisition Regulation (FAR), Subpart 15.101–2. 1974 (updated annually). Office of Federal Procurement Policy, Office of Management and Budget.
6. Manuel, K.M. & Maskell, J. 2013. Insourcing functions performed by federal contractors: Legal issues. Washington, DC: Congressional Research Service.
7. Ries, M. and Summers, D. 2016. *Agile Project Management: A Complete Beginner's Guide to Agile Project Management*. CreateSpace Independent Publishing Platform.
8. Rumbaugh, M.G. 2010. *Understanding Government Contract Source Selection*. Fairfax, VA: Management Concepts.
9. DoD Instruction 5000.02. 2017. Operation of the Defense Acquisition System. Office of the Under Secretary of Defense for Acquisition, Technology, and Logistics (August 10).

Chapter 4

Funding and Procurement of Solutions

The criticality of obtaining funding in order for the source selection process to proceed is explained in Appendix B. To fund a RFP, the government formulates an estimated cost for the contract and establishes a budget that matches that cost. Therefore, those presenting solutions to government agencies need to understand the availability of funding so that the solution can be successfully crafted to fit within the framework of what the government can afford. In the official evaluation of proposals, the price presented by the offeror is always a factor in the evaluation methodology. For LPTA RFP solicitations, the lowest price is the primary method of selecting the winner from those proposals that have been evaluated to be technically acceptable. For best-value RFP solicitations, the weight of the proposed price will often be stated in Section M of the RFP. If the price is below the government cost estimated, then the offeror will save the government money. However, if the price is far below the government cost estimate, then the government might conduct a price realism analysis and determine associated risks to performance. In cases such as LPTA procurements, the government could be so confident that minimum acceptable performance will be gained through the selection process that the RFP requirements language on price is that it only has to be reasonable but not realistic. In other words, risks in proposals being underpriced are accepted as long as the prices are not absurd.

Knowing the source selection team's price evaluation position is important and knowing the program office acquisition team's cost estimate will help
in establishing a price to win strategy. Government cost estimates are closely
guarded acquisition-sensitive information for many source selections. So, the
solutions development teams and business development leads may have to be
creative in piecing together such government baselines. One approach is to match
the government's cost modeling process. Another approach is to extrapolate from
the value of prior government contracts that are for the same work or similar
work. In RFPs where the price is the least important factor, the solutions development efforts can seek to maximize performance even though costs will increase.
The offeror must, however, be absolutely certain that outcomes pushed above government RFP expectations will garner value-added scores that justify the higher
price.

This chapter is actually not about pricing for proposals. Instead, it is about
pricing solutions well in advance of RFPs and crafting solutions for government
affordability and government acquisition planning. The timing for early pricing
should be aligned with each solution offeror's opportunities for influencing the
government's acquisition process. If the relationship with a government organization is strong enough, earlier awareness of available funds is an opportunity to
present innovative ideas for projects. Once a set of requirements and associated cost
estimates has received funding, the constraints of the funding profile, if identifiable by the solutions offeror, should immediately drive all engagements with the
program office. The concept presented in the RFI response should fit within this
funding profile. The staffing capacity presented to the government should match
this funding profile. Finally, the pricing in the submitted proposal should be within
the scope of this funding profile.

For RFPs to the follow-on work of existing contracts, the value of a current
contract in the Federal Procurement Data System (FPDS) is an indicator of the
government budget. Even when the RFP is a consolidation of contracts, the combined value of prior contracts would provide a likely ceiling for future work. The
most challenging situation in government engagements is when one believes that
one's solutions are so important that the government must go and find funding. In
such a situation, the government senior leaders can be supported in their quest for
funding. To support this quest, the solutions offeror must understand how government funding works.

As Figure 4.1 shows, there are several paths to finding funds for systems development and service contracts. To find enough funds to match the estimated cost of
satisfying requirements over the course of the contract base and option years, multiple funding paths might have to be pursued. Before we discuss integrated funding
strategies and the potential role of companies in helping government organizations
navigate funding challenges, the following are the general processes for acquiring
funding along each path.

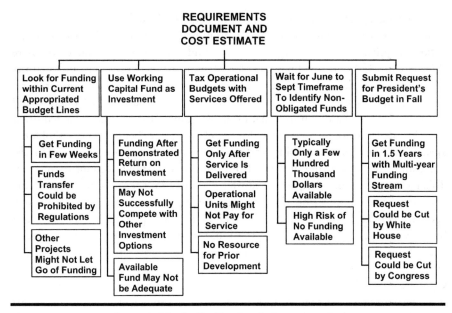

Figure 4.1   Key paths and risks in finding funds for new solutions.

4.1 Look for Funding within Current Appropriated Budget Lines

Sometimes, the quickest way to get funding is to take it from other programs. As funding for programs are authorized and appropriated through Congress, the taking of funds for a new solution must stay within the limitations of statutory guidance and agency financial management regulations. The congressional budget is organized by appropriation accounts, often associated with a "color money" to designate years for spending the money and budget lines associated with specific programs. The easiest way to fund a new solution is to justify the solution as being within the scope of a specific budget line with adequate funding. Then, other activities in that budget line can be down-scoped as the contract to pursue the new solution is awarded.

If funding must be pulled out of a budget line or even an appropriation account for the new solution, then there are only two mechanisms—reprogramming or transfer.

Reprogramming, according to regulations, is the use of "funds in an appropriations account for purposes other than those contemplated at the time of appropriation." Money is moved from one budget line in the account to another budget line. The action must comply with 31 U.S.C. § 1301, specific language in the Appropriations Act, and agency regulations for congressional reporting and congressional approval [1]. For example, previously budgeted funds that were at one time denied by Congress cannot be reprogrammed once received. Reprogramming actions requiring congressional approval include (1) those with values of more than $10 to $20M depending on color of money (i.e., operations and maintenance; research, development, test, and evaluation [RDT&E]; systems procurement), (2) money used to start new programs not yet authorized by Congress, and (3) money moved based on termination of programs. The threshold for requiring congressional approval is cumulative for each budget line. Below this threshold, the agency's comptroller has flexibility and discretionary authority over the use of funds.

Transfer is the moving of funds from one appropriations account to another. This requires statutory designated transfer authority for specific types of accounts and congressional reporting [2]. Transfers can be between accounts within one agency, such as from DoD O&M to DoD military personnel. Transfers can be between agencies, such as from the DoD to the Department of State. Broad authority is generally given to move money from working capital funds, and specific authority is given to the Secretary of Defense to move money from the Army Operations and Maintenance appropriations account to the military pay account to be responsive to the highly dynamic needs of global engagement. There is also authority to transfer money from DoD RDT&E to the procurement appropriations account.

Based on the above two mechanisms, there are some cases where transfer authority exists and an increase to a specific appropriations account will enable the solution to be funded. In most cases, however, it is easier to reprogram funds, such as from an RDT&E budget line, at a level that does not require congressional approval. Further, the use of the funds can be explained as acquisition planning, investigation of options, and other efforts that are preludes to starting a new program. The actual funding for the program would then be added into the President's budget for official congressional appropriation. If the urgency of need demands that a program be initiated and completed prior to the next congressional budget cycle, then approval by the appropriate congressional committees and subcommittees must to be pursued.

As the process shows, most ways of taking money from other programs will require substantial authority within the agency. Programs losing money will present their impact analysis. Other unfunded efforts in the agency will question the priority and importance of one's effort. As the solutions offeror, we can craft the description of our solution to support the best way to justify taking money from other programs and to defend against competitors.

4.2 Use Working Capital Fund as Investment

Beyond money held in congressional budget lines, money held in working capital funds can also be allocated to support new solutions. The intent of working capital funds is to pool financial resources from across an agency to enable the agency to be competitive in commercial market environments [3]. For example, an agency can buy materials and supplies in bulk or in advance to take advantage of best commercial pricing. An agency can invest in a way that offers clear downstream financial advantages similar to commercial business models. The Department of Labor, Department of Justice, and General Services Administration have used working capital funds to finance their administrative services in more efficient ways. The DoD has a broader working capital funding that is guided by statutory language, but the principal business investment approach is the same.

10 U.S. Code § 2208—Working-capital funds [4]: "(a) To control and account more effectively for the cost of programs and work performed in the Department of Defense, the Secretary of Defense may require the establishment of working-capital funds in the Department of Defense to—(1) finance inventories of such supplies as he may designate; and (2) provide working capital for such industrial-type activities, and such commercial-type activities that provide common services within or among departments and agencies of the Department of Defense, as he may designate."

Given the nature of working capital funds, new solutions that can save an agency money are eligible for such sources of money pursuant to the regulations and policies associated with each fund. An offeror seeking to implement a proposed solution by using this source of money needs to understand the historical patterns in the utilization of the fund, the customers and their agency process for expending the fund, and the realistic amount of funding that can be acquired. Then, the solution concept must be crafted to explain how the customer organizations across the agency will achieve cost savings by collectively investing in this solution. This argument for funds will be a competition between the government advocate for one's solution concept and the advocates of other government projects. From this competition that precedes any source selection, one's government advocate can end up with complete funding, no funding, or partial funding to get efforts started. Because of the speed in which such funds can be acquired, even partial funding is important as it could produce results that enable the program office to get the rest of the funding from the congressional budget cycle.

4.3 Tax Operational Budgets with Services Offered

Some government operational budgets allow for the payment of commercial services based on level of use. For government organizations that serve large user communities, this form of money can be large enough to sustain the development of new solutions. For example, the Veterans Health Administration of the Department of Veterans Affairs provides services to millions of veteran patients [5]. If a critical IT service can be added as a usage/transaction-based fee in patient bills, the resulting funds could be greater than funds from IT program budgets. A company must take the risk of investing in its own solution in order to tax the operational budget. Commercial product companies tend to build their capabilities for larger markets and push the government to adopt commercial processes. In cases where commercial products are simply inadequate, a company willing to invest in building for the unique requirements of government organizations could gain competitive advantages.

The challenge of this approach is that no funding will be received until the solution is deployed and operational. Also, the government will pay for service but not prior development. The company's investments will therefore have to be recuperated through a long-range pricing model. If the government stops purchasing the service any time before the recuperation of investments, the company will probably face financial losses. This path should therefore not be pursued unless one has absolute confidence in one's solution or some form of government commitment to the use of the solution.

Another way to tax operations is to provide professional services to headquarter organizations that control funds going to programs. Such organizations may not be able to use money from the program budget lines to conduct new systems development. However, this can justify the taxing of funds as conducting headquarter services that are integral to the success of the programs. Solutions offerors wishing to use this level of funding must craft the service solution to be appropriate for implementation at headquarter organizations. The benefits to the programs must be clear, and any perception that a solution is diverting funds away from the intent of the programs must be avoided.

4.4 Wait for June to September Time Frames to Identify Non-Obligated Funds

As the end of each fiscal year approaches, there will be programs that cannot obligate all their budgeted funds before the funds expire. Thus, between June and September, headquarter/oversight organizations across all agencies start to assess the obligation risks across their programs. If the risks are too high, they will start to pull out funds as "fallout money." This money can then be used to initiate unfunded requirements. The competition for fallout money can be fierce, but it will be very fast. Those who can present affordable solutions to the right government leaders and have appropriate mechanisms for receiving funds could quickly end up with several hundred thousand dollars or even millions of dollars to implement solutions. The solutions, as limited by funding, can be studies, prototypes, or services of definable scope. Follow-on competitions can then be held to build upon the solutions.

As failures in obligating funds are often connected with delayed source selections and the protesting of awards, government organizations seeking to realign fallout money and obligate the funds before September 30th will be very concerned about additional procurement risks. The following strategies can be used to eliminate procurement risks for the government.

- Strategy 1—Some indefinite delivery indefinite quantity (IDIQ) contracts prohibit offerors from protesting task order awards with values below a set dollar amount such as $10M. Thus, if the solutions offeror can present an appropriate IDIQ contract vehicle that they are on, a task order RFP can be issued with a contract awarded in a matter of weeks. The RFP must still be established for fair competition. However, this should not be a problem if one's solution is what the government wants.
- Strategy 2—The government can award sole source contracts up to a statutory limit to select types of small businesses with disadvantaged status, such as service-disabled veteran-owned small businesses (SDVOSB), 8(a) minority-owned small businesses, Alaskan Native corporations (ANC), and HUBZone businesses. The contract value limit is typically a few million dollars, and the government must in some cases justify that no other small business of a similar status can implement the presented solution.
- Strategy 3—The government can increase funding to an existing contract if the proposed work is within the scope of the contract. The easiest way to add funding is if an existing contract has unfunded options that call for the proposed solution. Then the additional funds can be passed to the managing program office to exercise the option.

The receipt of fallout money depends heavily on relationships with senior government leaders and paving a path for the award of money. The winning of IDIQs that are accessible across government organizations (governmentwide acquisition contracts [GWACS]) is thus very important, and leveraging small disadvantaged business status can lead to both sole-source awards and gaining small business set-aside IDIQs. Most IDIQs have either a small business track or a separate small business contract award. Companies that are not small disadvantaged businesses must therefore consider being subcontractors to such businesses or forming joint ventures with such businesses in order to create paths for funding. Since such subcontract arrangements typically mean that at least 51 percent of the work must go to the prime contractor in a set aside procurement, large businesses will first try to steer funding to its own contract vehicles for full and open competition. In the case of capturing non-obligated (fallout) funds, the simplest and lowest-risk path to award typically prevails. The quality of the solution is almost secondary as long as the contract for obligating money can be quickly established.

4.5 Submit Request for the President's Budget in the Fall

All other sources of funding draw upon funding appropriated by Congress. Therefore, it is a zero-sum game unless someone asks for additional funding from Congress. The process to gain funding through Congress is to gain priority within one's own agency so that the funding request can go into the President's budget. Then, one's agency leader must continuously defend the request first to the White House Office of Management and Budget (OMB) so that it competes well with other agencies' budget priorities. Then, the request must be defended in front of Congress as mission critical discretionary spending. The debate on entitlements, budget deficits, and the growing national debt are all a part of the funding decision.

While politics plays a major role in getting congressional funding, the advantage for the solutions offeror is that the competition is largely open except for the highly classified programs. This means that one can weigh one's solutions need against others. While contractors do not participate in government resource allocation panels, strong arguments can be presented to one's program advocates for why the solutions need/requirement must be funded. After funding has been acquired, the explanation of one's solution should be on how the solution is the best alternative to meeting requirements. In the quest for funding, the first argument is that the requirement is critical to the mission of the agency and the second argument is that the requirements can be satisfied with an affordable solution. The second argument must be made in a way that does not imply that the government has already selected a performing contractor without fair competition. Thus, solutions offerors wishing to support their government program advocates need to develop whitepapers and briefings with a government needs perspective.

Unlike other sources of funding, getting funding through the official budget process can and typically is for multiple years. There is an urgency to get the requests into the President's budget in the fall. However, it is also important to lay out all the required funding for the following fiscal years in the agency's budget-planning process. For programs with congressional reporting requirements, the planned cost for the entire program life cycle must be presented. For smaller programs, the agency's independent government cost estimates (IGCE) must still cover the totality of funding across multiple years to achieve the solution. This does not eliminate the annual need to defend one's budget in front of Congress. However, defending the budget for an existing program, particularly if it is performing well, is easier than arguing for the start of a new program.

4.6 Integrated Funding Strategy

The objective of the solutions offeror is to get funding, and the objective of a senior government professional is to fund a combination of solutions to optimally achieve the agency's strategic mission. This difference in priorities with common interests can cause gaps in communications. To bridge those gaps, the solutions offeror must try to fit the solution and the requirements into the government's strategic plan. This requires a high level of objectivity, which might include prioritizing other solutions as being more important if so merited. This impacts some of the strategies for acquiring funding that involve taking from other programs. Some business development professionals have convinced government leaders to take from other programs based on the strength of relationships. My suggestion is that if such actions can be objectively justified as being good for the agency, then the solutions offeror will be viewed as the trusted agent. Trusted agents act for the good of the agency and the government instead of for short-term gain. Their profitability comes from consistently delivering products and services at best value to the government.

Given the financial strain faced by the government and the tendency to use the LPTA source selection evaluation methodology, some may argue whether the government will recognize value and great solutions. My counterargument is that to every level of funding there is a best solution for satisfying requirements. The problem is that the government program office may not completely understand how to spend the available funds to get the best value. In the case of services, LPTA, when combined with set staffing levels in the government requirements, will often lead to the lowest quality of personnel. This is because after offerors trim back fee and overhead costs, the final step is to lower salaries and perhaps even benefits. Fewer high-quality staff will very often outperform a larger number of lower-capability staff while still being at lowest cost. However, the government must recognize this potential and remove set staff levels from LPTA RFPs. As trusted agents, we need to help explain to government leaders how acquisition strategies can be designed for best value under any pricing condition. Even when prioritizing lowest price, best value should not mean lowest quality.

References

1. Office of Management and Budget. 2013. Circular No. A-11: Preparation, Submission, and Execution of the Budget (July).
2. DoD Regulation 7000.14-R. 2015. Financial Management Regulation. Volume 3 (May).
3. GAO Report. 1994. Working Capital Funds: Three Agency Perspectives. AIMD-94-121 (May 31).
4. 10 U.S. Code § 2208—Working-capital funds.
5. Department of Veterans Affairs. 2016. 2016 VA Agency Financial Report, Section II—Financial Statements, Net Program Costs by Administration Before Changes In Veterans Benefits Actuarial Liability Assumptions (November).

Chapter 5

When and in What Format to Develop Solutions

In the previous chapter, we argued that the only real limitation on solutions is available funding. We also suggested that great solutions, when combined with trusted relationships with the government, can lead to the identification of funding. Solutions must respond to government requirements, but great solutions can also help government organizations realize their needs—their pain points. This leads us to the question of when to begin developing solutions. The trivial answer is when the RFP asks for a solution. This reactive approach, unfortunately, places the responding company at a severe disadvantage. One can always assume that the program office releasing the RFP has talked to some potential offers and heard ideas on how to structure the competition.

The alternative answer to when is as soon as a solution can be applied. If we look at the process from government need to the release of RFP, there are specific entry points for solution products, as shown in Figure 5.1. Each entry point poses challenges in business development and has an effective way and format for solutions to be presented. The business development challenge is not just to have the relationship to present a solution but also to have the relationship to gain a deeper understanding of government needs. Once a solution has been presented, the company must continuously defend the solution across the acquisition process until an award is made. The format of the solution must be changed to match the audience at each point, and the solution content must evolve to align with the thought processes of the program office acquisition team. The rest of this chapter discusses

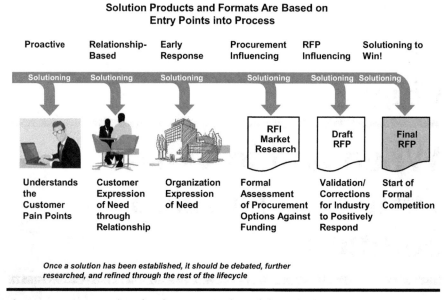

Figure 5.1 Entry points for the presentation of the solution.

how to present solutions at different entry points, and later chapters will discuss the solutions development process. While it is advantageous to present solutions at the earliest entry point, the government contracting environment and the breadth of one company's business relationships do not always permit such a scenario. There will be times when we must scramble to respond to an RFP with no prior engagement of the government program office. Despite the disadvantages, companies have been known to win through the strength of proposals and due to the sloppiness of competitors. Thus, the last entry point cannot be trivialized as much as the first entry point cannot be ignored.

5.1 Proactive Solutions Development

The hardest and most rewarding entry point for presenting a solution to the government is when government leaders do not realize their needs. This could be when one knows a government organization so well that one can find hidden problems and weaknesses in the current state of government operations. This could also be when one has such an improved technology, process, or personnel capability that there is an overwhelming opportunity to transform government operations.

The attempt to discover pain points within government organizations will require substantial collaboration between business development and the solutions development team. Understanding of current government operations must be achieved through interactions with government leaders, direct involvement in government activities, and review of government documents. Key documents to review include agency and organizational level strategic plans, technology modernization road maps, system architectures and concept of operations, policies and procedures, and directives. Agency and program funds can be identified through appropriated congressional budgets as well as prior contract expenditures as presented in the FPDS. Upon analyzing this information, the solutions development team might ask business development leads to further investigate specific areas in greater detail to determine the magnitude of pain points (low, some local inefficiencies, to extreme, agency-wide process disruption). There are situations where organizational processes have been broken for many years without people realizing. Organization databases could be filled with systematic errors from a flawed process of use, such as multiple records for one index reference and multiple competing index references pointing to one record, and nonsystematic errors from user randomness, such as mistyped names and numbers. Organization testing and auditing procedures might be missing critical risks such as design and manufacturing flaws. Organization workforces might be downplaying issues in front of leadership such as schedule delays and below-threshold performance, and organizational metrics might not be tracking true performance for fulfilling strategic objectives.

If the solutioning objective is to get in front of the government, then there is a finite period before the government realizes its own problems. At which time, the proactive entry point is lost. In the case of improvement opportunities where the government does not have a huge existing pain point, the challenge of creating the government pain point through recognition of how much better the operational state can be might require more time. This extended period of advocacy yields the vulnerability that a competing company will take advantage of the entry point one is trying to create. Thus, there is always a sense of urgency when one is trying to be the thought and capabilities leader.

Before we get too enamored with our solution, the business development leads need to investigate funding reality. If the nearest source of funding is in the President's budget a year-and-a-half away, the presentation of the solution needs to be quite different than when there is a stack of non-obligated funds sitting in a beleaguered program. Even though the initial funds might be limited, the solution development endeavor should focus on the overarching problem. If one is approaching the government without a big problem, the government is simply not going to care about small matters. No matter whether one is explaining a discovered problem or a transformational improvement, the first step must be to help government leaders feel the pain. Then, the solution must present unique innovations and preferably proprietary products, technologies, and processes. When presenting personnel capabilities, the resumes/bios must be specific and ideally recognizable by government leaders because everyone can see the weaknesses in a resume but personal familiarity can help highlight the strengths. At this point, a government leader is either interested or not. If interested, then our presentation of specific solution details, team members/partners, and relevant past experience goes to convincing government leadership to proceed.

There are two delivery strategies for proactively developed solutions. The first strategy is to engage government leaders with whom we have strong relationships. The solutions should then be developed as high-level whitepapers or briefings with due consideration of the busy schedule of government leaders. For very technically oriented government organizations, we can also submit unsolicited proposals to explain the details of our technical approaches. Unsolicited proposals are typically used in organizations where one has limited relationships. Therefore, the imperative is to present everything about a solution in a single try.

If relationships with government leaders are unavailable or ineffective, the second presentation strategy is to expose a government need and the solution in a public forum, such as at a conference. If a professional community sees great benefit in the presented solution, then the conversations about the solution can encourage government leaders to investigate its adoption. If the solution is big enough and if our company has the resources to hire lobbyists, attempts can be made to get Congress to state the need for the solution in statutory language. Although funding earmarks in the budget are no longer allowed, congressional language for agencies to satisfy specific requirements and investigate specific technologies can be a significant driver for implementing our proposed solution. This latter approach is somewhat brute force and could be received by government leaders poorly as it circumvents their internal planning processes. Some government leaders will respect the authority of Congress and embrace the pursuit of statutory requirements. Others could decide to only minimally comply with any congressional guidance. Thus, relationships with government leaders who have control over sources of funding is still the preferred means of proactively presenting solutions.

5.2 Relationship Solutioning

Any strong relationship with a government leader is an opportunity to figure out what solutions are needed. At this entry point for presenting solutions, we are not trying to convince the government to see the value of our solutions. Instead, we are trying to understand the pain points that government leaders already recognize and their progress in pursuing funding to resolve their pain points. Has the government made a decision to satisfy the solution need? Have requirements been developed? Has a cost estimate been formulated? And, have funding sources been identified? At some point, the details of government activities will become categorized as FOUO and acquisition sensitive. The business development lead must respect this status and honor their government friends' unwillingness to discuss future procurements even when they are well before the release of any formal RFPs.

Thus, leveraging relationships is about timing, careful listening, and knowing when to provide a solution idea to help the course of the acquisition strategy. It is better to influence an acquisition strategy before its development has started and after the decision to acquire has been made. In that window of opportunity, even before the first market research RFI has been released, presentation of a solution to address a recognized need could be well received. In crafting the solution, it is worth knowing whether our situational awareness is unique because of the relationship or whether other contractors have been able to gain the same awareness. If there is already competition at this phase, then the presentation must not only focus on the strengths of one's solution but also the weaknesses of other solution options.

Another detail that we need to find out about our awareness is how much of the awareness will eventually be shared with all potential offerors. If some awareness, such as information possessed by incumbent contractors, will not be publicly available, then the solution must exploit such awareness. There is no equal knowledge among offerors in a source selection and demonstrating superior customer knowledge is a part of the competition. If our awareness is incomplete, then the business development lead who understands the customer must help the solutions development team figure out what is written between the lines. Probably the most important interpretations beyond the actual problem statement are anticipated availability of funding and the acquisition timeline.

Armed with such awareness, solutions development must focus on a short and clear presentation. The solution must resolve customer perceived pain points and be achievable with available budget and required project life cycle/schedule. The perfect solution five years late and three times over budget is not the perfect solution. Since the acquisition strategy has not been developed, the presentation can suggest a contract vehicle, such as an IDIQ, and restrictions, such as a set-aside award for a class of small disadvantaged business. The suggestion obviously has to be to one's advantage, but it also has to be for the benefit of the government. If the government agency is below their goals in participation by a category of small business, and if the agency has a preferred contract vehicle, then such factors must be considered. The most important recommendations to make are discriminating language that can be used for the PWS/SOW/SOO and for the evaluation methodology. Such language, if adopted, gives one's solution competitive advantage in the proposal response and in the evaluation. As with other recommendations, the language must be clearly beneficial for the government in communicating desired solution paths and eliminating confusion among offerors. Such recommendations will create protest concerns for the government if one's solution is not the best for the government. So, the game is to be the best and then to sell/present the best.

The presentation format for this type of solution can be a whitepaper or a briefing. The whitepaper format works well as a standalone document for concisely explaining the solution, and the whitepaper can contain language usable in the acquisition strategy and PWS. A briefing format can be advantageous when helping government leaders argue for the solution as a part of their own strategy briefings. Either way, brevity and respect for the customer's position is critical to success.

5.3 Early Response Solutioning

Sometimes a government organization will express a solution need to all the companies that have gained their trust. This elite group has demonstrated capabilities and prior accomplishments in a way that the government believes one of them will be ideal for earning the contract for system or service. One earns this status not just by personal relationships but also by company relationships.

When receiving this type of awareness and ability to influence the government's acquisition strategy, the presentation can be less subtle than responding to awareness based on personal relationships. However, there is a field of competition, and our business development leader must figure out the terrain of competition. A key aspect of intelligence is whether one has been given slightly more or slightly less awareness than other selected companies. Rarely is the competition among equals, but even a slightly weaker position can be turned into victory if there is a chance to engage. This type of engagement must be done with the understanding that the government has not officially committed to the acquisition and that material provided to the government can give up some advantages even when it is marked as company proprietary. Thus, the response must match our gut feeling regarding whether the government truly views our company as a top contender. Then, the content of our response to the government must be shaped to both hide some competitive advantages until the formal proposal and to push the acquisition strategy toward one's advantage.

Because the government can be very serious about the solution at this point, we must be able to defend any material presented to the government. If the government wants to have follow-on meetings, our attendees must be able to provide more details. One does not have to and may not want to present the complete solution at this point. However, one must inspire confidence among government representatives.

The format for the presentation to the government can be a proprietary or publicly releasable whitepaper/briefing. A company capabilities package tailored for the needs of the customer and formatted leadership biographies should be available. The key to success, at this entry point, is not selling but inspiring confidence that we can solve the problem. The ability to influence comes when our company has risen above others in gaining confidence.

5.4 Procurement Influencing Solutioning

Market research is a required government activity when developing the acquisition strategy and preparing an RFP package. During the market research phase and particularly in response to an RFI, a company can formally influence the development of the acquisition strategy. At this stage in the process, if our company has had no prior opportunity to present a solution, the hard question of whether we should bid must be asked. We can assume that some other company has already been talking and presenting to government leaders. Even when hit by surprise with an RFI announcement, our business development leads can still try to gather more intelligence and even build relationships. Despite the formality of an RFI, informal engagements are not officially banded until the RFP is formally released.

The decision to bid or maintain the ability to bid at this stage should be based on (1) whether establishing a win theme is feasible, (2) what a winning team would look like, (3) availability of relevant contract past performance, and (4) whether the competition can be influenced in our favor. If the RFI is for a competition of existing work, we can try to find out whether the incumbent contractor has performed well, what is the value of the prior contract, and to what extend the scope and requirements of the new contract will remain the same as the prior contract. Even when the incumbent has performed well, government policies, such as making a competition a small business set aside when there are at least two qualifying small business companies, can force a large business incumbent into a poor position. If the incumbent consists of a large team, there may be subcontractors on that incumbent team who could be courted to our team.

Once a decision to respond to the market research has been made, the presentation should

- Follow the format of the RFI.
- Explain how we have the capability to meet schedule, reduce cost, lower procurement risk, and lower contract performance risk.
- Propose how the acquisition can be best done through a specific contracting mechanism.
- Propose limitations and constraints to isolate the best group of offerors.
- Include language that can be used in PWS/SOW/SOO which subtly favors our solution approach.
- Include language that can be used in Sections L and M that latently favors evaluation of our proposal.

What should not be in the presentation is our complete solution unless there is the possibility that the government will pursue a sole source contract award. Presenting too much at this point could cause the government to state details in the PWS that reduces our advantage. Even when the government is protecting proprietary information, ideas are hard to protect once revealed. In fact, some RFIs will specifically ask responders not to include proprietary information.

5.5 RFP Influencing Solutioning

Once the acquisition strategy has been established and the PWS/SOW/SOO has been drafted, an offeror's ability to change the strategic course of the source selection is very limited. The solution at that point must match the stated requirements and instructions. If the government asks for comments on the PWS/SOW/SOO, responses can still tactically shift the language of the RFP package and the evaluation methodology in one's favor. The firmness of the government requirements in the draft PWS/SOW/SOO will permit the formulation of a more detailed solution. This then allows us to understand exactly how to nudge the RFP language through comments to align with our solution that is saved for the formal proposal response.

At this stage of engagement, the decision to bid or not bid is generally finalized. Teaming arrangements are made through the efforts of capture managers and formalized with signed teaming agreements (TA). And, the competitive landscape is assessed. With the draft PWS/SOW/SOO, a formal solutions development process can be initiated based on the process of storyboarding. Instead of writing the proposal, storyboarding seeks to outline the main story of how we will support all the requirements in the PWS/SOW/SOO. If our solution has already been researched at the RFI stage, that solution needs to be refined given the new awareness. The important challenge at this point is safeguarding our solution while teaming discussions are occurring left and right.

At this stage, we also cannot become too attached to our solution because the final RFP released for the competition could be very different than draft documents. While potential offerors should not expect to change the government acquisition strategy, senior government leaders have been known to greatly change the acquisition strategy proposed by the program office during the approval process.

5.6 Solutioning to Win!

Ultimately, our solution in the proposal submitted in response to a formally released RFP is what matters, unless we are able to get a sole source (noncompetitive) award. Everything prior to the real competition was just to gain competitive advantage within the bounds of statutes, regulations, and policies. The process from the RFP release to the proposal submission due date is tightly controlled by the assigned proposal manager. From the perspective of the participating solutions developer, the proposal manager will provide the following:

- A writing template for the technical volume or section of the proposal.
- Section structures based on RFP Section L Instructions and Section M Evaluation Factor.
- Notes on content requirements based on a decomposition of the PWS/SOW/SOO.
- Notes on how the content will be evaluated in each proposal section.
- Solutioning considerations such as minimal technical acceptability at lowest cost or optimal trade-off between technical and cost.

The solutions development lead for the technical volume then needs to take ownership of both the solution and the volume itself. This means that if volume structure needs to be changed to fully express the solution, the solutions lead must work with the proposal manager to make the change. The proposal manager will endeavor to keep the content of all volumes compliant with the RFP. However, the solutions lead must develop a technical proposal that is both compliant and compelling. The solution must be designed to win and so the solutions lead must continue to work with the business development lead to understand who else might bid. The strategic position of competitors, their relationships with government, their technologies and processes, the level of incumbency experience in other proposals, and competitive cost models must all be considered in the solutioning strategy.

In this final solutioning to win endeavor, the proposal manager will coordinate activities based upon a schedule. If the Shipley proposal development method is used [1], the schedule will have due dates for Pink, Red, Gold, and Final Drafts of the proposal volumes. Each complete draft will be reviewed by others and refined for the next draft until the Final Draft is white-glove reviewed and submitted. As Figure 5.2 shows, the solutioning effort must be fully completed by the Gold Draft and the solution concept must be established in the Pink Draft. The purpose of the Pink Draft is not to debate the completeness of content, but to determine whether there is a winning path forward. Many believe that the content must be at least 60 percent presented in rough form in order for the right path to be even debated. The reviewer can recommend adjustments to the solution path or even major changes in direction. In some cases, this initial step into the proposal process might uncover

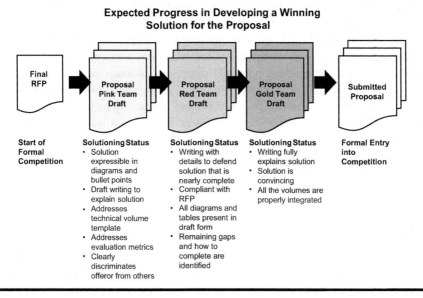

Figure 5.2   Integration of solutions development with proposal development.

enough issues that the decision to bid should be reversed. In most cases, however, the solution concept merely needs to be refined. While it is useful to have well-written content in the Pink Draft, the objective can be achieved if a solution can be diagrammed and described in bullets. The review should focus on whether the solution addresses the requirements and the evaluation factors and on whether the solution can beat the competition.

Based on Pink review recommendations, the Red Draft should present a complete solution that is compliant with the RFP, defended with capabilities and experience, and written to the intended evaluating audience. The diagrams and writing must be well-structured and close to page limits. This then allows for the determination of gaps in the proposal, such as additional diagrams, selling points, and defending information. If these gaps are not identified during the writing, they should be identified during the review of the Red Draft. The review of the Red Draft should help guide the authors to complete the solution in the Gold Draft. The Gold Draft is about making sure that every requirement is satisfied, and that the solution connects beginning to end. The solution should be challenged in developing the Gold Draft and efforts to evaluate the solution from the perspective of the government should be conducted to ensure that it will be well-received. While the authors of the technical, past performance, and cost volumes should be communicating with one another throughout the proposal process, the volumes should converge at the Gold Draft. Thus, reviewers must validate that technical, past performance, and cost presentations are consistent in the Gold Draft, and final trade-offs between cost and offered services and products should be done with recommended adjustments. Once the specific changes identified in the Gold Draft review has been addressed, the solutioning team should back down and let the proposal management team complete and submit.

Throughout this chapter, we have advocated the early evolvement of solutions development in engaging current and potential government customers. However, there are situations when the opportunity to present solutions exceeds a company's business relationships. For example, if one is a prime contractor for an IDIQ or BPA contract, the task orders from government organizations using the contract vehicle could overwhelm the ability of business development teams fully engaging government organizations. With a lack of complete situational awareness, we might still wish to bid by relying on pure solutions development capability. Regardless of how complex or simple the RFP is, all proposals must contain a solution. However, the solution does not have to contain technologies. Building a solution based on incomplete government customer awareness automatically has a low probability of win (P-Win). In fact, the lack of understanding might require one to wait for the final RFP to explore solution options because guessing at what the RFP might look like at the point of RFI release could be a waste of time. Even with a low P-Win, a business can operate based on careful selection of a substantial number of bids, rapid development of solutions, and sustained low percentage of wins. In this strategy of mass attack instead of precision strike, success depends on the solutioning team's capacity and selection of RFPs that will not waste capacity. Consistently winning 10 percent of all bids could sustain a business while letting the P-Win drop below 1 percent will mostly likely lead to exhaustion and defeat. Much of this text is devoted to crafting the best solution. What is the best, however, depends on the strategic position of each company and the specific circumstances for each bid.

Reference

1. Newman, L. 2011. *Shipley Proposal Guide,* 4th ed. Poolesville, MD: Shipley Associates.

Chapter 6

Learning from Tragic Outcomes for the Government

The history of federal acquisition has many success stories, and it is also littered with cancelled programs, terminated contracts, and systems plus services that failed to perform against expectations. While some programs have been cancelled due to political decisions and some contracts have been terminated for convenience, others are due to tragic failures in the government's requirements, source selection, or oversight processes. Most certainly the contractor will not be free from blame when money is spent without results, and some contractors can be legitimately accused of deceiving the government. However, if we are not the type of contractor who would consciously leverage false information in proposals and in contract reporting, then we must deeply understand how to avoid being drawn into the potential paths of tragic government failure as we develop solutions for proposals and implement solutions in contract performance.

At the end of the day, the one who makes the decisions is always accountable. In the case of determining what to acquire, selecting who will do the work, and whether the work is incrementally approved, the government is the owner of the process. Thus, this chapter is devoted to learning about the mistakes of government. When it comes to decisions on whether to bid and how to bid, our solutions presenters are accountable. Thus, the next chapter is devoted to learning about the mistakes of contractors/offerors. Out of respect for the government, this chapter will not use case studies, accuse government leaders, or expose specific faults. Instead, we will explore the conceptual framework of different types of mistakes.

This is done not so that we will immediately reject the idea of working on specific opportunities. That will be too trite an approach for companies desperate for government contracts. Instead, the goal in studying government mistakes should be to figure out through the solutioning process a strategy for knowing when to accept, when to fix, and when to run away through no-bidding. Companies have made great profits by pursuing high-risk contracts knowing that such contracts will most likely end in failure. Companies have also been heroes in rescuing government endeavors that are in deep trouble. And, companies have evaded great blows to their reputation and CPARS ratings by knowing when to leave the work and revenue behind. Let us explore some scenarios formulated through a combination of historical cases to see what lessons can be gained for those developing and implementing solutions.

6.1 Scenario: There Are Changes in the Mission and Requirements before the Completion of Development

In the 1940s, 1950s, and 1960s, system designs were led by visionary men with unique personal insight into how things need to work. Wernher von Braun as the leader of rocket design [1], J. Robert Oppenheimer as the leader of the Manhattan Project [2], and Admiral Hyman G. Rickover of the nuclear navy are among those who have personally driven programs to succeed [3]. Then, the growth of computing power enabled system designs to become more complex, and the incorporation of onboard computers for controlling systems demanded increasingly more lines of code. In this transition from individual insights to processes, models, and simulations, the nature of system acquisition programs began to shift. Program managers (PMs) with training in coordinating large teams, designing schedules, and managing costs took over. Work became more delegated tasks. Each system was then built as a result of collaboration, component integration, and successful management. Then, as great engineers and software developers are overshadowed by armies of average engineers and programmers, system designs and components became at times unnecessarily more complex and even sloppy. One can argue that this is an unavoidable reality of having modern computer-driven systems. However, the risk is that (1) program schedules can slip with the cause buried within thousands of interdependent tasks, and (2) program schedules are inherently so long that systems could become obsolete before completion of development.

Managing a program's schedule to the proposed baseline is the contractor's responsibility, but accepting a large multiyear schedule or even establishing requirements that demand a large multiyear schedule is the government's decision.

Today, we sometimes acquire systems that take more than a decade to build and deploy systems with an anticipated life of many decades. As the United States is using systems built decades past, this might be an acceptable acquisition lifecycle. This prolonged systems development process did not exist during the rapid technology advances of World War II and it was not acceptable during the rapid information technology advances of the 1990s and 2000s. A series of large development efforts that could not keep pace with technical advances led to a congressional mandate for completion of major automated information systems (MAIS) in less than five years as states in U.S. Code Chapter 144A of 2009 [4]. Even before then, the concepts of fielding rapid prototypes and building systems through usable increments had already been introduced in acquisition planning.

Despite such awareness of the dangers of prolonged development, the dangers of development becoming obsolete as mission and requirements change still lurks for every major program. Thus, before any company starts to develop solutions for government requirements, it should study the mission driving the requirements and the natural pattern of technology advances that enables the satisfaction of requirements. In doing so, the contractor may discover that the government's acquisition schedule is misaligned with projected technology advances. For example, if the acquisition is to be delayed a year or two, new technical breakthroughs and products would transform the capabilities of the system. The contractor may also discover that the government needs are based on domestic or global situations that will change soon. For example, a sudden shift in a political situation could lead user demand for the system to increase many folds. Knowing these potential outcomes that the government has not foreseen and captured in requirements, the contractor can find ways to

- Build flexibility into the development process beyond what is required.
- Convince the government to delay the acquisition until the risks and opportunities are better realized.
- Convince the government to change the requirements to allow for system evolution.
- Convince the government to adopt a stop solution.
- Design the system for new technologies and scope as value added for government.
- Conduct development based on government requirements and accept program cancellation or restructuring without accepting blame.

Then again, the contractor always has the option to not bid on inherently risky ventures. What is important as a lesson is that those who develop solutions cannot blindly follow. Effective solutions must take into account even the flaws in the government's understanding of need.

6.2 Scenario: The Requirements Are for the Last War

As a corollary to the conceptual framework above, the government's military requirements can be flawed from the beginning. Even before studying what new technologies might appear and what geopolitical situations might emerge, the requirements may simply be based on our understanding of how to fight the last war instead of the war occurring now. These requirements can be based on what we did right last time and what we did wrong. For example, if precision bombing caused a prior nation state adversary to yield, we might be convinced to only develop better precision bombs even though our current adversary has no infrastructure, key leaders, or heavy weapon bases to protect. Also for example, if our troops and their weapons faced difficulties in stopping the enemy in urban environments, our strategies and requirements might be pushed to avoid urban conflicts all together. This could be at the expense of allowing urban threats to grow. While these are only hypothetical scenarios, potential offerors on requirements for the development of future combat systems have a vested interest in studying the performance of those systems not in wars of the past but against today's and tomorrow's adversaries. This includes understanding how the adversaries will think and adapt to the deployment of our systems, such as applying improvised explosive devices (IEDs). Yet, even IEDs are now from the last war. A new billion-dollar weapon that can be countered by a new hundred-dollar technique and technology is a tragedy. If such vulnerabilities are discovered prior to development completion, the program will most likely be cancelled and if such vulnerabilities are discovered after deployment, lives can be lost.

So, when we are developing solutions for the battlefield, we should not focus on just meeting requirements but also on whether the solution can win current and further wars. We can get very attached to the capabilities of complex technologies. Instead, the solutions developer needs to assess the effectiveness of the capabilities in real scenarios. Real scenarios take into account how solutions can be defeated. In the case of software solutions, black hat assessments take on the role of attackers in discovering system vulnerabilities. For physical systems, war gaming simulations can test the outcomes of engagements. Even as we test for vulnerabilities, those who are executing these tests must be very careful to not place their preconceptions on the role of adversaries, overlook hidden patterns in real adversary behaviors, and underestimate the randomness of technical advancements.

So, the designer of a system based on requirements may come to realize that the system will be defeated in combat. At such a point, the company performing the work can keep on developing until the system is delivered with government acceptance consequences, introduce the system weakness results to the government with recognition that program cancellation is possible, or back away from the contract while letting the government come to their conclusions. Unlike situations where the requirements have changed, there is not much that can be done in fixing the solution when a set of requirements is wrong. It is hard for a contractor to say that the government should return to reevaluating needs and requirements, but this at times must be done.

6.3 Scenario: What Is Good for the Commercial World Is Good for the Government

The government is clearly still the primary buyer of weapon systems. In the case of IT systems and perhaps even for space systems, commercial markets have emerged over the years that equal and surpass the government market. Companies developing software for business and personal use have long been more innovative than companies developing software for government use. Thus, companies such as Apple, Microsoft, Google, Facebook, and Amazon did not grow based on studying requirements documents, preparing proposals, and having armies of lawyers and business developers. Instead, Silicon Valley companies live and die based on innovation. Their accomplishments became so immense that the government, in most cases, yielded to the idea that what works in the commercial world must work for government users. Leveraging COTS products became a government mantra and many commercial products have been used to satisfy government missions. Some can be used out of the box and others may require some customization to include configuration changes, additional code development, or database adjustments.

There has, however, been cases where the commercial product functionalities appear close enough for government needs, but the inflexibility of the application does not allow government requirements to be satisfied. In fact, the effort to leverage commercial products often increases even when disconnects appear small. Much resources have been spent working in futility on connecting products to requirements with hundreds of millions of dollars wasted. Commercial products must meet federal security standards, support disabled user access, perform against user groups of several million people, and have the correct functional features for government application. Security, disability access, and user community size are non-negotiable metrics. This leaves application functionalities and functional requirements as the two ends where flexibility can enable convergence.

As solutions developers, we might encounter situations where the government wants to use COTS products but did not affirm that either the requirements or the COTS functionalities are flexible enough to sustain the utilization. Flexibility in the application can be seen in (1) how much of the functionalities can be configured by the users, (2) whether third-party components can integrate into a modular architecture, (3) to what degree custom codes can be added to the application, and (4) to what degree the database can be realigned. Flexibility in the requirements can be seen in (1) the user community's willingness to adjust to new workflows, (2) the leadership's willingness to accept different metrics, and (3) the flexibility of dependent systems. The recognition of flexibility as being more important than how well the functionalities and requirements are initially aligned is critical for the solutions developer. Even when the application and requirements are well aligned in the beginning, this alignment will eventually break apart if both sides are completely rigid. This is because a COTS product is advanced for the commercial market, and every new release could break their connection with federal requirements unless the federal market is considered in product upgrades. This is also because the government does not have much control over commercial IT developers and any change in the government's mission could cause the application to misalign. The lesson learned is that when a solutions developer is facing a situation where the required application technology and the required functionalities and features are all completely rigid, he or she might be better served to walk away.

6.4 Scenario: We Can Do It Better, Faster, Cheaper

The National Air and Space Administration (NASA) confronted reduced funding in the 1990s while still desiring to maintain a broad collection of programs for space exploration. Thus, NASA Administrator Daniel Goldin presented the concept of *better, faster, cheaper* [5]. When a series of four out of six unmanned missions to Mars failed, this concept became controversial. The concept of better, faster, and cheaper comes from each program officer's ability to control performance, schedule, and cost. So, why not seek to increase performance, shorten schedules, and reduce costs? The dilemma with this strategy from the government is that it will work only if a systems acquisition program has been poorly designed and managed. Thus, efficiencies can be gained through management and technical correction. If a systems acquisition program is being competently executed, then attempts at increasing performance, shortening schedule, and lowering cost all at once could destabilize the program and place all tasks at risk.

Despite the controversy with NASA, the demand for transformational solutions where the outcomes must be better, faster, and cheaper might still appear in government acquisitions. When confronted with this demand, the solutions developer must find a pivot point. In other words, for programs that have been relatively well managed, squeezing more from performance, schedule, and cost will require a firm position to apply additional force. Without that firm point for us to get the right footing to apply force, pushing one set of metrics forward can cause other metrics to slide backwards. If force can be applied, even the best-managed programs might have more to give. For example, the solution may be to first compress the schedule and then use the revised schedule as the anchor. Then, performance-increasing strategies can be implemented within the task structures of the schedule and cost reductions can be implemented in the task structures. In doing so, from the greatest level of schedule detail, the schedule tasks can tell us whether we have gone too far. The savings might be a little everywhere, but such is better than pushing the program to the point of instability without realization.

6.5 Scenario: The Government Wants the Cheapest

Unlike the idea of better, faster, and cheaper, the concept of just wanting all contracts to be of the lowest price has been a movement in federal acquisitions ever since the Great Recession of 2008 [6] and the withdrawal of troops from Iraq (2009 to 2011) [7]. From 2011 to the present, the DoD has issued a vast portion of its RFPs for services based on the evaluation approach of LPTA awards. Through the LPTA process, inflated prices for contractor staff achieved during the war years were eliminated and staff of lesser capabilities were placed into a variety of key positions. Since most contractors have structured their labor categories to allow for great variabilities in quality, the strategy to win LPTA competitions is literally to operate at the lower limits of staff acceptability and the offerors may yet have to sacrifice profit and reduce overhead to be competitive. If the labor category calls for a college graduate, everyone is racing to find the colleges with the lowest post-graduation employment success. If the labor category calls for years of experience, everyone is trying to figure out how to align the experience of the most junior candidates.

Ironically, LPTA RFPs can still provide government organizations with the highest-caliber staff if the program office established the acquisition strategy correctly. For the lowest price, the government can ask for quality and not quantity by raising the standards for technical acceptability. If a solutions developer is confronted with a situation where the government has not raised the standards so that an effective team can be formed to complete the tasks, then the decision is to (1) design the best team/solution within the limits of the lowest price and assume the risk of the team not being good enough to perform, (2) design the team that can perform regardless of price and absorb the additional cost as lost overhead so that proposal price is still low, or (3) walk away from the bid. Hiring lower-quality staff will immediately degrade companies. Cutting back on overhead expenses, such as employee benefits, office space, and support staff, will degrade companies slower. Finally, giving up on LPTA work could lead to unacceptable loss of revenues. None of these are good options. So, perhaps the decision should be based on a path where companies can most easily recover when LPTA is no longer a driving force in government contracting.

6.6 Scenario: The Government Can Develop Information Technology Solutions

In the early to middle 2000s, the network infrastructure of the United States started to go through explosive growth. As a result, all manner of applications are suddenly able to be centrally hosted and accessed over networks. These enterprise solutions instilled some government organizations with great ambition. Complex requirements for massive systems that must support millions of users were established.

Then, the federal contractor community responded to these requirements. While some enterprise systems where successfully developed and deployed, others ran into developmental or operational difficulties. The problems included the following:

- Shifting requirements that caused the need to rework developed components.
- Excessive integration across many system components.
- Development cycles that did not allow for learning and process correction.
- Too many parallel development efforts with flawed coordination.
- Sloppy coding that was bulky and hard to audit.
- Lack of modularity that enables component level changes.
- Complex data structures that were easily corrupted.
- Poorly designed user interfaces that did not take into account the user experience.

The history of government-funded software development efforts continues to remain one of successes and major program failures. Even now, every contract for software development is filled with risks. The offering company and solution architects can determine the correct technology stack, quality of developers needed, processes for executing Agile development, and the testing methodology. Yet, the contractor cannot prevent government stakeholders from continuously changing requirements (user stories) because it is allowed in Agile, applying rigid requirements and oversight to hinder Agile development, demanding overwhelming levels of documentation, and funding developers at below commercial market rates. When a contractor sees such risks with an opportunity, it can (1) appease the government managers until the development is too far along to be cancelled despite delays and cost increases, (2) establish mechanisms in the proposal and contract that reduce risks, (3) find ways to pad the schedule and cost to account for risks, or (4) walk away from the risky opportunity. There are times when the risk of damage to a company's reputation due to program failure outweighs the short-term financial benefits.

6.7 Scenario: The Government Cannot Develop Information Technology Solutions

Fear of costly failures in government software development has caused some government organizations to delay IT modernization. Instead, contracts are issued to maintain software developed as early as the 1980s. Contractors are required to find staff who are still familiar with obsolete technologies and software development languages. Then, old and inefficient software are continuously patched up and kept running. As more system and database structural understanding are lost due to retiring and departing personnel, the sustainment effort becomes more challenging. As database structures are corrupted over time, avoiding the impact of data error becomes more challenging. Sustaining obsolete systems, therefore, cannot last forever, but the work can be very lucrative if one has the expertise.

The attractiveness of endlessly collecting money with one's team of old-generation technology experts can be a trap when the government realizes that IT modernization is unavoidable. At that point, the legacy system sustainment contractor could also be viewed as obsolete. The one strategy that the contractor can adopt is to leverage its knowledge of legacy data and how it must be migrated into the next-generation system. Had the contractor been the one pushing for modernization, then it might be in a better position to win the IT modernization contract. The willingness to risk current work for a better probability of winning future work is a difficult decision when the government is hesitant of IT development.

6.8 Scenario: The Government Has Too Little Money to Spend

In the financially constrained environment after 2008, there is often too little money for the mission needs of government organizations. The correct response is to scale back needs to match the availability of funds, and many contracts have indeed been cancelled or down-scoped because of fiscal realities. However, organizations once and a while cannot let go of their full mission needs and have thus issued RFPs where the PWS/SOW/SOO is completely misaligned with the government estimation on level of effort (LOE). This places potential offerors in a difficult position. One strategy is to over promise in the proposal and hope for the opportunity to renegotiate the LOE after contract award. This strategy has at times worked if initial performance is exceptional and the government has additional funds. Another strategy is to write the proposal with enough flexibility and vagueness in select areas so that one can offer less in the actual work. This strategy will most likely be defeated by the proposal that very specifically offers more details. Yet another strategy is to innovate enough to achieve government mission objectives but not necessarily to meet all incremental performance metrics. If the PWS is very specific about the solution path that the contractor must take, presenting a different solution path that affordably reaches the same endpoint could nevertheless be found to be noncompliant in the proposal evaluation process. Finally, the potential offeror can either decide to no-bid or protest the RFP. The protest will be stronger if the contractor had explained the non-feasibility of the solution given available funding in its response to the draft PWS released for comments. All of these options are better than accepting the government's misperception and failing in contract performance.

6.9 Scenario: The Government Has Too Much Money to Spend

During the 1980s when the Cold War arms race was at its peak, excessive amounts of funding were being appropriated for programs such as those in the Strategic

Defense Initiative (SDI) [8]. The funding increased so rapidly that engineers and scientists were challenged in coming up with ideas for advanced technology systems. While the system concepts of SDI drove the Soviet Union to match military spending and eventually collapse, very few of the concepts eventually became operational systems. During the Iraq War and the war in Afghanistan, excessive amounts of funding were appropriated for contracts that support combat operations [9]. The funding increased so rapidly that companies were looking for anyone who was willing to go to Iraq or Afghanistan as private contractors. Both these two periods of excessive funding and spending cannot be considered tragic outcomes. However, there were great inefficiencies that contributed to the national debt.

For companies experiencing such periods of growth opportunities, the temptation is to cast real solutions development aside and just focus on catching as much funding as possible. As a result, companies will grow but their capabilities might diminish. When the period of excessive funding ends and cuts must be made, companies might discover that they have failed to create real experts and build real intellectual property over the past years. This tragic outcome is amplified when companies further decide to cut staff in groups based on contract loss without considering individual capabilities to retain. Long-term sustainable capabilities and expertise should govern company priorities during good and bad years.

6.10 Scenario: It Is All Politics

Periodically, a program will emerge that is strictly aligned with the political position of either the Republican or Democratic parties of the United States. This usually occurs when one party both controls the presidency and has the majority in Congress. As a result, the mission need and requirements are not refined through party compromises and may even present extreme positions. In such a case, the program has until the opposing party wins the presidency and Congress to demonstrate its worth. Otherwise, the program will be quickly cancelled.

Companies confronted with the opportunity to win such a program can (1) design the solution to appeal to both parties even though one party is driving the funding, (2) accelerate the development and implementation schedule so that the program has demonstrated results before an election, (3) create enough flexibility so that the opposing party can restructure the program instead of cancelling it, or (4) create enough funding cushion so that the program can still survive under heavy budget cuts. Companies that are pursuing or working on heavily politized programs might consider the employment of lobbyists. While lobbyists can no longer help in acquiring earmarked funds, they can help present a contractor's solution in such a bipartisan way that it becomes the national solution.

References

1. Ward, B. 2009. *Dr. Space: The Life of Wernher von Braun.* Annapolis, MD: Naval Institute Press.
2. Bird, K. and Sherwin, M.J. 2006. *American Prometheus: The Triumph and Tragedy of J. Robert Oppenheimer.* New York: Vintage Books.
3. Duncan, F. 1989. *Rickover and the Nuclear Navy: The Discipline of Technology.* Annapolis, MD: Naval Institute Press.
4. Ren, C., Busch, S. and Prebble, M. 2010. Improving the initiation of acquisition activities for automated information systems. *Defense Acquisition Review Journal,* Defense Acquisition University. Vol. 17, No. 4 (October): pp. 420–435.
5. Murman, E.M., Walton, M. and Rebentisch, E. 2000. Challenges in the better, faster, cheaper era of aeronautical design, engineering and manufacturing. *The Aeronautical Journal.* Vol. 104, No. 1040: pp. 481–489.
6. Grusky, D.B., Western, B., and Wimer, C. (Eds.) 2011. *The Great Recession.* New York: Russell Sage Foundation.
7. Sky, E. 2011. Iraq, From Surge to Sovereignty: Winding Down the War in Iraq. *Foreign Affairs.* Vol. 90, No. 2 (March/April): pp. 117–127.
8. Reiss, E. 1992. The Strategic Defense Initiative (Cambridge Studies in International Relations). Cambridge, UK: Cambridge University Press.
9. Bacevich, A.J. 2017. *America's War for the Greater Middle East: A Military History.* New York, NY: Random House Trade Paperbacks.

Chapter 7

Learning from Tragic Outcomes for the Contractor

The previous chapter focused on the dangerous decisions and misperceptions of government and how a contractor can avoid being drawn into tragic outcomes. Many tragic outcomes are, however, of the contractor's own doing. So, we need to also understand how to avoid our own misperceptions, poor judgment, and self-aggrandizement. The following are examples of mental traps in the solutions development process. Despite how obvious these traps appear, business development activities and solutions development efforts continue to be crushed by their inescapability.

7.1 Scenario: The Government Needs Our Perfect Widget vs. We Can Resolve the Government's Pains

The first lesson of business development is to sell to the customers' pain points instead of trying to increase their desires [1]. Yet, companies continuously fall in love with their products and lose objectivity regarding what pains potential customers. Instead, they blindly devote more resources to refining and selling products based on their individual vision for what government organizations want. Government organizations will at times appear as if their needs are based on desires for the best capability, but that is an illusion. Instead, the number-one pain point for all government officials is risk. In a federal employment system that has salary limits and rewards longevity, the way to advance as a government official is to avoid failures. The way to avoid failures is to do what is expected and not necessarily what will achieve the greatest success. At the strategic level, doing what is expected includes:

- Aligning one's decisions to higher strategic visions and priorities. For example, the White House National Security Strategy drives DoD Joint Staff vision statement, which drives service requirements.
- Adopting commercial industry standard processes. For example, if top companies are doing Agile development, then the government should be doing Agile development.
- Buying market-leading commercial products. Applications used by millions of public consumers must be good for government users.
- Selecting brand-name companies. If the biggest company has failed in a high-risk program, then it cannot be the government's fault.
- Selecting a disadvantaged small business. If the decision is based on satisfying a small business participation policy or statute, then any failures are in part due to the policy or statute.

Within the strategic framework of risk avoidance, government organizations then procure products based on requirements. The requirements must be based on tangible benefits to users, and the federal user communities are more monolithic than commercial entities. Federal workflows are often less adaptive to new solutions, and user dissatisfaction can spread quite rapidly across an office environment.

A product that succeeds with the government and most satisfies the government decision-makers needs to avoid or at least control risks. Then, the product must be part of a solution that resolves a problem or potential problem in the government's operational state. This means that unless the selling company understands different government user community workflows and how those workflows can be advanced with the product, their chance of success in proposals is low regardless of how beautiful, powerful, and functional the product is.

7.2 Scenario: Our Solution at the Wrong Time or with the Wrong Cost

The availability of government funding is based on different cycles as discussed in Chapter 4, and there are few solutions great enough to bend the cycles and political realities of funding. If the funding need requires congressional appropriations and the President's budget has already been submitted to Congress, the solution will require massive levels of lobbying in order to have a chance at getting Congress to add funding guidance to the appropriations bill. Even with added funding, the prohibition on earmarks means that the receiving government organization must still conduct a competitive procurement process to award the funds. If the solution is against the current political realities, such as downsizing the defense infrastructure or ending environmental protection projects, then getting initial funding and even retaining funding commitments is a nearly impossible battle.

If one has a solution that gains the interest of a government organization and user community, that solution must still make its way through the complex environment of funding and political support. The cost and distribution of funding requirements must align with sources of funding. The nature of the solution must either align with current political realities or avoid political debates. Thus, there are great programs that began as small projects and some projects that are kept alive at levels that do not attract political attention during the years when political priorities are not aligned. If a company truly believes that its solution is to the benefit of the people, then it must find its way through the maze of appropriate timing and cost structures.

7.3 Scenario: We Have a Solution When the Government Does Not Care

There are situations where targeted government organizations do not want our solutions even when our solutions are clearly needed. A user community can become completely attached to the current systems, business processes, or support staff. A decision-maker can be absolutely confident in his or her preference of another solution. A government organization can be committed to a near-term cost-minimizing strategy. In all these cases, the government's position may not be best for the government and operational states can eventually go into decline or hit major problems. However, if the government refuses to see the emerging problems or does not care, there are times when the contractor is completely powerless. Pushing against a hopeless situation may just annoy the government and the better strategy might have to wait until government operations fail.

Even when a government organization must conduct a source selection to award to a preferred contractor and continue incumbent/trusted provider activities, that source selection package can be filled with signals that it is intended for a specific company. These signals include the following:

■ A very short solicitation response time.
■ RFP key personnel requirements that have a very extensive list of specific qualifications.
■ RFP technical requirements that can only be addressed by detailed incumbency or product-specific knowledge.
■ RFP technical page count that is so high that only companies with advanced preparation can complete it.
■ RFP technical page count that is so low that only companies who know the exact evaluation methodology can get it right.

- RFP guidance on demonstrating past performance relevancy that heavily favors incumbent work.
- RFP evaluation methodology completely hidden in Section M.

These signals individually do not always suggest that the RFP is "wired" for a specific company; an issuing government organization might simply be sloppy. Further, the government organization and its contracting office must still stay minimally compliant with Federal Acquisition Regulations. Nevertheless, the attempt to present a performance solution when the government does not care may be a futile battle. If our company wants to still bid and try for a low probability of win opportunity, then the solution must focus on leveraging government and opponent mistakes in the RFP and the response process. The unfairness of the draft RFP can be challenged through questions and comments. The unfairness of the RFP can be challenged through protests. In the response, the technical proposal can focus on how the axiomatic winner might get sloppy and noncompliant as well as how our cost proposal can be so acceptably low that the evaluators will take notice. The game in fighting for that 10 to 20 percent probability of win is to convince government evaluators that the preferred winner is not worth the risk of protest or even a violation of the Acquisition Integrity Act.

7.4 Scenario: We Will Recycle a Solution but Not Tailor It for the New Customer

Companies that submit many proposals can get sloppy in their processes. With every new RFP, they find related content in past proposals, glue it together, and then submit. If the content is not reworked to align with the PWS/SOW/SOO and if no energy is invested in understanding each potential customer's operations, then the proposal will be evaluated poorly. A solution can be advanced to support new customers, but a solution cannot be simply recycled unless government organizations and government requirements are nearly identical. The ultimate level of sloppiness is leaving references to the prior government organization in a proposal to a new government organization. Companies have also left in references to previous team members who are not on the current team.

At the very least, all proposals must go through a full RFP compliance review and copy edit. Even so, the win theme is hoping that other offerors are sloppier in their proposals. To truly present a solution, each proposal must show the government how our team, processes, and technologies will take the government from the current operational state to an objective operational state that aligns with the PWS/SOW/SOO and how this is of clear benefit (best value) for the issuing government organization. With this said, there are no simple proposals if one wants to win. There are efficiencies that can be gained with a company that wants to bid on many proposals because of similarities in government needs. However, more bidding means more work. The work can be relaxed a little if the probability of win is low, but this relaxation cannot further lower the probability of win.

The ultimate arrogance in recycling a proposal is blindly using our prior proposal from years ago to support a recompetition for our own incumbent work. Even when the PWS is identical to the prior PWS, our new proposal response must note our accomplishments, lessons learned, and innovations achieved over the course of the current contract. It is the belief that we cannot lose that opens the door for competing offerors. In fact, all incumbents should take a hard look at why they are irreplaceable when developing the solutions for recompetitions. One's staff can be stolen with competitors' conditional offeror letters, one's government-owned knowledge base will go to any winning offeror, and even the products one developed belong to the government if they paid for development. The only way we can achieve true leverage is to own government-needed intellectual propriety for which there are no good commercial alternatives. Microsoft, with its Office product suite, can make such a claim, but few other companies can. So, do not be arrogant and focus on the customer in all bids.

7.5 Scenario: We Will Agree to Meet Government Needs and Sell It as a Solution

As discussed in Chapter 2, repeating back to the government evaluator what is written in the PWS is not a solution. If the PWS is so detailed that it charts a solution path, our written commitment that we will do what is in the PWS only tells the government evaluators that we love their vision of a solution. There are situations where the government just wants to hear an affirmation of their tasks and approach, but those situations typically lead to price-only competitions (price shoot out) where solutions are unfortunately unimportant. More and more, the government is adding language to RFPs to specifically state that proposals should not be a repeat of the PWS language.

To overcome the tendency to repeat detailed PWS content, the solutions developer can summarize each PWS bullet and then ask the question of how it should be done. Even with highly detailed PWS bullets, there is typically still a level of execution detail that can be expressed in the proposal. When the PWS language vastly exceeds the page limit of the technical proposal, the solutioning effort must integrate PWS tasks into combined workflow descriptions and address how these workflows for different PWS sections can be innovatively accomplished. It is only by working with and decomposing the content of the PWS that proposal writers can truly begin to understand what government organizations want. SOWs and SOOs inherently do not contain government understanding of how to perform tasks. Therefore, RFPs with SOWs and SOOs compel the offerors to think about technical approaches and solutions. If an offeror still repeats RFP content back in the proposal, then the proposal effort or lack of effort is completely wasted. Starting the proposal process with a solutioning-driven story board exercise will help prevent massive amounts of writing without original content.

7.6 Scenario: We Will Present Past Performance and Let You Assume That We Have the Solution

A company's past performance could add significant confidence regarding the company's ability to perform all the tasks specified in the RFP. The past performance evaluation is specifically designed to establish relevancy of the proposed past performance exhibits to the RFP and validate that quality of past performance. However, the past performance exhibits do not represent solutions in the technical proposal. If the technical proposal simply asserts that a company has applied effective solutions on similar contracts in the past, then it is asking the government to evaluate based on trust. If the evaluators personally know the referenced past activities, then trust might work. However, trust that a solution exists is not the same as presenting a solution.

Solutions from past contracts can be used to build the solution in the technical proposal. But, that is a mapping of the past conditions to the conditions needing a solution stated in the RFP. The key question is, how are the starting operational states and the objective operational states between past government organizations and the government organization in RFP different? This helps the solutions developer adjust past solutions to meet the current need. Unfortunately, a solutions developer may find that a past solution has not been documented because past proposals did not win based on solutions. The performance of work on past contracts must have solutions, but those solutions could merely exist in the minds of those performing the tasks. The solutions developer must therefore at times go the extra mile and learn from people working on existing contracts to pull out current processes, technologies used, and architectures. These demonstrated capabilities can then be further innovated into true winning solutions. This is far different than saying we have done it before, so trust us.

7.7 Scenario: Our Solution Has Gaps and We Will Talk Really Fast through Those Gaps

Sometimes we do not really have a complete solution, but the attractiveness of the RFP compels us to bid. So, we bid by being vague in areas and hoping that the evaluators will not notice. We might even try to make exaggerated assertions to bridge the gaps in our solutions. The rationale is that the gaps can be resolved after we are awarded the contract. This strategy has at times worked and at times resulted in contract performance failures. Because of the risk associated with overstated claims in proposals, some government organizations are adding actual capability demonstrations as a part of the source selection process.

The alternative to arm-waving around gaps in the solution is to recognize the gaps as post-award work and to describe in detail how our winning team will bridge these gaps as a part of contract performance. By establishing a process for filling the gaps, we will be presenting a complete solution. The solution will have risks because of the gaps. However, recognizing these risks is better than hoping that technical evaluators can be fooled. If other offerors are struggling with the same solution gaps, our mature response to the gaps could actually provide a competitive advantage. If we cannot even formulate a process for resolving the gaps after contract award, a no-bid decision should be seriously considered.

7.8 Scenario: We Will Give the Government a Solution That We Do Not Really Believe In

The solutions developer must believe in his or her solution. Otherwise, the disbelief will be hard to hide in the writing. Words that hedge the possibility of us being wrong will slip into the writing, convincing arguments will be missing, and overcompensating language will be used to disguise our uncertainty. The first mission of any solutions developer is, therefore, to sell the solution to oneself. The solution must be worked and reworked until we believe in its effectiveness. We do not have to know all the details of the solution and, as noted above, we can have processes to resolve solution gaps. What we cannot do is go through the motions of applying a process, technology, architecture, or staff based on leadership direction.

The mission of solutions development is to achieve an effective solution and not to appease leadership. If the preferred process, technology, architecture, or staff must be changed to make the solution believable, then the argument must be made. If no real solution can be formulated, then the technical proposal is better written by people from sales. Before this conclusion, the solutions developer must be absolutely sure that the lack of an achievable solution is due to the position of the company relative to the RFP and not due to the lack of capability on the part of the solutions developer or a lack of business intelligence. Proposal development is a team effort and personal ego as a cause of poor solutioning also cannot be a part of the proposal process.

7.9 Scenario: We Have a Bold Solution That We Are Afraid to Show the Government

Foolishness is not a good quality in deciding when to bid and how to bid on government RFPs, but lack of courage in seizing opportunities can also cause a company's downfall. There may be times when our solution is so different and against conventional views that we are afraid that its presentation will damage our company's reputation. There may be other times when our solution is so complex that we think that it is never done. So, we keep working on the solution and miss all the opportunities to present it. We must recognize that timelines are a part of solutions. The timelines for presentation and execution are as important as the processes, technologies, architectures, and staff proposed in the solution. Therefore, when the time is right, the solution must be presented or it weakens. The time is right when an opportunity to apply the solution exists, when the solution is clear enough to justify funding, and when waiting longer will decrease our opportunity to gain funding.

When our solution is unconventional, we must objectively weigh the risks and benefits. In most cases, a rejection by the government will not have any lasting adverse impact if we have clearly presented the solution in the context of advancing the government's operational state. If the government decision-makers are visionaries, then the implementation of an innovative and perhaps revolutionary solution could transform the company. When our solution is complex, the challenge is to both unravel the complexity and to express the solution in simple conceptual frameworks. Not all the complexity has to be unraveled in order for the solution to be conceptually explained. Thus, once the conceptual explanation has been established, we should present it.

Finally, when the opportunity to get funding is rare and momentary, we must present our solution no matter its level of maturity. This presentation will require high confidence and a belief that the solution will work. Sometimes, if our solution is still at a very high and conceptual level, we must trust the capabilities of our people to complete and implement the solution. When the time is right, we just need to make the pitch.

7.10 Scenario: We Debate Our Solution and Are Late in Presenting

Occasionally, a company might have internal disagreements on what the solution should be. Different solutions developers working on an opportunity might generate competing concepts. In large companies with various products, divisions might fight over which product is best suited for a customer. Internal debate and competition done professionally is healthy for a company. However, the debate and competition cannot interfere with the timing and commitment for capturing opportunities. Thus, business development and the development of proposals should involve company leaders. Collaboration is great. A leader must, however, step in and make the critical decision when an opportunity has a deadline.

Once a decision has been made, the entire company must rally together and support the way ahead. For companies that have not experienced this level of challenge, the first time could be a traumatic experience. Unprepared companies can be fighting about proposal content down to the last minute with sloppy and confusing results. Without an accepted decision, different groups from the same company might approach the same potential customer with conflicting options. To prevent these tragic outcomes, the processes and chain of command for business and proposal development must be established and validated. The best way to validate our ability to come together as one company and team is to bid, make mistakes, learn from the mistakes, and bid more.

7.11 Scenario: We Let Some Other Company Steal Our Solution

Written content can be copyrighted. New processes and inventions can be patented. However, ideas are incredibly hard to protect. As Apple could not stop Microsoft from copying its concept of a graphical user interface through a 1994 lawsuit [2], there is little hope for other companies in legally protecting ideas that are not patented. The only real way to protect ideas is to prevent it from leaving the company. Employees and subcontractors can be asked to sign nondisclosure agreements (NDAs). However, if they express the ideas in their own words without handing proprietary documents to other companies, there is not much that can be done. Thus, the best protection is employee and team member loyalty as well as strict procedures for handling proprietary information.

The technical solution and pricing structure for a current competition can immediately cause one to lose if they are stolen by competitors. Therefore, key employees who have been recruited by competitors and team members who are cross-teamed with competing companies are real concerns. If a company's solution is so unique that it offers continuing competitive advantage, then that solution must be protected during competition after competition. Yet, that solution will still most likely be copied over time. Therefore, the strongest position for a company is to have the capability to continuously develop innovative solutions and the capability to protect those new solutions long enough so that they can be formally presented to the government buyers.

As we keep to heart the approaches for handling the risk of tragic outcomes posed by government decisions and the potential pitfalls in our own decisions regarding RFPs, we are ready to tackle solutioning challenges.

References

1. Suster, M. 2013. How to identify client pain points. Inc.com (June 17).
2. Myers, J. 1995. *Apple v. Microsoft*: Virtual identity in the GUI wars, *Richmond Journal of Law & Technology*, 1, 1/8.

Chapter 8

Analyzing the Problem or Opportunity

All the chapters prior to this point serve to help us prepare for the main event, which is to present an understanding of the government's problem or opportunity as defined by pain points and to present the best solution based on the government's evaluation metrics. We have explored the ways to influence the emergence of the main event, approaches for preparing the solution concepts prior to the main event, and techniques for avoiding tragic outcomes during the main event. Once we have done all we can to prepare for the win, we must develop the solution with the highest probability of win given our competitive situation. No solution is a guaranteed win when a competitive RFP is released. A bad solution, however, can cause a loss even when one is the incumbent offeror, when the customer has shaped the RFP to favor one's capabilities, and when one has all the knowledge of customer processes. Let us now study the art of creating solutions that meet or exceed our objective probabilities of win. If a competitive situation only allows for a 20 percent probability of winning, then our solutions development across multiple endeavors must reflect a 20 percent or greater probability of winning. If we have done our preparations correctly and have not lied to ourselves as in the scenarios presented, then our understanding of the P-Win should be fairly realistic as long as we keep it within the scale of 20, 40, 60, and 80 percent. It is better to be accurate in predicting P-Win over the course of many government RFP responses than to randomly hit major successes. This is because major successes that occur randomly make it hard for businesses to plan long-term growth.

Once the RFP is released and the main event starts, the proposal manager will focus on how to create a compliant response and the solutions developer/architect should begin by thinking about how to present the solution against the government customer's official statement of the solution requirements. This is typically the PWS, SOW, or SOO in Section C of the RFP package, the instructions in Section L, and the evaluation factors in Section M. No matter how much we are taught to follow standard proposal formats, the format for each proposal must serve the solution to be presented. The simplest format is when the evaluation factors and subfactors align one to one with the sections or tasks in the PWS as shown in Figure 8.1. Then, the proposal format should simply be based on evaluation factors and subfactors with the solution addressing the PWS. When a SOW or SOO is general enough that specific tasks are not well-defined in the RFP, then the proposal format should try to follow the evaluation factors.

The proposal format requires more thought when multiple PWS tasks all respond to a single evaluation factor/subfactor or when a single PWS task responds to several evaluation factors/subfactors. In such cases, also as shown in Figure 8.1, we must debate whether the PWS or the evaluation factors/subfactors offer a more logical structure for the solution. There are situations where it makes more sense to address the evaluation factors/subfactors as a part of another more logical structure if such is permitted by the instructions. It is important to check the compliance boxes and make it easy for the evaluators to validate compliance. However, the proposal must also embody an integrated solution. If the proposal format does not make sense for the solution, then the format must be changed.

Once we have determined a format, the next step is to study the requirements as reflected in the RFP or associated documents. Based on the current government operational state workflow and the requirements, we need to figure out what the solution should accomplish and what should be the objective state operational process as well as workflows through the process. The objective state is what the solution must accomplish through a combination of advancements in processes, system architectures, new technologies, and human capability enhancements. This state must clearly respond to

	PWS Task 1	PWS Task 2	PWS Task 3	PWS Task 4
Eval Factor 1	●			
Eval Factor 2		●		
Eval Factor 3			●	
Eval Factor 4				●

	PWS Task 1	PWS Task 2	PWS Task 3	PWS Task 4
Eval Factor 1	●			
Eval Factor 2	●	●	●	
Eval Factor 3			●	
Eval Factor 4			●	●

One to One Alignment between Evaluation Factors / Subfactors and Tasks

Varying Weight in Evaluation Factors / Subfactors Based on Tasks

Figure 8.1   Alignment between evaluation factors and the PWS.

the evaluation factors/subfactors and the PWS/SOW/SOO. This state must be clearly better than the original state in a beneficial way to government staff and external stakeholders. Finally, the objective state must be achievable through the allowed schedule and budget. Therefore, it will often make sense to start with a possible objective state that is refined through the solutioning process. The solution must be believable, but the results of the solution must first be the best way to resolve government pain points.

While most solutions will have a technology component even when the development of technologies is not required, some service contracts may require only an effective process and staffing solution. Process is always a part of the solution and staff is always a part of the solution unless the contract merely calls for the delivery of material goods. Even in the delivery of material goods, such as selling commercial laptop computers to the government, there are processes for ordering, shipping, tracking, receipt, billing, and so on. This simple series of processes/procedures can still be refined to reduce the number of steps, increase situational awareness, accelerate the completion of each task, decrease errors, and eliminate risks. If the solution is for the sustainment of current activities, then workflow and staffing changes might not be desirable. However, even a stable workflow can go through process enhancements at the procedural level. Slight improvements in the procedures for performing set tasks can lead to significantly better performance outcome. Equally, improvements in training of the current staff can also lead to better performance. Thus, process understanding is always critical to solutions development.

Conceptually, as represented in Figure 8.2, a process must have an entry point for users which may be controlled through a mechanism of checking user identity and

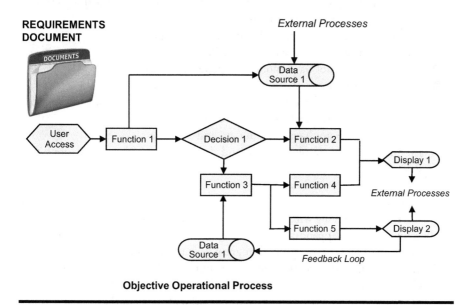

Figure 8.2 Understanding the purpose of the solution.

granting access based on the privileges assigned to the user during account setup. Then, the process will have functions that support actions to satisfy requirements or actions to enable other actions satisfying requirements. Some actions within functions constitute decision points in the workflow, and some actions within functions will require data sources. Data sources can be from external processes or one's own process with collected data on completed activities. Functions later in one's own process can also generate data for a feedback loop to support earlier functions and decisions that must be repeated. Finally, while all the functions can produce output products and effects, there comes a point where the accomplishments of the process should be displayed. This display can be reports, presentation of end products, new data sets, or a variety of new products for the government organization. At such a point, the process can end, feed into greater processes, or repeat itself to serve new users or changing current user needs.

Beyond being obvious about how our objective process in the solution will solve all pains, we must also be able to demonstrate that all the requirements and tasks in the PWS/SOW/SOO can be accomplished through specific functions and workflows across the process. Chapter 9 will discuss approaches for process design that enable the creation of the most optimal and continuous processes. Common challenges in the current state process could include the following:

- Too many separate processes to handle different workflows.
- The processes are only partially automated with many segments that require manual activities.
- The data in the processes are not all computable, such as scanned images and written notes that require human interpretation.
- The current control systems still require human operators.
- The data in the systems are not fully utilized.
- The processes do not have enough adaptive capability.
- The processes have too much unnecessary complexity.
- The processes do not have enough rigor and too many activities are improvised.
- The processes are too easily broken and too large to restore.
- The processes do not have enough data and awareness.
- The processes are simply obsolete and do not align with new missions and objectives.

If the processes or integrated common process are enabled by technologies, then the next step after studying what should be the objective state is to consider the technical architecture. In Appendix C, the four-plus-one views to represent a software architecture are presented as a part of program execution. While these views are key engineering artifacts, the solutions developer must be able to represent the objective technical solution in simple ways for potential evaluation by non-engineers. Processes must transition from the current operational states to the objective states because people involved in the processes cannot switch from old processes to new processes like machines. Technical architectures to sustain these processes, however, can be adopted through evolution (component upgrades), transition (component replacements with architectural advancements), and transformation (brand-new architecture with brand new technologies). In technical architectural transition, the old architecture is still recognizable as new components are added and architectural changes are made. In technical architectural transformation, the new can be completely unrecognizable from the old. It is then only by looking at the processes that one can see the connection. For example, if we compare the technical components of the first mobile phone demonstrated by Motorola in 1973 with the components of a modern iPhone or Android device [1], it is hard to identify the similarities. However, we can tell that they are all mobile phones once we see the devices in use. With this thought in mind, we should not let our understanding of processes constrain our thoughts on technologies and technical architectures. Approaches for developing architectural solutions are presented in Chapter 10.

In modern IT architectures there are some common concepts that can be further defined through specific technical products and techniques. These concepts, as shown in Figure 8.3, come together to enable enterprise-wide IT systems. Some locally deployed IT systems do not require all the concepts, and some concepts will eventually be replaced by new transformational concepts. For the enterprise system, it is the functionalities established in each application, the unique capabilities and

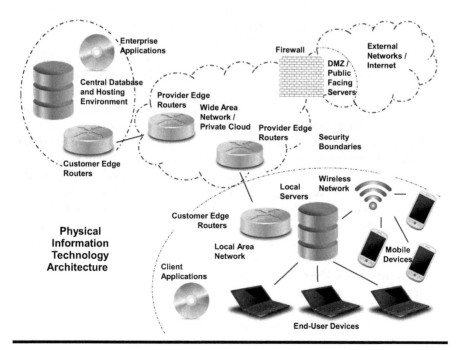

Figure 8.3   Conceptualization of IT architecture.

capacity in each hardware component, and the specific configurations for hardware and software that make the system unique. To describe the key concepts, enterprise applications and software components sustaining enterprise applications are hosted on servers. If an application is built for virtualized deployment in a cloud environment, then the application can be deployed across distributed servers with load-balanced operations to support users across the enterprise.

Whether servers are deployed as part of a cloud or as bare metal, they are set in racks and placed in data center facilities. The facilities provide power to the racks and servers as well as heating, ventilation, and air conditioning (HVAC) to prevent servers from overheating. Modern blade servers require extensive cooling, so other cooling techniques, such as by fluids, may be used. Data centers are connected to the local area network (LAN) as well as to the local wireless networks. This permits the hosted applications to support user devices connected to the network. At one time, user devices were largely desktop and laptop computers. Now, most applications are designed to be further accessed through cell phones and tablets.

If a local data center is acting as a distribution point for enterprise application services hosted elsewhere, then connection with a wide area network (WAN) is required. WAN connection is also required when the data center is hosting an enterprise application, or if the data center is hosting applications that mostly communicate with applications hosted elsewhere. Most of today's WANs are cloud networks where communications are transported across the cloud through Internet protocols (IP) that govern how routers control the traffic. Local data centers connect to the cloud through the customer edge (CE) routers, and the cloud connects to CE routers through provider edge (PE) routers [2].

The federal LAN and WAN must be secure networks with levels established in accordance with the Federal Information Security Management Act (FISMA) of 2002 for the nature of the mission and supporting system. The security controls, such as firewall, identity management, access control, data encryption, and active network monitoring, must be documented in the system security plan (SSP) and the system must pass assessment and authorization (A&A) before obtaining an authority to operate (ATO) [3]. Software applications, which will be discussed next, may go through their own A&A process after the network and datacenter infrastructure have already obtained ATOs. For infrastructures that use a secure commercial cloud purchased through a service contract, the commercial cloud must be FedRAMP-certified to be an infrastructure as a service (IaaS). If the systems must gain access to the open Internet, a DMZ zone can be established so that public-facing servers sit on the other side of the firewall to interact with users without secure access. Over time, the hardware components making up this infrastructure will have to change, and understanding when and how to change is a part of the solutioning process. When the concepts can be changed, such as when centrally hosted applications replaced locally hosted applications in the mid-2000s, the solution becomes revolutionary.

Revolutions occur more often in the realm of software. With cloud computing, the current trend has been toward the development of modular software components that permit easy reuse and easy replacement. Modularity requires exposed APIs, a standard communication format between modules, and standard taxonomies in the data to be communicated. This architectural transformation permits the creation of platforms with modular components that can be shared by multiple applications. The platform can be created for an enterprise, or an enterprise can purchase platform as a service (PaaS) from a commercial vendor. By using a commercial PaaS, applications can be built upon the PaaS with reduced levels of development. An enterprise can then pay for dedicated software development based on government-specific requirements, modify commercial or open-source software to fit government requirements, or adjust government requirements to accept commercial or open-source software out of the box [4]. Figure 8.4 shows basic modules in a technology stack of infrastructure, platform, and software services. The challenge of solutions development is to figure out what specific modules are needed for a government RFP, what existing technologies exist to support the acquiring of the modules, and what development is required to fill the gaps in capabilities to complete an integrated system. Chapter 11 discusses approaches to technology innovations.

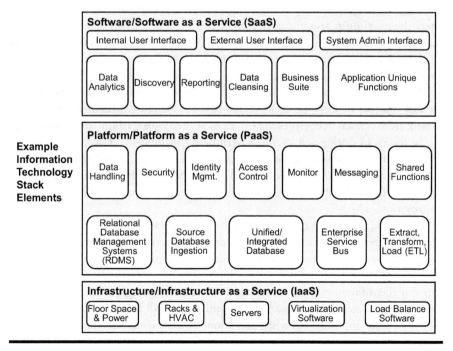

Figure 8.4 Conceptualization of an information technology stack.

Through the software modules, the solution defines functions, processes, data, data formats, operational performance, number of users, number of concurrent users, data tranport capacity, and so on. Also, software and platforms must have security controls and pass A&A to gain ATO. A part of the A&A process is the conducting of security scans to search for vulnerabilities across the integration of modules. The structure of databases are designed to match the operations of the software. In selecting the database technology, the first question is whether the database schema can be created by set relationships or whether the size and interaction of data is so large and dynamic that a non-relational database technology must be used. Relational databases create a set structure so that the application knows where to place and extract data that are needed for computations. Non-relational databases save data in cells where the association between cells can be defined and redefined based on computational need. Each current path of data storage has its own technology stack. Therefore, the software technology stack decisions must be made in conjunction with the database technology stack. Some commercial platforms are so inclusive that the software module, database technologies, and even programming language are all a part of a single platform. This one-stop commitment to simplicity ensures component integration. However, the government is then locked into a primary technology vendor. In contrast, using open-source components with licenses, such as Apache 2.0, enables one to do almost anything one wishes with the software code and offers the maximum amount of flexibility in choosing technologies to integrate. Adopting an open-source architecture, however, requires a great deal of expert knowledge on how components are compatible and how components are supported by the open-source community.

The vast number of competing software technology stacks in the market and the vast number of software components that can be reused, further customized, or built from scratch make software solutions very complex. Many software designs can be forced to work given a set of government requirements, but solutions development is about discovering the best design. What is best could have a favorable cost, fast schedule to deployment, minimal risk, better performance, scalability to future needs, modifiable to incorporate future technologies, or effortless process transition.

In the end, it is the successful transition of the users/stakeholder organizations from the current state processes to the future objective state processes that matters. Toward that end, user instructional training, self-training, and hands-on training are parts of the overall solution. Even with training, the complexity of the system and the difficulty of use could lead to continuously high user errors. If use is overly difficult, people are remarkably adaptive and will find ways to marginalize the system. The solution fails when user adoption has failed. So, all systems and all services should be designed with the end user in mind.

For physical systems, the concepts shown in Figure 8.5 are straightforward, but the technologies are more diverse. Physical systems serve many functions and

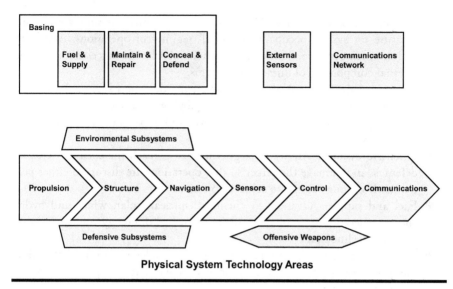

Figure 8.5 Conceptualization of technologies for physical systems.

travel through air, space, land, and sea. However, they are all governed by the laws of physics, and thus their concept of operations all have similar technology areas. The innovation comes in specific technologies and potential technological break-throughs in select areas [5]. The innovation also comes in engineering and design breakthroughs that maximize the way current technologies are being used. The search for innovations tends to have the following focus:

- Propulsion: Mechanism for generating propulsive force. The amount of fuel required to generate a specific level of propulsive force. The medium in which the propulsive force will work.
- Structure: System form strength that resists compressive, torsional, explosive, vibrating, or impacting forces. Material surface strength that resists heat, cold, friction, and corrosion.
- Navigation: Ability to chart geospatial paths from point A to point B. The challenge is greater when there are threats along the travel path and when the system has to cross regimes, such as from jungles to deserts.
- Sensors: Ability to detect all threats and targets at effective distances and with sufficient details to enable proper response. Detection across key parts of the electromagnetic spectrum.
- Control: Ability to control the system at the extreme operational ranges of design. Understand all the forces acting on the system and how to solve the differential equations that link the forces to implementing control theories.
- Communications: Transfer of information across great distances in a secure, accurate, high-bandwidth, undetectable, and low-latency manner.

- Environmental subsystems: Ability to sustain internal air supply and temperature for system occupants across all regimes of operations. Ability to maintain temperature, humidity, pressure, and other factors essential for the internal components of unmanned systems.
- Defensive subsystems: Ability to avoid enemy detection such as by stealth, evading attacks, deflecting projectiles, deploying decoys, countering attacks, absorbing or reflecting energy weapons, and repairing damages during operations.
- Offensive weapons: Ability to target the enemy, reach the enemy, overcome defenses, and damage the target so that operations are disrupted either permanently or long enough to achieve objectives.
- Fuel and supply: Advances in chemical, nuclear, solar, wind, and hydro energy generation technologies. Advances in fuel or energy storage and distribution technologies.
- Maintain and repair: Techniques for detecting needed repairs just before failure of subsystems. Optimize components use while reducing the number of system breakdowns.
- Conceal and defend: Base concealment and defensive technologies and techniques. Passive fortifications and active-point defense weapons.
- External sensors: Breadth of worldwide coverage, continuity of worldwide coverage versus revisit times, fidelity of coverage, spectrum of coverage.
- Communications network: Geographical reach, key nodes, key pathways, capacity, latency, packet loss, security, physical robustness, adaptiveness against local and regional outages, monitoring capability, and traffic control capability.

The scientific breakthroughs in these areas may take years of investments with uncertain results. Thus, the government often sets aside such investments as basic research and starts programs based on demonstrated technologies that can be incorporated into systems through more controlled development. This development is to first mature the technology and then to apply the technology. The challenge of developing solutions is to deeply understand and explain this path in a convincing way.

For both systems development and service contracts, staffing to perform the work is a key part of the solution. Staff to perform service contracts can have a broad collection of responsibilities that may or may not be interrelated. Thus, their qualifications, capabilities, and performance are measured by the individual tasks to which each is associated. These tasks could produce deliverables that can be measured as performance, or they could simply produce effects/outcomes based on completing tasks. Staff-produced systems are ultimately measured by the quality of the systems produced and their ability to maintain schedule and cost while producing the systems. If the government is buying completed systems, then the composition of the staff that produced the systems does not matter. When the government is paying for the development, then the contractor-proposed staffing mix and qualifications to execute the development tasks provide the government with the confidence that the system can be completed on schedule and within cost. The confidence is further increased when individual staff and entire teams have completed the proposed tasks before on similar projects. For staff working in high-demand professional areas, the solution needs to explain how the contractor will recruit new staff and retain those staff when the market makes them job offers [6]. For staff working in rapidly advancing technology areas, the solution needs to explain how staff will be trained or self-educated to stay current with use of new technologies. For staff who are junior, the solution needs to explain how they will be mentored to become effective members of teams. While there is a tendency for the government to want senior staff at junior staff prices, such is a capabilities trap where the senior staff hired may have the paper qualifications but will not have the capabilities to succeed. Even for LPTA proposals, seeking people who have the required degrees, certifications, and years of experience but are willing to work for the lowest salaries is never a good solutioning idea. Approaches for creating an effective staffing solution are presented in Chapter 12.

Assuming that we have formulated the right team, the remaining piece of the solution is how that team will be organized to complete the work. Figure 8.6 shows how a team for developing and deploying a system can be organized. This organization is based on functional groups. These groups must then work together to complete the tasks. How these groups work together for specific programs is a solutioning endeavor. Key concepts in formulating these interactions include the following:

■ What information and products are handed over from one group to the next?
■ How are subgroups, such as Agile development teams, formed within broader operations?

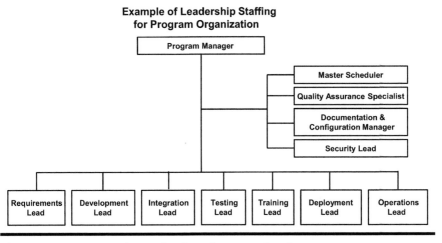

Figure 8.6 Conceptual organization of systems development team.

- When must groups interact with one another?
- What are the dependencies between groups?
- Who controls the interactions between groups?
- What are processes within each group for completing tasks?
- How should the composition of groups change over the life of a program?
- How should the structure of groups change over the life of a program?

Now that we have discussed how to look at RFP problems or opportunities and asked the right questions, the following chapters will explore ways to answer these questions in processes, architectures, technologies, and personnel capabilities to complete solutions.

References

1. Seward, Z.M. 2013. The first mobile phone call was made 40 years ago today. *The Atlantic* (April 3). https://www.theatlantic.com/technology/archive/2013/04/the-first-mobile-phone-call-was-made-40-years-ago-today/274611/.
2. Rosenfeld, L., Morville, P., and Arango, J. 2015. *Information Architecture: For the Web and Beyond* 4th ed. Newton, MA: O'Reilly Media.
3. Gantz, S.D., and Philpott, D.R. 2012. *FISMA and the Risk Management Framework: The New Practice of Federal Cyber Security.* Rockland, MA: Syngress
4. McConnell, S. 2004. *Code Complete: A Practical Handbook of Software Construction,* 2nd ed. Redmond, WA: Microsoft Press.
5. Challoner, J. (Editor). 2009. *1001 Inventions That Changed the World.* Hauppauge, NY: Barron's Educational Series.
6. Phillips, J.M., and Gully, S.T. 2014. *Strategic Staffing,* 3rd ed. Boston: Pearson.

Chapter 9

Developing Solutions that Improve Processes

In the previous chapter, we discussed the importance of determining the original state workflow and formulating the objective state workflow. Process change then enables the transition path from the original state to the objective state. Even when the workflow must stay the same, process and procedural advancements within existing functions could still increase performance. Finally, when current state performance is threatened by adverse external forces, increasing adaptiveness within the business process can sustain the integrity of the workflow. Solutions development, therefore, involves improving the process in most situations. Even when just making changes in personnel, new training and new management tasks in the overall process might be required to yield a complete solution. Even with the replacement of one technical component in the architecture, that replacement is only a solution if it improves speed, quality, duration, or some other performance metrics. The act of replacement involves a process. But if nothing has changed, then the replacement activity is just maintenance. Some processes are designed with such self-adaptiveness and self-organization capabilities that the solution is to find better ways to technically support the existing patterns of change. Other processes may be designed with such rigidity to prevent errors that all changes must be heavily validated and cautiously adopted. No matter the system or service requirements, the heart of solutions development starts with understanding the process with architecture, technologies, and people supporting the process [1].

In contrast, a solution can be formulated even by keeping the same system architecture, legacy technologies, and incumbent staff. Process improvements alone can yield cost savings, compressed schedules, better products, and lower risks. To understand how to improve the process behind the workflow, we start with an assessment of functions. Functional analysis organizes the process into major blocks of activities that yield specific outcomes. From the point where the user initiates or enters the process, functions are completed through series of tasks and new functions are initiated through decision/control activities. Some functions will depend on specific sources of data and some functions will generate data for shared databases. Some functions and data sources depend on external processes, and the completion of a functional path in the workflow typically yields displayable results that can support external processes. When functions have more direct interactions with external processes, then the system enabling the workflow can be considered a system within a greater system.

If we want to achieve process innovations at the functional level, we begin by looking for (1) missing functions, (2) unnecessary functions, (3) functional interdependencies that can be reorganized, (4) new and better data sources, (5) where new feedback loops be established, (6) new gateways/filters, and (7) new decision/control points. Since few processes work in isolation, we should never propose any changes to functional structures until we fully understand all the internal and external forces as well as interdependencies affecting the process. For adverse forces, we need to adjust functions in a way to reduce their effects. Adverse forces in the information realm can be erroneous data, poor controls, conflicting commands, intentional false information, and incorrect dependencies. For critical interdependencies, we need to advance functions in a way that they are sustained or properly replaced. Fixing one thing while breaking something else is a risk in process change that must be managed.

Once we start to truly understand all the subtle effects in a process and how some processes are more vulnerable to forces than others, we will recognize that many process innovations can only be discovered through task flow and procedural analysis. Functional analysis identifies the bigger changes, such as adding blocks of new tasks. Task flow analysis helps us to understand how to affect the performance of specific functions. This is because all functional blocks can be defined as a series of tasks. The execution of these tasks then completes the function. For complex functions where many workflow paths are supported by a single functional block, the tasks can have different dependencies and directions based on the nature of work. The tasks can also have different results based on the data and material used to perform each task. Process improvements can therefore be made by changing functions that automatically change the tasks, changing the tasks, or changing how the tasks are executed. Procedural changes within task execution generally do not require major changes in the tasks and interdependencies. Thus, process improvements at the procedural level can be applied to virtually any workflow and even when the workflow overall cannot change. We will now discuss process improvements at this most basic level.

To improve procedures, we need to understand how tasks are structured. Figure 9.1 conceptually presents the broad nature of tasks and interdependencies between tasks. The conduct of tasks requires resources such as assigned personnel,

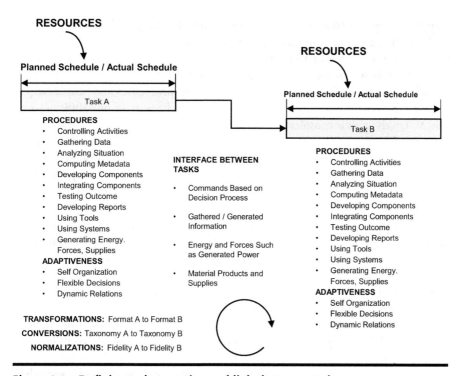

RESOURCES

Planned Schedule / Actual Schedule

Task A

PROCEDURES
- Controlling Activities
- Gathering Data
- Analyzing Situation
- Computing Metadata
- Developing Components
- Integrating Components
- Testing Outcome
- Developing Reports
- Using Tools
- Using Systems
- Generating Energy. Forces, Supplies

ADAPTIVENESS
- Self Organization
- Flexible Decisions
- Dynamic Relations

INTERFACE BETWEEN TASKS
- Commands Based on Decision Process
- Gathered / Generated Information
- Energy and Forces Such as Generated Power
- Material Products and Supplies

RESOURCES

Planned Schedule / Actual Schedule

Task B

PROCEDURES
- Controlling Activities
- Gathering Data
- Analyzing Situation
- Computing Metadata
- Developing Components
- Integrating Components
- Testing Outcome
- Developing Reports
- Using Tools
- Using Systems
- Generating Energy. Forces, Supplies

ADAPTIVENESS
- Self Organization
- Flexible Decisions
- Dynamic Relations

TRANSFORMATIONS: Format A to Format B
CONVERSIONS: Taxonomy A to Taxonomy B
NORMALIZATIONS: Fidelity A to Fidelity B

Figure 9.1   Defining task execution and links between tasks.

equipment, material, and facility. The activities must be governed by a set of procedures. These procedures can be for a variety of potential activities as listed, and the nature of the task can demand rigid immutable procedures or procedures that allow personnel to be adaptive. Rigid procedures force personnel to perform a task according to design. This prevents errors particularly when a task must be repeated many times or be conducted by different people. In order for rigid procedures to work, the environment in which the task is performed also has to be the same each time the task occurs, or the environment has to vary in a predictable way so that the procedures can include decision steps.

When the environment affecting task execution is complex or when the task itself requires complex reasoning, the procedures may need to allow for adaptiveness on the part of personnel performing the task. One type of adaptiveness is the ability of the person to organize his or her procedural knowledge in creative ways to handle each task execution uniquely against the situation of occurrence. For example, a martial artist's skills are defined through standard kicks, punches, flips, and turns. However, his or her capabilities are expressed through the combination of these moves in response to the opponent. The same can be true for other skill sets associated with a task.

Adaptiveness can also be in deciding which path of procedures to follow. For some tasks, procedures can be less a combination of tactical moves and more of a strategic path with flexibility in how the path can vary. For example, a sculptor chipping away at a block of marble is constantly thinking and deciding on how to shape the outcome. Similarly, a programmer or product designer might have to make a series of decisions to satisfy requirements. Finally, the task can allow for flexibility in how it associates and interacts with other tasks. If so, this dynamic behavior in relationships must translate down to the procedures and people executing the task. Adaptiveness is associated with people because of our ability to reason. When the task is completely executed by a machine, the computer can mimic human reasoning but cannot be truly adaptive. Computer decisions are made within programmed boundaries and the boundaries can grow through machine learning. However, the computer will always have limitations in responding to unforeseen situations until true artificial intelligence is eventually invented.

We have said that procedures can be improved while maintaining the purpose of tasks and the original workflow. In doing so, we can accelerate task completion, increase quality of task outputs, and correct performance issues. Common issues and mitigation approaches at the procedural level includes the following:

- ■ **Issue:** Too much variation in the implementation of procedures leading to incidents of performance deficiency.
  - – **Mitigation:** Establish standard operating procedures (SOP) and increase training plus performance evaluations until execution converges on standards.
- ■ **Issue:** Too much variation in the outcome of procedures despite standardize execution.
  - – **Mitigation:** Isolate and eliminate variation in environmental factors, such as changing temperature, forces, material quality, and power levels.
- ■ **Issue:** Too slow in the completion of tasks.
  - – **Mitigation:** Streamline procedures down to only those that are definitely required for tasks, simplify procedures through user-understandable descriptions, employ graphics and videos to help users grasp execution, and make SOP easily referenceable. Then, increase training.
- ■ **Issue:** Complexity of procedures causes delays in execution.
  - – **Mitigation:** Use process-management tools with automated features to reduce the challenges of human execution. Design the rules engine to handle complexity if the complexity can be bounded—known scope of what is to be done.
- ■ **Issue:** Too many resources required to execute procedures.
  - – **Mitigation:** Reassess the need for parallel executions and combine skill/capability levels for fewer resource types required to execute. Allow for longer task duration to have fewer resources.
- ■ **Issue:** Too many unpredicted environmental changes that cause misalignments with procedures.
  - – **Mitigation:** Create flexible ranges in the execution of procedures and allow human judgment to choose how to execute flexible procedures.

- **Issue:** Forces affecting procedural execution changing in unpredictable ways.
  - **Mitigation:** Create modularity in the procedures so that human awareness can organize procedures to respond to shifting forces.
- **Issue:** Changing relations with other tasks causing interdependencies in the conduct of procedures to change.
  - **Mitigation:** Create procedures that allow personnel to dynamically change interdependencies in the course of execution.
- **Issue:** Systematic errors continue to appear in task execution results despite standardization and training.
  - **Mitigation:** Test different procedural steps and different environmental situations to isolate steps and conditions that are introducing errors.
- **Issue:** Nonsystemic errors continue to appear in task execution results despite standardization and training.
  - **Mitigation:** Establish error filters in the procedures so that correction can be made immediately during time of execution. Some complex procedures may need to be done several times before one can move forward.

The above mitigations are for sustaining the original design of tasks so that process improvements can be made at the procedural level while the workflow is maintained. If this constraint is not required, we can change tasks to improve the process. A task can be changed by changing its procedures with corresponding changes in input requirements and output results. A task can be changed by how it is interlinked with other tasks. And, a task can be changed through the elimination or addition of surrounding tasks with effects traveling across the links. Even for existing tasks, the change can be significant if they are executed at different times, with higher or lower frequency, or under different functions. Figure 9.1 also shows how tasks are linked to one another. A link can be defined as the passing of commands, information, energy, forces, or materials from one task to another. In an assembly line, for example, the worker at each station conducts the task of assembling a specific part until the component is complete. The design of the component and the parts create a common reference frame for completing tasks. When the reference frame is different from one task to another, one function to another, or one system to another, then the link must perform procedures to connect the reference frames.

One procedure is transforming what is passed across the link from the format of one task to the format of the other task. To develop the transformation functions for passing data, we need to know the definition of data elements on both sides and the organization of data elements on both sides. Then, equations must be formulated for data elements from one side to be transformed into data elements on the other side. The transformation could merge data elements, break apart data elements, or change data altogether. When the taxonomy for describing something in one task is different than the taxonomy for describing the same thing in another, the ability to link the tasks requires taxonomy conversion. The conversion can be a part of data structure transformations, but it is hard to formulate data transforms until taxonomy differences are understood. Similar to taxonomy differences, information from multiple tasks could be at different fidelity levels when supporting follow-on tasks. If so, then the fidelity must be normalized to achieve a consistency of process. One normalization method is to reduce all data to the fidelity and scalar definition of the least-accurate dataset. This sacrifices the quality of other datasets. Another method is to pick an in-between fidelity and spread out the lower-fidelity data into the higher-granularity scale by repeating data to fill the gaps. When lower-fidelity data must be placed into the scale of the highest-fidelity data, just spreading the data out might introduce too much inaccuracy for the follow-on tasks. To reduce the inaccuracy, we can take a range of low-fidelity data and test hypotheses for how the data should vary across that range. If the data should be increasing or decreasing, we can test behavioral curves for expressing the likely change. Tasks in designed functions and workflows should not have such challenges in linking to form a continuous process. Nevertheless, legacy technology, databases, and procedures used in one task and not others are a key reason why connectivity issues exist.

Once tasks can be linked correctly so that the required interdependences can be achieved, the next level of analysis is understanding how tasks should be linked. Figure 9.2 shows the types of links between tasks. The standard linear dependency between tasks is that the completion of the first task provides what is needed to begin the second task. If Task A cannot be completed on time, then Task B cannot start on time unless a cushion to absorb the delays has been established in the schedule between Task A and Task B. The inverse of the linear relations is when the start of Task B forces Task A to end. For example, Task A could be filled with personnel preparing for a mission and Task B is the start of that mission. Two or more tasks can sometimes be conducted in parallel. Even with schedule overlap, there could still be dependencies. One dependency is when a task must start before other tasks can start. For example, the start of Task A could take down a barrier that Task B cannot take down. After the barrier is taken down, Task B could begin anytime and even end before or after Task A. The dependence can be in the inverse direction where Task A must start after Task B takes down a barrier. If the dependency is both ways, then both tasks must begin at the same time. Like back-to-back relations, front-to-front relations can exist. The completion of Task A enables Task B to be completed, and Task B can be completed at any time thereafter. Inversely, Task B may enable Task A to be completed. If the dependence is both ways, then both tasks must be completed at the same time. For example, if two teams are working to finish a common list of product requirements and neither team can complete their task until the common list is done, then the two teams working on two tasks will have to finish together.

In the design of complete workflows, the types of links between tasks can be used in a variety of ways to constrain and control task execution. Two or more tasks can be forced to start together and end together. Two or more tasks can be forced to follow one another in a continuous series. Any single task can further be linked to

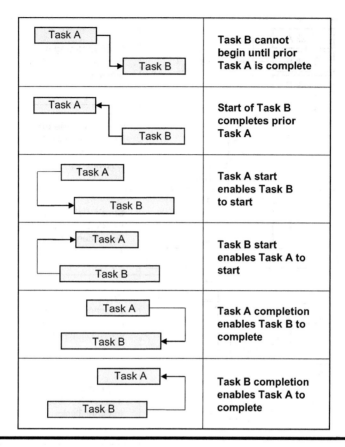

Figure 9.2   The types of interrelationships between tasks.

many other tasks and many tasks can converge to support a single task. Some tasks contain decision processes and specific links are activated based on decision results. Other tasks provide information and even commands for the repeated execution of prior tasks, so the links become feedback loops.

Beyond the ability for the execution of tasks to guide the process flow along different paths, some tasks can have the ability to control the velocity and acceleration of the process. Tasks can tell other tasks to begin sooner, complete quicker, and abandon dependencies. This control can be based on tasks that monitor the workflow, and monitoring can be based on filters, pattern recognition, searches, and projections. While our objective should be to design the tasks and the interlinking of tasks correctly, processes can reveal execution issues and risks. Some common issues and risks in the interdependence of tasks are presented in Figure 9.3. This is particularly true when one has inherited an existing process and is trying to evolve it toward objective performance levels. Regardless of how issues and

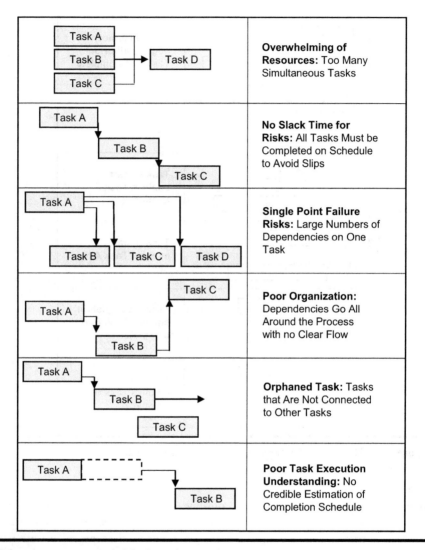

Figure 9.3   Issues and risks in task structures.

risks emerged, they can be corrected by changing the nature of tasks or the linking of tasks. Common corrective approaches are as follows [2]:

- **Correcting the Overwhelming of Available Resources:** We can try to decrease task durations through procedural efficiencies and try to spread apart the tasks so that they are not conducted completely in parallel. We can determine whether some tasks could be linked with later tasks to be completed later.
- **Correcting the Lack of Slack Time:** We can reevaluate dependencies to see whether some tasks can be linked with later tasks to free up a tight series.

Once a few tasks are allowed to reconnect, the remaining tasks can be spread apart to allow slack time. Ironically, the effort to reduce task completion time through procedural efficiency can increase the risk of task schedule slips. Taking out slack time between procedures to gain slack time between tasks may not always be wise.

■ **Correcting Single-Point Failure:** Any time when the failure of a single task can cause the entire process to be disrupted, we have a major risk in the workflow. This risk can be reduced through a set of backup tasks and links for when the primary task fails or is significantly delayed. Alternatively, the primary task can be executed in a redundant and parallel manner. However, the parallel execution must be designed so that there are no mechanisms that can cause both tasks to fail. Often times, this implies physical distance between two teams, systems/network isolation, or separate sets of independent capabilities.

■ **Correcting Poor Organization:** When links are extending across a process and the schedule to yield confusing configurations, the tasks are often not grouped and organized correctly. When tasks are grouped to logically satisfy functions, then there is a set of links between tasks in a function and links from tasks that represent connectivity between functions. By organizing the tasks and links according to these layers, a complex process does not have to be confusing.

■ **Correcting for Orphaned Tasks:** In large processes, how tasks are linked do not always appear in engineering and schedule documents. Some tasks may appear to be on their own. To verify that a task is truly an orphan, we must follow the trail of all its input and output parameters. If the trail leads to no other tasks, external activities or process level outputs, then the task may indeed be a legacy from prior processes. The final test is to remove an obsolete task and see whether the process or environment reacts. The test is best done in a simulated environment and not on deployed systems. The task must be quickly added back to the process if any kind of adverse reaction occurs because removing obsolete tasks should only improve efficiency. The replacement of legacy systems with many associated tasks is thus very challenging because each of the removed tasks can have hidden dependencies despite careful planning.

■ **Correcting for Poor Task Execution:** At times, the links between tasks are affected by the ability to perform tasks according to plans. Even with set procedures, the execution of a task for the first time and the statistical variation in the execution of a task over time could defy plans. The options for addressing this uncertainty includes (1) design task interdependences to be adaptable to greater variations in task performance, (2) redesign task execution procedures to reduce variability, (3) evaluate task execution resources as potential causes of instability, and (4) allow operations to be delayed when task performance issues emerge. At times, there is a trade-off between maintaining schedule and maintaining quality. This priority helps to determine which option to select and refine as the solution.

Based on the previous discussion, process innovations and corrective solutions can be at the procedural level within tasks; task design level, which includes the design of enabling procedures; task interdependence level, which includes linking within functions and across functions; and the functional level. Functional-level innovation is based more on better understanding of what the users really want to do than on the technologies and techniques that go into designing tasks and procedures. Functional innovation can integrate workflows, consolidate subordinate tasks, simplify processes, establish new capabilities, integrate data, increase awareness and controls, support more users, support broader missions, accelerate activities, and improve presentation. These functional changes that extend to the tasks and procedures must be designed for specific processes. While solution models for similar processes can be used as a starting point for innovation, trying to reuse solutions without considering specific customer needs is a very dangerous approach.

In summary, innovations and corrective solutions at all these levels can be expressed in the form of system diagrams that explain the process level by level. All the levels can be further expressed in the form of a hierarchical schedule. For rigorous operational processes, the integrated master schedule (IMS) represents an auditing standard for taking corrective actions when performance ranges are exceeded. For schedules of processes that require a great deal of learning and adaptation, the manager should use the IMS as a mechanism for controlling process activities. Tasks can be redefined and relinked over the course of performance. When there are downstream schedule risks, the manager should use the IMS to test out potential solution scenarios and associated impacts to the schedule. Testing should be a part of the process/schedule design step and testing should be a part of process/schedule validation. Common testing techniques include the following:

- **End-to-end testing:** This test executes all the workflows in a process design from beginning to end in a controlled environment where there are metrics and mechanisms established to assess performance. The first validation is to make sure that the workflow is not blocked at any specific point. The second validation is to make sure that all the operational requirements are met. The validation of requirements can be converted into test scripts. The test scripts can then be organized to test capabilities by functions utilized in the workflows.
- **Operational load and range testing:** This test executes the tasks based on the projected maximum number, diversity, and distribution of users for the system and process. Automated tools can be used to help simulate the breadth of users and the level of repeated execution. However, there is no substitute for representative human testers when measuring how human learning and adaptiveness will impact the process. The natural performance pattern for human users is a bell curve. With process improvements, we can reduce the standard deviation in the bell curve. When performance starts to cluster into different peaks, then we have to question whether certain categories of users are being disenfranchised by the designed process. Depending on age,

disabilities, geography, and numerous other factors, the human user may face task comprehension and learning problems. These problems can be solved through human capabilities improvements, to be discussed later, or process improvements. Finally, when performance is at all levels randomly spread across a metric, process adoption is essentially broken. At that point, either the process must be simplified for the users or we will have to figure out how to help users learn and converge their capabilities around a standard.

- **Regression testing:** For processes that are changing either due to redesign or adaptation, testing the process each time a change has occurred is recommended. Intentional attempts to improve the process in one area can cause operational and performance issues in other areas. The modeling of the entire process to help with design could reduce the risk of adverse effects. However, the only complete way to manage risks is to conduct regression testing. Process changes due to adaptation is less planned, but the flexibility built into the process to allow for adaptation hopefully also prevents the process from hitting adaptive dead ends. Nevertheless, regression testing after a permanent adaptive step could help determine whether the process should be reverted to its original states. Temporary adaptations are better tested through gaming simulations.

- **Gaming simulations:** Processes that flexibly interact with the environment or other processes can only be fully tested in a simulation that reactively or proactively applies external forces to the process. These forces can test how the process responds, what range the response can be, how much stress can be tolerated, and whether the desired results can still be achieved. Corrections made based on simulation results are complex because weaknesses are not just about points of vulnerability or capability limitations. The corrective solution must consider the totality of the process and how it engages the intended environment and opposing processes.

- **Security testing:** All processes, both physical and IT, may contain vulnerabilities to adversary or criminal attacks. When the process is not very adaptive, security testing is critical in identifying all the points of vulnerability. The identification of vulnerabilities starts with the boundaries and how the boundaries are protected. On the network, boundary protection includes firewalls and gateways. In the physical world, we have fences, guards, and gates. As people, things, and information must travel across boundaries, the test must address the effectiveness of managing identities and granting access. Within the boundaries, the test would validate the effectiveness of monitoring, detection, and response. At specific points, where high-value assets are stored, the test should focus on effective protection of the assets, such as by the encryption of data, bodyguards for people, and sensors for the storage of goods.

As we test process improvements and innovations, it is hard to divorce the process from the technical architecture when the process is enabled by technical products. Sometimes, architectural changes must be made to complement process innovations; other times, new technology-enabled architectures will encourage improvements in process. Therefore, the next chapter is on developing solutions based on architectural innovations. While process and architecture are clearly coupled when the process is enabled by technology, the strategy for innovating the process and the architecture simultaneously carries risks in execution complexity. To manage these risks, solutions architects have at times endeavored to complete the redesign of the process before figuring out the architectural solution. When new technologies demand architectural change, it is often safer to first conduct the transition with the currently known process. After the technology-driven architecture has achieved stable operations, then the process can be advanced under the new architecture.

Finally, the idea that process improvement is needed but cannot be accomplished for the proposal to the government due to a lack of information or operational readiness has led some solutions developers to present processes for improving the process. These processes might be anchored to validated methodologies such as Six Sigma, Balanced Scorecard, and Total Quality Management [3–5]. However, we must recognize that this is presenting a capability along with a contract delivery promise instead of a process improvement solution. As long as we are not fooling ourselves, we can then properly explain the process for improving the process to increase customer confidence.

References

1. Ren, C.H. 2017. *How Systems Form and How Systems Break: A Beginner's Guide for Studying the World.* Switzerland: Springer International Publishing.
2. Lewis, J.P. 2010. *Project Planning, Scheduling, and Control: The Ultimate Hands-On Guide to Bringing Projects in On Time and On Budget,* 5th ed. New York: McGraw-Hill Education.
3. Pyzdek, T., and Keller, P. 2010. *The Six Sigma Handbook,* 3rd ed. New York: The McGraw-Hill Companies.
4. Kaplan, R.S., and Norton, D.P. 1996. *The Balanced Scorecard.* Boston: Harvard Business School Press.
5. Martínez-Lorente, A.R., Dewhurst, F., and Dale, B.G. 1998. Total quality management: Origins and evolution of the term. *The TQM Magazine,* 10, 5: 378–386.

Chapter 10

Developing Solutions that Improve Architectures and Designs

The decision regarding whether to evolve, transition, or transform an architecture should depend on how we should improve the architecture and system designs to support the comprehensive solution. At times, the needed improvements will automatically dictate an evolutionary, transitional, or transformational path. Other times, performance, cost, schedule, and risk trade-offs are required to determine the best-fit architectural path. Just as understanding the current operational state is essential to improving the process, understanding the current architectural state is critical to improving the architecture. Appendix C.3.1 on Configuration Management explains how to document an IT architecture through the 4 + 1 view [1]. The physical and logical views include all the hardware and software in the architecture, the facility and network infrastructures, the network and security boundaries, and end-user devices. The process view links all the architectural components from the perspective of operations and the development view provides insight on the construction of the components. Finally, the use case scenarios connect the architecture with the system process and user workflows. Architectural constraints include industry-accepted products/technologies, communication/interface standards, common data formats, compatible database base schemas, and interdependent security controls. The 4 + 1 view approach for developing architectural/engineering artifacts is effective for all software-intensive systems. In modern times, this includes many physical systems with software modules. For other physical systems, traditional engineering designs remain valid.

The logical and process views enable the improvement of the architecture to be integrated with the improvement of the operational process as explained in Chapter 9. This integration starts with the functions sustaining process workflows and how the functions are achieved through architectural components. Component-level improvements, such as new technology products, configuration changes for software and databases, interface adjustments, and establishing or enforcing standards, are ways to advance architectural performance without major architectural design endeavors. However, component changes in one part of the architecture must be compatible with other legacy components in the architectural as well as the overall operations of the architecture. Any component change further raises security concerns, and may require a reassessment and authorization of the architecture. A well-established configuration management process prevents mistakes in component updates and upgrades.

This chapter focuses on IT architectural improvements through redesign with new configurations, links, and nodes. The new design can be to support required process improvements that need more than just component-level upgrades. The new design can bring greater efficiency to the current process. And, the new design can yield additional process improvements. To understand how to improve the design of a current IT architecture, we will review some popular design concepts. While the improvement of architectures for physical systems can also benefit from these concepts, the complexity, flexibility, and pace of technology advancements for IT architectures make these concepts a key factor in solutions development.

The following design concepts do not represent the totality of architectural innovations. However, these examples can be used as starting points to think about the architecture. When there is no initial architecture to constrain a transition path or when the current architecture can be torn down for an enterprise-wide transformation, our ability to select an architectural concept is less constrained. Either way, the ultimate constraint or focal point in architectural design should be the objective operational state.

10.1 Designing the Architecture for Systems Federation

When systems have been developed and deployed in isolation at separate locations, the federation of these systems through a network architecture, as shown in Figure 10.1, could enable the coordination of activities/workflows across the enterprise. The easiest systems to federate are those that started with a common software foundation. Network capacity and speed prior to the mid-2000s were not high enough to sustain centralized enterprise applications. Thus, large complex systems had to be deployed at regional locations/data centers. Once deployed, modifications of these systems by local IT departments over years caused architectural variations in many situations. Bringing system configurations back to an agreed-upon standard

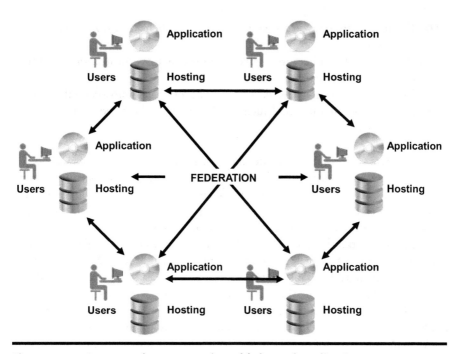

Figure 10.1   Conceptual representation of federated applications.

is then the technical challenge for federating systems that once started from common software.

In modern times, multiple commercially competitive systems can end up being deployed at various locations. Competing electronic health record (EHR) systems at local hospitals across the country is a good example. When data integration across hospitals became essential for improving patient quality of care, the challenge of federating completely different system architectures, data structures, and technology stacks emerged [2]. Finally, systems with different missions may need to be federated to support a new greater mission. For example, different government agencies could have systems that collect human intelligence data, satellite imagery data, airborne reconnaissance data, measurement and signature intelligence, signals intelligence, and so on. While these systems support different missions, some missions, such as the Global War on Terrorism [3], are so complex that only true federation across a common network can support integrated analytics.

Before we discuss federation techniques, the reasons for federation include the following:

■ The users are migrating from system to system, so the data must migrate with the users and the processes must be standardized.
■ The users need information from other systems in an improved process.

- The users can rely on other systems when their primary system is not performing.
- The federated architecture enables the systems to perform as an enterprise system under a single process.
- The systems contain related data that can be integrated into a central database.
- The systems contain complementary data that can be fused for greater analytical insight.

Once there is a reason to federate, the process of designing for a federate architecture starts with ensuring that there is network connectivity between the system locations. The connectivity must be reliable enough and with low enough latency to support operations. Then, the capacity of the network must match the capacity needs of federated operations. Once the applications are connected, they must be able to pass data. This means that APIs on all sides must be configured to pass data and that a communications standard must be established. Once data can be passed, the data must be usable on the other side. If both sides can be baselined to a standard database structure, then data utilization is not a problem. Otherwise, the data will have to be transformed from one database to another. The transformation might have to include a mapping from one taxonomy to another and a converging of values to a common scale. Once usable data is moving across a federated architecture, the systems can continue to operate independently with the advantage of utilizing shared information, process coordination, and functional redundancies. Alternatively, federated systems can integrate processes with the architecture enabling process steps in one system to hand off to process steps in another system. Process connectivity may have greater operational demands for system hardware and software. Delays in data migration or synchronization, for example, could hinder process connectivity. Thus, performance modeling and issues resolution is a key challenge in designing a federated architecture.

10.2 Designing the Architecture for Systems Consolidation

The maintaining of independently operated datacenters and applications at various locations can be costly and inefficient. If these deployments can be brought to a centralized location, then the number of hardware maintenance and software administration staff can be reduced. Also, the amount of equipment can be reduced through better optimization. Architectural consolidation does not require the hosted software systems to be integrated. In fact, the systems do not even have to be federated if the sharing of information is not required. Consolidation is about changing the architecture to use less resources, and the advancement of network technologies allows for physical consolidation while supporting a distributed user

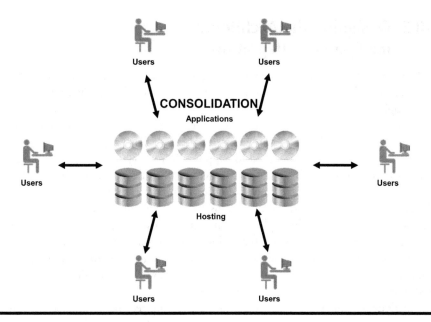

Figure 10.2   Conceptual representation of consolidating the architecture.

community. As Figure 10.2 shows, consolidation does not seek to change user access and their workflows. The objective is to maintain the user experience even as the hosting environments are moved away from their regions.

The consolidation of the infrastructure seeks to reduce floorspace and supporting HVAC requirements. The consolidation of servers can be done with higher-capacity equipment such as blade servers. The consolidation of applications deployment seeks to use as many back-end shared components as practical. This is facilitated by the applications using modular architectures. If the applications are sharing data, then the use of a common database could facilitate data sharing. In select cases where all the applications being consolidated are the same, then the number of application deployments can be reduced if each deployment can be scaled to multiple user communities.

The design challenge of architectural consolidation is figuring out where to consolidate and how to consolidate. If cloud hosting can be used and is cost-effective, then location is less of a concern. However, dedicated cloud virtual servers mimicking bare metal servers will still need to be provisioned if the applications are not designed for distributed cloud deployment. If the consolidation still requires the management of racks and servers, then there needs to be a decision regarding whether to reuse existing hardware. If new hardware is required, the transition may need to be done in parts with hardware installation, validation, retirement, and transfer of the applications. This coordination requirement encourages consolidation when hardware is facing retirement.

10.3 Designing the Architecture for Systems Integration

When users across the enterprise are relying upon many local applications that are common or related in nature, the need can alternatively be satisfied by an enterprise application as shown in Figure 10.3. This transformation generally requires an enterprise application development effort where the functionalities of current applications are combined into requirements for the enterprise application. The enterprise application must be designed to support the totality of the user community across the enterprise, be able to sustain all existing workflows, and be able to control user access based on roles and responsibilities. For large enterprises, the application should be cloud-based with an operations load that is balanced across servers on the cloud. The design of the application should embody a modular architecture and leverage the latest technologies. Technology innovation is, however, not required for systems integration. The development can simply use existing technologies to address an integrated set of requirements. The improvement then lies in the design and development of the enterprise application.

In figuring out what needs to be developed, the requirements analysis must converge similar user processes to achieve an acceptable standard process. At the same time, unique features needed by user subgroups must be preserved. And, process improvements/innovations can be adopted through the design of the new application. Appendix C.2 provides a description of different methodologies for

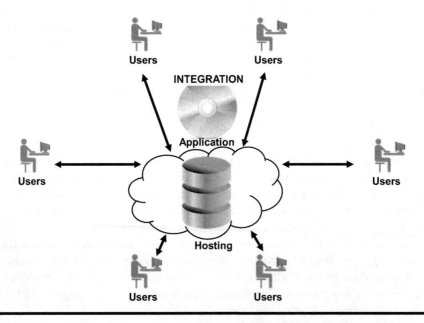

Figure 10.3   Conceptual representation of an integrated enterprise application.

software development. Thus, the innovation in moving to an enterprise application includes adopting a development approach that matches the challenges in design. If the architecture can be designed perfectly from the beginning, then the development can be done in rigorously scheduled increments. If the architecture needs to incorporate new technologies, then rapidly prototyping the technologies and making adjustments prior to full development could reduce risks. If the architecture is not perfectly aligned with user needs, then an Agile development process can fine-tune the architecture through the sprint testing and planning processes. All these approaches are well-established, but their utilization have at times been flawed. Incremental waterfall development efforts have been poorly planned with massive schedule delays and cost overruns. However, this does not mean that waterfall is an obsolete approach. Agile development efforts have led to continuous user involvement in changing designs and endless development. However, Agile development can be highly effective for a mature user community. Understanding how to develop an enterprise application within cost, schedule, and performance objectives is the key to having an integration-based architectural solution. Being able to explain this understanding is the key to having a winning proposal.

10.4 Designing the Architecture for Systems Segmentation

At times when a single enterprise architecture is supporting many types of users through many hosted applications on the network, we might want to ask the question of where the architecture should be segmented, as represented in Figure 10.4. If sets of applications and groups of users do not require tight integration, we can create logically separated boundaries to establish segmented communities. We can also reorganize the architecture to make existing segmentation clearer and more optimized. The advantage of creating segments is that the architecture will be easier to manage, the security controls can be more effective, and the implementation of advancements might not require adjustments and testing across the enterprise. Segments can have different security levels, and communications across segments will need to pass through firewalls.

In identifying segments, we can consider geography, missions, and systems interconnectivities. In geographical segmentation, the determination is that the user community stretching across the country and the world is too large to manage from a single monolithic architecture. Instead, if the users do not need to heavily interact across the world, they can be supported by regional hubs. In mission segmentation, the determination is that organizational missions have different criticality levels, reliability standards, and security requirements. Instead of raising all the systems and network elements to the criticality, reliability, and security level of the most demanding mission, segmentation could make operations more efficient. Some segments can integrate separated communities, allowing communities to

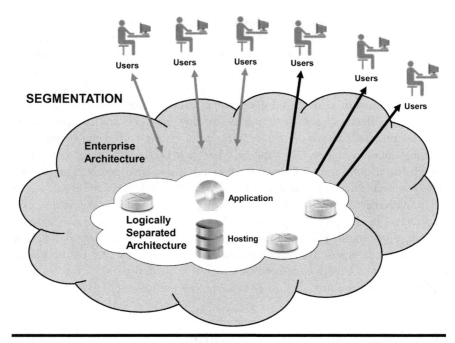

Figure 10.4 Conceptual representation of a segmented sub-architecture.

share information while blocking direct access by each side into the domain of the other side. Logical segmentation based on instructions for the servers and routers further allows for the reallocation of physical resources between segments. The risk in segmenting an architecture is that the boundaries could be selected incorrectly. Poor boundaries create barriers in parts of the enterprise architecture that should be integrated. To manage this risk, simulations can test design solutions and potentially discover hidden dependencies.

10.5 Designing the Architecture for Layering of the Systems

When the enterprise is supported by many systems with interdependent functionalities, an architecture that organizes these systems into a system of systems could improve operational efficiency, as represented by Figure 10.5. One system of the systems-design approach is to organize the architecture into layers. This is similar to designing a single application with a layered modular architecture of middleware web services and front-end UIs. In fact, many modular application architectures include other third-party applications. The slight difference between a system of systems and a modular system is the level of application coupling. In a system of systems architecture, applications can be organized based how interactive they are

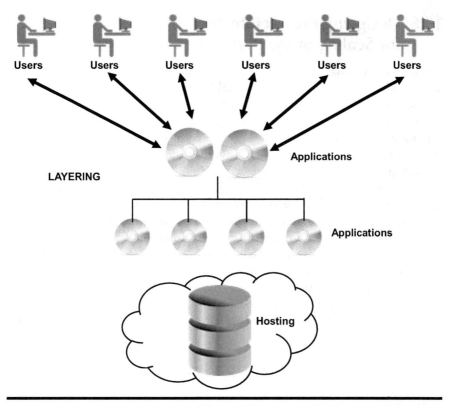

Figure 10.5   Conceptual representation of application layers.

with user groups and with system-to-system processes. The organization can actually match the hierarchy of user groups with applications that support senior leadership decision-making at the highest level. From that point, we can have applications that support information gathering, applications that conduct data analytics, and applications that perform business processes.

The purpose of layering is to better manage the flow of information from system to system in a more structured way. Filters and security controls can be established between layers. Communications capacity can be designed based on layers. And, coordination can be increased within a layer before there is communication across layers. Instead of passing separate streams of non-validated information across layers, for example, additional capabilities can be added to the architecture to determine discrepancies between data streams and authoritative sources. Applications within a layer can also be redesigned to reduce their footprint. Other architectural design techniques such as federation, consolidation, and integration can all be used within the structure of layers. Layering is different than segmentation largely because of a lack of boundaries. Layers should be designed to better integrate and not separate operations.

10.6 Designing the Architecture for Scaling of the Systems

For architectures that might be required to support many more users or higher levels of user activity in the future, scalability must be a part of the solution as represented in Figure 10.6. Scalability generally refers to network capacity, database size, and application transactional capacity. Scaling network capacity is about making sure that the LAN and WAN have adequate planning for future states. Future LAN capacity can be gained by installing additional fiber or having enough conduit space so that additional fiber can be installed in the future. Future WAN capacity can be gained by leveraging the full capability of an IP-based network that optimizes traffic flow for all users on the physical infrastructure. Then, the capacity of the network or the cloud is based on the total amount of fiber. Different parts of the physical infrastructure can be continuously upgraded as traffic is being routed across other parts of the infrastructure. Even when investments have not been made to the WAN infrastructure, the use of the infrastructure can be reprioritized among shared systems.

The scaling of the database can be done by growing relational database structures to the maximum size allowable by database technologies. When performance

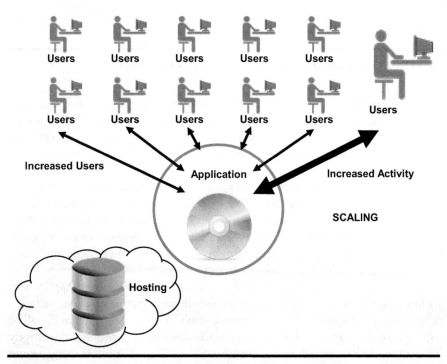

Figure 10.6   Conceptual representation of scaling operations.

starts to decline with terabytes of data stored in a continuous manner, the data can be broken apart into multiple interconnected databases, or Big Data technologies can be applied. In breaking apart data, we can archive old data beyond a set number of years into other databases or we can reduce the fidelity of data by moving data between set increments into other databases. Archiving old data limits longitudinal studies where complex analytical equations need to be applied on data that extend into history. Reducing the fidelity of data will require analytics to done at a higher order to isolate areas of concern. For those areas, the data can be integrated back to full fidelity to sustain in-depth analysis. Switching over to non-relational database technologies, such as Hadoop, resolves the database scaling issue [4]. However, setting up a Big Data infrastructure requires a dedicated group of experts, and operating on a non-relational data structure requires an understanding of how to dynamically organize data to match analytical needs.

Finally, scaling an application is based on how the application can operate across multiple servers (server farms) in a load-balanced way. Load balancing permits the support of a vast community of users with no appearance of separation. Alternatively, if a single user needs to conduct complex high-computational capacity operations, this is at times better done by a single high-capacity server than by chopping apart the operations for server farms. Thus, server technology is still very important in architectural design. The introduction of blade servers dramatically increased server capacity [5]. The introduction of technologies in the future, such as superconducting quantum computing with near-zero resistance energy flow [6], will again change the concept of scale in IT architectures.

10.7 Future Architecture Design Concepts

The architectural improvement approaches that have been presented are popular within the IT communities. However, solutions architects at times do not debate the best approach for their situation, but instead embrace the most popular approach. The true solution must fit the architecture to the needs of the object-state and not the end-state to the limitations of the architecture. Even popular architectural concepts have room for innovation, and those dedicated to finding the best architectural solution must always be aware of the opportunities offered by emerging technologies. Some future architectural design approaches might be

- Highly distributed microsystems imbedded across a web architecture with IT components integrated within all types of devices, machines, and computer hardware.
- Dynamically morphing architecture with self-forming and self-adjusting communication links that shift the architecture based on changing needs.
- Low infrastructure networks that can be established in remote regions to create complex architectures.

■ Low connectivity architectures with high systems autonomy and adaptiveness, essential coordination and synchronization, and reduced dependence on networks.

These and other architectural advancements will depend on technical innovations and breakthroughs. Understanding the nature of technology innovations and breakthroughs is thus the purpose of the next chapter.

References

1. Kruchten, P. 1995. Architectural blueprints—The "4 + 1" view model of software architecture. *IEEE Software*, 12, 6: 42–50.
2. Blumenthal, D., and Tavenner, M. 2010. The "meaningful use" regulation for electronic health records. *New England Journal of Medicine*, 363: 501–504.
3. Law, R.D. *Terrorism: A History (Themes in History)*, 2nd ed. New York: Polity.
4. Mayer-Schönberger, V., and Cukier, K. 2014. *Big Data: A Revolution That Will Transform How We Live, Work, and Think*. New York: Eamon Dolan/Mariner Books.
5 Goldworm, B., and Skamarock, A. 2007. *Blade Servers and Virtualization: Transforming Enterprise Computing While Cutting Costs*. Hoboken, NJ: Wiley.
6. Rieffel, E.G., and Polak, W.H. 2014. *Quantum Computing: A Gentle Introduction*. Cambridge, MA: The MIT Press.

Chapter 11

Developing Solutions that Improve Technologies

The U.S. General Services Administration (GSA) published a list of what they consider to be leading-edge information technologies needed by government agencies as a part of the Alliant 2 Request for Proposal in 2016. This list represents technologies that are at different stages of maturity, but all these technologies have crossed the line of fundamental breakthroughs. Thus, engineering investments are what is needed to turn these technologies into operational solutions. This investment can be made by commercial entities and recovered through the sales price of complete products for the government, or this investment can be made by government organizations so that products can be developed based on specific requirements. Alliant 2 is a service IDIQ contract that issues task orders that implement government investments. The government's decision in making the investment should consider (1) when a technology is needed, (2) the benefits/value of the technology, (3) the maturation path and remaining cost at specific points, and (4) the development timelines. At times, competing technologies must also be considered with an analysis of alternatives. One alternative with or without competing technologies is to wait and see how a technology is matured by the commercial community without government investment.

During the Cold War, mission priorities, classification requirements, and a lack of commercial markets encouraged the U.S. government to invest heavily in many technology areas. With the modern commercial IT market and severe constraints on government funding, government investment decisions are far more complex. Maximizing return on investment has overridden maximizing total capabilities within most government agencies. Once an investment decision has been made, perhaps with the support of our business development leads, our solution development endeavor must determine the objective features and performance of the technology once development is complete, the approach for implementing the technology into the architecture and process, and the IMS. When the government is not certain about the technology investment path to take and issues a SOO, our analysts must take on the challenge of both selecting the technology and creating the technology development path. When a technology is already in use by commercial enterprises, integrating the technology into a government system architecture might still require the tailoring of the technology through development and configuration changes. Finally, when we own a proprietary technology that is of benefit to the government, the adoption of this technology should be pursued across the business development life cycle, as explained in Chapter 5.

It is beyond the scope of this book to do justice to all the leading-edge technologies interested by the government. Thus, only a quick summary of the technologies is provided as a starting point to help solutions developers investigate their continuously advancing status. In these technology areas, secret commercial investments can suddenly yield new products, new investments by other government agencies can be exploited, and breakthroughs can unexpectedly emerge. The solutions developer must understand the complex environment for each technology area. Following the government's determination of leading-edge technologies increases our ability to gain funding. However, it is a reactive approach for developing solutions. Reactive approaches present the risk of overlooking unpredicted technology breakthroughs and sudden leaps in capability. Also, we become part of a pack all chasing after the same technology-driven outcomes.

11.1 Understanding How Technologies Advance

While following the government's decision is important in many situations, understanding how technologies advance will help our solution to break away from the pack and capture real innovation. Figure 11.1 summarizes the advancement path of computer hardware technology. First, we see the miniaturization of computer technology from the vacuum tubes of the 1940s with Colossus and ENIAC to transistors after 1955 [1]. Then, Jack Kilby at Texas Instruments and Robert Noyce at Fairchild Semiconductor invented the integrated circuit (IC) in 1958 [2]. The IC, in the form of a microchip, uses structures of semiconducting material (i.e., silicon) to achieve the functions of millions and eventually billions of transistors. IC designs eventually enabled the creation of miniaturized sensors and micromachines. More importantly, ICs immediately became the backbone of modern computers. By the late 1960s, the processing functions of a motherboard with microchips had been compressed into a single IC called a *central microprocessor*. Since then, engineering advances in the design of microprocessors and supporting memory chips have been fast and steady. What history teaches us is that scientific breakthroughs are vastly more dramatic than engineering advances. Better

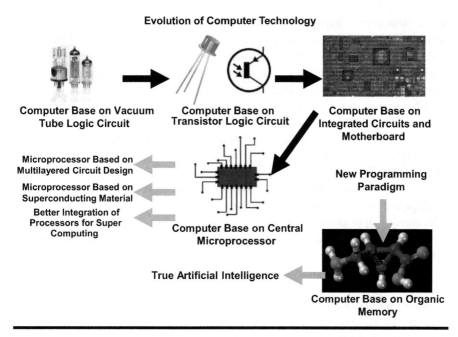

Figure 11.1   Breakthroughs and advancements in computer technology.

vacuum tubes cannot come close to transistors and better transistors cannot come close to microprocessor chips.

As we look toward the future of computers, the layering of circuits in the microprocessor or the use of superconducting materials, which requires less electrical current, can dramatically increase computational capacity [3]. Supercomputers are already integrating tens of thousands of microprocessors, and keeping these processors cool is a key part of supercomputer design [4]. Thus, engineering advances for integrating microprocessors could make massively powerful computers easily assessible. Yet, these known opportunities are not necessarily breakthroughs. In fact, the concept of the computer as a system that operates on data, rules, and mathematical formulas through a linear series of binary code has not changed since the invention of the first computer. The next major leap in computing is therefore a breakaway from linear operations to match operations similar to the way the human mind processes information. To do this, organic memory or similar technologies need to be developed to store and process information three dimensionally [5]. While this breakthrough may be years away, the point is that the world will change once this technology comes. We as solutions developers must not be so focused on immediate needs that we completely overlook greater opportunities. Computers based on molecular activities is obviously an extreme example. The lesson in solutioning for technical advances is that whenever we invest heavily in a technology, we must obviously question when that technology will be obsolete.

At the same time, whenever we want to be early adopters of potential technology breakthroughs, we must also objectively question whether we are being premature.

Unlike computer hardware technologies, software technologies are not always about one type of software design replacing another, as shown in Figure 11.2. For example, programming languages, such as FORTRAN and C, which are compiled for implementation yield applications, run much faster than programming languages, such as BASIC and MUMPS, which are interpreted in real time for execution [6]. With much faster computers and the need to operate a great variety of light codes across the Internet, newer interpreted languages, such as Java, Python, and Ruby, have gained popularity. As software became more complex, the creation of coded objects based on functional capabilities helped accelerate development and code integration. As software component reuse became desirable, creating applications as an integrated collection of loosely coupled software modules gained popularity. Then, many programming endeavors became exercises in understanding which existing components could be reused and modified. The bundling of reusable software components into platforms or market places is now the trend in developing collections of enterprise applications [7]. Many commercial software products for knowledge management, customer relations management, and business process management have built platforms around their core business software to greatly expand utility. The solutions developer then faces the challenge of selecting which platform technology to adopt as multiple products can be used to satisfy the same set of government requirements. In fact, as software technologies continue to expand, solutions development is increasingly about making the right software technology choices. The mismatch of software technology with government requirements has led to major program failures. Common misalignments include choosing a program language that is too slow for the desired operations, a program language with very limited shared components, or a software platform that is too restrictive for customized development.

Like hardware technologies, software technologies can have breakthroughs. For example, programs can be developed to alter their own coding to automatically refine their capabilities, new program languages may no longer need to use linear branching logic and loops, and programs may be formed through natural language interpretation. Also like hardware technologies, potential software breakthroughs help us to maintain a strategic focus while addressing immediate solution needs. Immediate solution needs obviously cannot wait for technology breakthroughs. However, we can design the engineering advancement of technologies to encourage breakthroughs, adapt to breakthroughs, avoid the threat of breakthroughs, and find breakthroughs. We note finding breakthroughs even though all our examples have been dramatic. This is because technology breakthroughs are not always about size, but about introducing non-standard concepts and not following the given path. While hardware breakthroughs are hard to quietly achieve because of the investments involved, some software breakthroughs may already be present in niche commercial markets. As we proceed to look at the technology paths

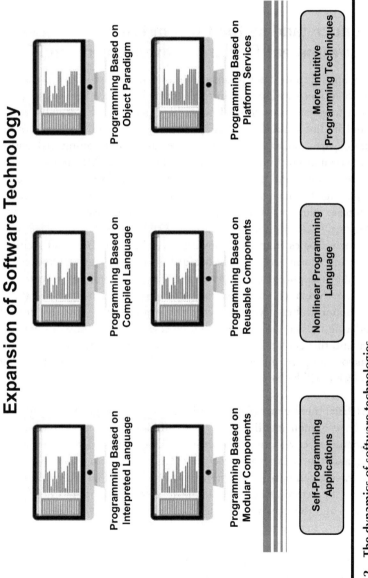

Figure 11.2   The dynamics of software technologies.

that current researchers and developers are already pursuing, please allow room for innovations. The last thing this book should be is a template for stuffing written content into proposals. That defeats the importance of solutions development, creativity, and customer understanding.

11.2 Understanding the Current List of Government-Declared Advancements in IT

The following are short descriptions of leading-edge technologies as identified by the GSA. Solutions development in these technology areas involves adapting new capabilities to government needs, finding high pay-off and acceptable risk investments, and finding capabilities that are not obvious to other federal contractors. Sometimes, partnerships with academic, research, and commercial entities are required to establish technical capabilities. Alternatively, SMEs in each technology area can be recruited and hired as consultants and employees for inhouse capability. As lead-edge technologies implies limited contractor past experience, developing a complete solution that presents a clear path from government investment to technology utilization is critical to success. As solutions developers assess how to integrate technologies from the following areas into processes and architectures, the temptation to arm-wave must be avoided. If there are gaps in knowledge, those gaps should be recognized and plans for resolving them must be presented. If there are risks in performance, those risks should have mitigation strategies. If there are potential opportunities beyond government requirements, the steps for refining and validating those opportunities must be elucidated. Because of the pace of IT advancement, this book cannot tell solutions developers where to look to improve the technology for government customers. Nevertheless, the strength of a technology-driven solution will be based on discovery.

- ■ **Artificial Intelligence (AI):** Techniques and technologies for getting machines to have human intelligence–type capabilities, such as decision-making in unbounded environments, learning and self-adaptation, uncertain reasoning, and natural language processing. Until the development and maturation of organic computing with nonlinear processing that truly mimics human thought processes, AI capabilities must be achieved through alternative techniques and the massive application of computing power. Current uncertain reasoning analysis techniques include [8] the following:
  - – Fuzzy Logic: Set theory that deals with the vagueness instead of the randomness of data. A fuzzy variable belongs to different sets with varying levels of enclosure. Set boundaries are therefore elastic with logical constructs based more on degrees than binary true or false. Insights gained through an inference engine with possible conclusions are associated with a knowledge base.

- Bayesian Networks: Node and link networks where the propagation is based on the probability of each uncertain condition being one state or another. This is often the case when given inadequate knowledge for a definitive diagnosis. The network then presents patterns of beliefs for understanding of outcomes and consequences.
- Rough Set Theory: Set theory that defines what data clearly falls within specific sets and what data falls within the region between sets. It then uses a reductionist approach to determine how to be lenient with inconsistent data and to create rough boundaries. For the reductionist approach, information is decomposed down to indiscernible elementary granules of knowledge that can form elementary sets (concepts). Concepts can then integrate into compound concepts to be a crisp set or to become part of rough sets.
- Genetic Algorithms: Data search algorithms based on completing candidate approaches associated with a knowledge base. The approaches are then selected and altered (controlled variation) for further searches based on each generation of results (fitness parameter) in an evolutionary process. Next-generation searches are created through genetic operators which can create hybrid approaches. They are highly successful in probing an unknown search space.
- Neural Networks: A layered interconnected network of subsymbolic (no rigidly defined symbolic meaning) elements (neurons) that abstractly models a problem space. The neurons have design weighting, and connection strengths can receive positive (excitatory) and negative (inhibitory) environment inputs such as from a change dataset. The network structure then morphs through iterative learning to provide insight.
- Agent-Based Modeling: An explorative tool that regards the problem space as unbounded—the space is bigger than the data that has already been collected. The available data is then used to help define behavior constructs for agents. Agents are simple abstract representations of actors in the problem space, such as people, things, forces, and so on. The theory is that interactions by agents over time or across a large population sample can explore the data-deficient parts of the problem space and gather new insights on problem scope, hidden forces, and extended consequences. These models are very useful in studying complex systems with self-organizing and self-adapting behaviors.
- ■ **Autonomic Computing:** Systems that operate across their range of functions and complete missions without human involvement. Self-driving cars are a prime example of emerging autonomic computing technology. In theory, a broad range of devices can have embedded computing that automates operations and reduces the need for human control and decision-making. These pervasive devices can further coordinate activities across networks, and the range of their capabilities is only constrained by each device's ability to

perform high-order situational analysis functions. As no computer can yet match the human mind's ability to handle unbounded situations, autonomic computing tends to be more successful for functions with defined ranges such as established road systems and limited behaviors for surrounding vehicles.

■ **Big Data:** Data sources or integrated data sources at the high terabyte level that should be stored in a continuous manner within a single data structure is a Big Data problem. Continuous storage is required for high-speed advanced analytics across a great volume and potentially high diversity of data. If this is not a requirement, then the terabytes of data can be stored in clusters of relational databases. Currently, the only way to store massive volumes of data in an unlimited database is through non-relational technologies such as Google's Big Table approach, where data is stored as cells tracked by row string, column string, and time stamp [9]. Once data is ingested into a single non-relational database, the relationships between data can be dynamically formed to match the needs of analysis. Advanced data-mining techniques that can take advantage of a Big Data technology stack include [10] the following:

  − Deductive Decision Tree Mining: Multistep tool-based searches into datasets driven by dependent rules and incremental search outcomes. Results from start to end are organized into tree structures.

  − Agile Characterization of Data: Tool-assisted dynamic organization of data into summary groups, such as groups based on ranges, with sufficient generalization for comparisons and contrasting between groups. This technique can also be used for data compression and abstraction in macro-dynamic analysis.

  − Complex Classifications: Tool-based identification of properties that are common across all or portions of the data and interrelationships among data elements based on these properties.

  − Regression Analysis: Graphical tool-based discovery of functions that map to data such as through curve-fitting techniques across approximate ranges or statistics-based linear regression. The representation can further be used to identify hidden patterns and trends.

  − Inductive Data Association: Graphical tool-based node and link constructs in data based on discovered associations. Association type and strength can be reflected in the definition and distance of linkages. The representation can also be used to identify spatial gaps in data and future collection requirements.

  − Clustering Analysis: Tool-assisted artificial grouping and regrouping of data to discover collateral datasets where knowledge discovery can be better made. Meaning of a cluster is understood after analysis, whereas the meaning of a classification is more connected with the classification process.

  − Baseline Pattern Searches: Tool-assisted searches for entire patterns, groups, and states in data. These entities may sometimes be obscured by other data elements intermixed into the patterns and groups.

- State Change and Deviation Filters: Tool for the continuous monitoring of state changes and pattern deviations in data based on user-defined markers and indicators.
- **Biometrics:** All information gathered about a person can be used for identification, tracking, authorization, and behavioral prediction. Information that are considered biometrics include fingerprints, eye retinas and irises, voice patterns, facial patterns, and hand measurements. Technologies associated with biometrics analysis include sensors, encryption, Big Data store, and analytics that coordinate multiple types of data. Identification is done by key metrics and baseline points from an authoritative data source. Then, data from other sources are matched to the authoritative source to yield a probability that the person at a location is of a specific identity. This probability increases with multiple points of validation, such as voice and fingerprint recognition. For security, biometrics technology is critical in confirming and granting access. For intelligence, biometrics technology can help find and track people, such as from CCTV cameras. Biometrics can further be used to screen people for diseases, identify irregular behavior within a crowd, and find hidden associations among people due to gene expression.
- **Cloud Computing:** Cloud-based IaaS, PaaS, and SaaS are now common commercial practice. However, the full potential of the cloud has not yet been recognized. On the cloud, applications can grow to support ever-larger user communities, data sources can be integrated in new ways, and user/ social organizations self-form and continuously morph. New technologies and techniques on the cloud will therefore continue to emerge for years to come. Some of the innovations can have federal applications. Other innovations may pose threats or introduce vulnerabilities to federal operations.
- **Cybersecurity:** Technologies and techniques must be continuously developed to keep pace with advancements in adversary capabilities such as hacking into networks and systems, developing new viruses and worms, designing Trojan horses and malware, and discovering identity information based on available sources [11]. Standard methodologies include firewalls, encryption, network and system monitoring, system scanning, identity management and access control, enforcing information management procedures, and physical security at data centers and across networks. However, effectiveness depends on the ability to stay ahead of the cleverness of adversaries in finding ways to penetrate security boundaries. Black hat testers playing the role of adversaries can discover hidden vulnerabilities. Yet with fiber running across all parts of our infrastructure, it is hard to prevent someone from tapping into a network. Thus, cybersecurity is forced to focus on point defense as well as broad security boundaries. With so much data on the open Internet that can be used through advanced analytics to cause damage, cybersecurity is in turn also forced to focus on crisis/damage response.

■ **Health Information Technology (HIT):** Modern EHR systems and medical process business systems are generating substantial amounts of computable patient and caregiver data. The data, when used, can effectively improve the quality of care, support medical discoveries, and achieve cost savings at hospitals and clinics [12]. Software-driven components are further being added to medical devices. The components increase the precision of procedures, conduct real-time diagnostic support, help share information and situation awareness, and improve data gathering. Thus, HIT stretches from central databases to the hospital bed and even to the home through telemedicine. HIT includes health informatics which advances ways to use health data. Currently, new cures are being discovered using genomics, proteomics, and oncology data. In the future, the totality of data could be used in new ways through advances in analytical techniques. As IT devices continue to become miniaturized, implanted devices in patients can further regulate body functions, monitor physical status, and support machine-to-body integration.

■ **The Internet of Things (IoT):** The integration of wireless technologies, micro-electromechanical systems (MEMS), and machine-to-machine (M2M) communications software permits objects, animals, and people with embedded devices, such as biochip transponders, to form an interactive automated network. This network can report on the status of failing machines, the whereabouts of animals, and the health of individuals.

■ **Mobile IT:** Continued advances in the computational and storage capacity of cell phones and tablets should broaden the utilization of mobile IT. Mobile IT will increasingly be used for functions traditionally handled by desktop/laptop devices. Mobile applications can provide real-time decision support and knowledge access to users. Ultimately, mobile IT can be the extension of people, and the management of mobile devices can enable the dynamic organization of communities.

■ **Virtual Networking:** A class of products that enable the control of software over networks. These tools promote remote systems administration and can take over local system operations. They can control the flow of data, manage system-to-system interactions, test operations, and remotely resolve problems. As systems and networks become more complex and as problems become more complex, these products will have to keep pace.

11.3 Understanding Technology Advancements in the Non-IT World

Until the dominance of the information age, technology advancement was all about heavy investments into propulsions, structures, energy generation, navigation, sensors, control, communications, and other elements of physical systems [13].

The technologies in these areas are vast, complex, and still advancing. However, their advancement can often take years of scientific research and engineering work. These technologies come together to form different types of systems with missions ranging from weapons to support of day-to-day societal operations. For physical systems that support day-to-day business operations within the federal government, procurements tend to be for buying commercial products without solution requirements. Government investments into unique solutions for physical systems are thus largely for national security systems, disaster response systems, and exploratory systems. Most of the investments made by the U.S. National Aeronautics and Space Administration (NASA) are disclosed to the general public to the degree where the technology is still protected from adversary exploitation. NASA's budget is, however, very small. The DoD's investments into physical systems have declined since the Cold War, but it still has the greatest budget by far. Appendix A presents DoD's successes and challenges in developing physical and IT systems over the past several decades. Most of DoD's physical technology investments are highly classified and it is inappropriate for us to discuss solutions development for those technology areas in this book. The following descriptions are therefore merely high-level considerations for the solutions architect as he or she enters the classified world.

- **Propulsions:** Propulsion technologies focus on how to move systems in their designed realm of operations—on land, at sea, in the air, and in space. The effectiveness of the technology is measured in the amount of total force, fuel used to generate a unit of force, achievable maximum acceleration, achievable sustained velocity, and duration of propulsive travel. Force is generated through mechanical interactions (i.e., an engine and wheels), chemical reactions (i.e., a rocket), electromagnetism (i.e., some trains), and nuclear/ionic energy (i.e., some ships and spacecraft). Propulsion technologies are aligned with the environment of operations because the environment generates forces opposing the motion and may also supply the material used for propulsion. For example, jet airplanes use oxygen from the atmosphere to burn fuel, which then propels air to create propulsion. Car motors burn gasoline with oxygen in the air to generate mechanical force. Nuclear vessels use desalinated water from the ocean to run the nuclear power–heated steam turbines and propellers. Innovations in propulsions tend to focus on efficiency (minimizing fuel mass per unit thrust) or total propulsive force through engineering designs. Breakthroughs in propulsions can be made by discovering new and better energy sources.
- **Structure:** Structural technologies focus on the utilization of material to form the physical container for systems. The resulting structure must be able to maintain a fixed or controlled shape, resist environmental effects, and withstand the forces of motion and action. Structural materials are defined by their substances (i.e., aluminum, steel that is an iron/carbon alloy, graphite that is a crystalline formation of carbon), complex molecular constructs (i.e., organic

and nonorganic polymers), and physical constructs (i.e., honeycomb, trusses, fiber weaves). Structural configuration characteristics include the ability to withstand strains, stresses, and torsional forces on the structure. Structural surface characteristics include the ability to withstand electromagnetic radiation that can be absorbed or dissipated, friction that generates heat and material stress, and impacting forces that can cause deformations and internal vibrations. Innovations in structures tend to focus on creating new complex polymers, new configurations, or new form designs. Increasingly, lightweight high-strength structures are critical to systems design. Also, structures for micromechanical devices and nanotechnology systems are areas with high potential for continued innovation.

- **Energy Generation:** Technologies for energy generation can be used to power systems or create weapons. The prime example is nuclear power where controlled nuclear energy release can run cities and uncontrolled energy release from an explosion can destroy cities. Beyond nuclear reactions, energy can be gained through chemical reactions, electromagnetic interactions, biomolecular interactions, and mechanical forces. Innovations in energy generation tend to come from finding new sources of energy and achieving higher efficiency in existing ways to generate energy. As total energy is conserved in a closed environment, efficiency in energy generation means the percentage of energy that is successfully converted into a useful form. For example, in using chemical reactions to generate mechanical energy, a part of the released energy is lost as heat. As the nuclear age disclosed the amount of energy stored within the atomic structures of matter, the future of energy source discovery may be in finding ways to get energy from the atom without fusion or fission reactions.

- **Navigation:** Modern terrestrial navigation is typically based on the global positioning system (GPS), cell tower triangulation, magnetic compass, or terrain identification. The challenges of navigation are accuracy and continuity across great distances to permit precision travel. As vessels, such as drones, become faster and more capable of traveling greater distances, the ability to navigate these vessels across the world and across tight city environments become additional navigation challenges. Navigating in areas where signals cannot be received and where maps do not exist is difficult. Human operators have been very adaptive in such situations, and advances in artificial intelligence could enable automated machines to figure out how to travel without prior flight plans, set rules, or clear coordinates.

- **Sensors:** Sensor technologies focus on gathering information from environmental sources through detection of electromagnetic radiation, fast-moving particles such as neutrons, slow-moving particles such as odors, sound waves, and other changing activities in the environment. Sensors can be passive, receiving only what is emitted into the environment, or active, sending energies and disturbances into the environment to get measurable results.

Detection of light in the visible and near-visible regime can be used to form static and video images of terrestrial conditions and situations from great distances. These images can be built by a photo sensor array where the density of the array structure governs the digital resolution. When the light is faint and spread apart, lens and parabolic mirrors can be used to focus the light at the photo sensor array. However, technical advances have been on developing new sensor material for detection of fainter radiation, better detection of radiation beyond the visible ranges, and compactness of the sensors. In the future, breakthroughs in sensing technologies could be in the areas of long-range detection of odor trails to determine number and types of people miles away, detection of environmental situations based on minute vibrations emitted by objects, and detection of gravity waves to study distant stellar objects.

■ **Control:** Control theory is an extension of mathematical constructs for dependent variables, and the application of control theory uses computing capability to isolate all the environmental and internal forces governing the system being controlled. The computer then uses control equations to converge all the forces so that the system will move along intended paths. As forces can cause a system to go into unstable motion with dangerous oscillations, achieving system stability is a key challenge in control. Another challenge in control is achieving high maneuverability in systems. For systems that must combat other systems, maneuvering the system at the extreme ranges of forces is often the difference between victory and defeat. Even with modern computing power, solving the differential equations associated with control can be challenging. Some equation states can be solved deterministically, and other states require computational methods. When automated decision-making needs to be added to the control process, control technology extends from advanced mathematics to information technology and AI.

■ **Communications:** Current communication technologies all center on encoding messages into a waveform that is transmitted a great distance. Verbal communication between people is the encoding of sound waves. Waves in the electromagnetic spectrum, as shown in Figure 11.3, in contrast, can travel far faster and greater distances than sound waves. The way to encode a wave is to either modulate the amplitude (AM) or modulate the frequency (FM). Amplitude modulation requires changes in energy levels across the waveform. Thus, it is used for long wavelengths where frequency modulation is less practical. In frequency modulation, the rate of data transmission is directly tied to the shortness of the wavelength/highness of the frequency. High-frequency transmissions also yield beams that do not spread apart as much. When the frequency is high enough to be in the range of light, a beam of coherent light waves (a laser) can propagate great distances with minor diffraction. Thus, modulated laser beams have been used for high capacity point-to-point communications across the atmosphere and in space. If communications between a point and a broad region is desired, an expanding beam can be transmitted

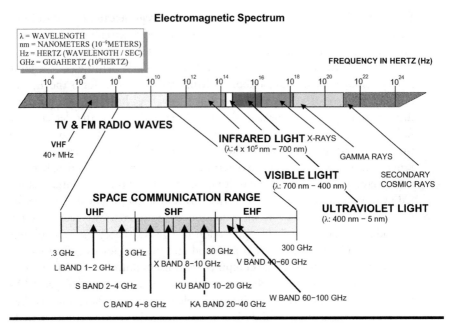

Figure 11.3 Waveforms used for communications.

from a satellite, radio/TV tower, or cell phone tower. For communications within a societal infrastructure, copper wires have been used to carry encoded electrical waves, and fiber optic wires are now being used to carry encoded light waves. Historically, communicated information is encoded directly into the waveform as analog signals. With the convergence of computers and communications technologies, information is first consolidated into digital form. The digital information is then encoded into the waveform in a compressed manner.

11.4 Technology in Solutions Development

Our brief review of technology areas reveals the immense scope of potential technologies that can be used for solutions to the government. Some government procurements require the offerors to provide the best paths for obtaining new technologies. In the proposal response, we must be extremely competitive in performance, cost, and schedule if our technology solution is in the same direction as everyone else's solution. Alternatively, we must find a better path as suggested.

Not all procurements require technology development, but most procurements will expect the offeror to at least incorporate the most modern technologies and products from the commercial market place. As best practice, all solutioning endeavors should start by identifying the current technologies used in the customer organization. Then, even before we explore process changes and architecture redesign, we should conduct market research to determine which technologies are obsolete. If modern commercial products can be used to update the technology stack, then we might wish to adjust processes and architectures to enable such instant improvements. The last piece of a solution after process, architecture, and technology is human interface. With human users, operators, workers, and leaders, the system becomes a more complex system. The solution becomes a more complex solution.

References

1. Burks, A., and Burks, A. 1981. The ENIAC: The first general-purpose electronic computer. *Annals of the History of Computing*, 3, 4: 310–389.
2. Lécuyer, C., and Brock, D.C. 2010. *Makers of the Microchip: A Documentary History of Fairchild Semiconductor*. Cambridge, MA: The MIT Press.
3. Salman, E., and Friedman, E.G. 2012. *High Performance Integrated Circuit Design*, 1st ed. New York: McGraw-Hill Education.
4. Murray, C.J. 1997. *The Supermen: The Story of Seymour Cray and the Technical Wizards behind the Supercomputer*, 1st ed. Hoboken, NJ: Wiley.
5. Giordani, A. 2012. Is organic computer memory on the horizon? *ScienceNode*. Sep 5.
6. Petzold, C. 2000. *Code: The Hidden Language of Computer Hardware and Software*. Seattle, WA: Microsoft Press.
7. Klimczak, E. 2013. *Design for Software: A Playbook for Developers*, 1st ed. Hoboken, NJ: Wiley.
8. Chen, Z. 2001. *Data Mining and Uncertain Reasoning*. Hoboken, NJ: John Wiley & Sons.
9. Marz, N., and Warren, J. 2015. *Big Data: Principles and Best Practices of Scalable Realtime Data Systems*, 1st ed. Greenwich, CT: Manning Publications.
10. Han, J., Kamber, M., and Pei, J. 2011. *Data Mining: Concepts and Techniques*, 3rd ed. Burlington, MA: Morgan Kauffman.
11. Franke, D. 2016. *Cyber Security Basics: Protect Your Organization by Applying the Fundamentals*. Amazon Digital Services LLC.
12. Glaser, J.P. 2016. *Glaser on Health Care IT: Perspectives from the Decade that Defined Health Care Information Technology (HIMSS Book Series)*, 1st ed. Boca Raton, FL: CRC Press.
13. Trefil, J. 2017. *The Story of Innovation: How Yesterday's Discoveries Lead to Tomorrow's Breakthroughs*. Washington, DC: National Geographic.

Chapter 12

Developing Solutions that Improve Personnel Capabilities

The fourth area of solutions development is by no means the least important. In fact, some might argue that with the right team to develop the processes, architectures, and technologies after contract award, the incompleteness of the solution in the proposal can sometimes be overlooked by evaluators. Offerors frequently default to the conclusion that the right team is one where key personnel are people favorably recognized by government customers. While this strategy has worked, only adopting this strategy without thinking about how the people, the proposed staff, will work together in meeting PWS/SOW/SOO requirements reflects laziness on the part of solutions development.

Starting with a strategic view, people are a part of a government agency's solution need as users of systems, government stakeholders of processes, government procurers of capabilities, contractors supporting the program office, contractors developing the solution, and contractors or government personnel implementing the solution. As contractors developing the solution, our solution must include a process that addresses the roles and responsibilities of all the people involved. We further support the successful implementation of roles and responsibilities through providing training products, system operations support, system administration, and system maintenance services when tasked. For people who are not directly under our management, the effectiveness of our solution lies largely in developing user interfaces (UI) that encourage new process adoption, designing multimedia user training that is appealing and traceable to objective workflows, and establishing feedback mechanisms for all types of people involved to support continuous process improvements.

In user-centric UI design for solution-specific tasks and workflows, the design team should use system screen mockups to apply a scientifically validated model for saliency-based visual attention. Such a model maps a screen to show the degree to which its specific objects and locations draw a user's attention. The UI design can then leverage this mapping to keep user attention on the most important screen items to support the workflow. Screen elements not critical to the workflow but draw user attention, such as logos, should in turn be considered for elimination or modification. After initial assessment, UI prototypes can be developed to test user interactions and refine usability. In the testing process, contextual inquiry with representative user groups can be further conducted through structured interviews to better understand how to optimize user interactions. Even before this human-centric design process, it was assumed that user needs and inputs were a part of the requirements development process. After the start of systems development, it was assumed that user evaluations were a part of the testing process, particularly in the case of Agile development. However, user-centric designs reflect a positive commercial approach to solutions development that is very often overlooked in government contracts.

For all the people directly under the authority of our program manager (PM), the solution to improve the capabilities of the staff must be more comprehensive. Our personnel developing a process, architecture, or technology solution are part of the acquisition process. Our personnel responsible for operating and maintaining a deployed process, architecture, or technology solution are part of the sustainment process. For each process, there should be an established workflow with functions, tasks, standard operating procedures, and performance metrics. The workflow can be designed to be rigorous to prevent errors or adaptive to handle situational changes. Some parts of the workflow can be anchored to established methodologies, such as Agile development, and other parts of the workflow must be tailored to the specific policies and regulations of the supported government organization. To improve the staff's capabilities in executing these processes, the solution needs to address (1) recruiting and retention, (2) training and evaluations, and (3) organization and management.

12.1 Recruiting and Retention

The staffing process for a solution begins with determining the work that must be performed and projecting the types and number of positions required to accomplish the work. Each position should have well-defined roles and responsibilities, and the position should then be associated with a labor category that allows for the hiring of staff with adequate levels of education, certification, security clearance, and experience to satisfy roles and responsibilities. When lower cost is a critical factor in winning a proposal, the strategy can be to find ways to conduct the work with less but more capable staff, find positions that can be filled with minimally qualified staff, and find places other than salary to cut expenses. Contractor fee, general and administrative expenses, overhead expenses, and even fringe benefits can sometimes be reduced for the sake of competition. Once positions and salary objectives have been formulated, the challenge of innovatively recruiting candidates to maximize capabilities under controlled cost must be confronted.

The standard questions all offerors ask are whether there are already incumbent personnel supporting the work being pursued and whether those people are well-liked by the government customers. Being well-liked does not automatically mean that incumbents are the most qualified for the positions. Misalignments between incumbent qualifications and position needs create solution opportunities. If the incumbent personnel are truly the most qualified, then solution development must focus on getting contingent incumbent commitment letters or convincing the government that incumbent staff can be adequately captured after contract award. Making assertions of incumbent capture is not a solution. However, presenting arguments about the attractiveness of the employment package, the lack of alternative employment options in select position locations, and back-up plans for when incumbent capture drops below threshold requirements are starting points for a convincing solution.

If incumbent capture is not required or desired, then creativeness in recruiting and staffing becomes a part of the total solution. The government buyer is always concerned about whether positions will be filled on time and with qualified people. One way to alleviate this concern is to fill key positions with elite personnel who are overqualified for their positions. If these people can start on day one of the contract and lead essential processes, their heroic efforts can resolve delays and challenges in staffing for other positions. One team dynamics concept is that a senior expert can lead four-plus junior/mid-level staff and cover for their deficiencies in skills. Therefore, in challenging staffing situations, a strategy is to make sure that at least 20 percent of one's staff is truly the best. To find these best candidates, the solutions developer cannot merely hand position requirements to human resource (HR) recruiters. Most recruiters operate based on checklists. The checklist approach is acceptable as a first-level filter. However, it has two major deficiencies in even creating a short list of candidates. The first deficiency is that the unique qualities associated with the way each checklist criteria is satisfied and how credentials work together to yield capabilities greater than the sum of the parts cannot be understood. The checklist might require a bachelor's or master's degree, but it is hard for a checklist to identify the strength of where that degree comes from to include quality of school and education curriculum. The checklist might require 10 years of experience, but it is hard for a checklist to appreciate all the accomplishments and skills gained in those 10 years. The second deficiency is that a checklist cannot restructure a resume given the content presented so that a candidate appears more qualified than how the resume was originally written. As a result, candidates with exceptional qualities in other areas might be eliminated by human resource recruiters in a fine cut simply because one criterium was not written well enough for the position. Given these concerns, the solutions developer should get deeply involved in the evaluation of a broad group of candidates after the resumes have been gathered with only the clearly unqualified people eliminated.

In the candidate identification process, the recruiter should leverage current employee referrals, personnel networks, employment websites, social media sites, advertisements, professional conferences, and business intelligence. The top candidates will often require proactive engagement with courting endeavors by the recruiter. If the recruiter lacks the experience to communicate at a level that impresses a top candidate, the solutions developer might need to get directly involved in recruiting. Normal candidates can be hired through a standard process, such as through the following steps:

- Candidate Qualifications Screening: For each candidate resume received, the HR recruiter screens the candidate's resume against the job position description developed earlier to make certain that high-caliber experience, expertise, education, licensure, certifications, and other requirements are met.
- Internal Rating and Ranking of Applicants: The HR recruiter and program manager rate and rank candidates for each job description based on experience, availability, and other factors. They can call upon senior-level advisors for assistance when positions involve specialized capabilities or significant experience. Candidates rated as superior receive priority attention for follow-up qualification steps.
- Capabilities Validation: The HR recruiter or program manager conduct extensive screening to validate functional and technical expertise, the number of years of experience, the status of certifications and credentials, and any other specific requirements listed in the job description. The HR recruiter and program manager will also utilize extensive interview questions or tests to determine the aptitude and potential success of each applicant and develop a list of top candidates.
- Preliminary Security Discussion: The HR recruiter and security manager discuss security requirements and inform candidates of background, issues, or activities that could result in a clearance being denied, thus eliminating candidates who may be unlikely to clear security.
- Reference Check: Employment references are contacted to verify employment and gain further insight regarding the candidate. The HR recruiter pays special attention to the duration each candidate stayed at a given job and any information about their job satisfaction during his or her employment.
- Candidate Interviews: The program manager identifies and arranges in-person interviews for the exceptionally qualified candidates for each job description. To ensure that qualifications are validated, the HR recruiter can reach back

to corporate SMEs with understanding of the candidate's specialty area and arrange separate interviews. Additionally, the HR recruiter will ask behavioral questions to ensure that the candidate is an exceptionally qualified and highly motivated fit for the program.

■ Candidate Selections and On-Boarding: Working together, the HR recruiter and the program manager will select the best candidates and they will be approved to receive contingent employment offers. The program manager further seeks out customer inputs on key candidates when appropriate to prepare the program for a shift in new staff resources.

Candidate resumes are seldom written exactly to fit targeted positions. Therefore, the resumes of all selected candidates must be adjusted to further explain relevant experience and highlight key education and certifications before inclusion in proposals or presentation to customers.

The candidate retention process begins immediately upon start of employment and should be explained in proposals as such. Employees often determine quickly whether they have long-range futures with companies. To retain the best employees, the managers must achieve the following tasks:

■ Provide new employees with a full orientation of company processes.
■ Assign buddies to new employees to help them integrate with company culture.
■ Offer training and educational assistance to help employees advance their careers.
■ Provide career mentorship with genuine endeavors to help each employee achieve his or her potential.
■ Create strong team structures that thrive on performance, interdependence, and mutual support.
■ Recognize loyalty and commitment as a part of the company culture.
■ Have a fair and understandable system of rewarding performance and accomplishments to include financial awards and bonuses.
■ Instill a sense of job security for those who have achieved and are maintaining acceptable performance.
■ Offer superior benefits in medical insurance, dental and visual insurance, life and disability insurance, retirement plans, and leave plans.
■ Help each employee achieve an acceptable level of work–life balance with recognition that some employees might accept long work hours when fairly compensated.
■ Provide feedback mechanisms for employee suggestions and concerns.
■ Sustain annual raises that, at minimum, account for inflation and growing experience.
■ Maintain paths where employees can be promoted to leadership positions from within the company.

As employees are vulnerable to public perceptions and the opinions of others, the retention process should be aware of how the company is represented on social media sites and in news articles. The senior leaders of the company must further maintain public personas that garner trust and respect. Above all, the senior leaders of the company must truly care about their employees. Small acts of caring in the day-to-day work environment will resonate across the workforce.

12.2 Training and Evaluations

Preparing new employees for positions and current employees for new assignments always require training. The strategy for training is to leverage commercially available training courses, often with associated certifications, to fill gaps in basic skills. This enables company-designed training to focus on the needs of specific customer programs and workflows. The first step in designing training is not actually content but whether the employee must be trained to follow rigorous processes or to be independent and adaptive in executing tasks. In rigorous process execution, the training content must be very procedural with exact details of what must be done. Volumes of standard operating procedures can be made easily accessible through indexing, knowledge management tools, color-coded sections, reference tabs, and graphics. In adaptive execution, the training content must support employee decision-making and activities under different operational outcomes. The content needs to include essential situational knowledge, decision trees on options for courses of action, and scenarios/case studies for how decisions have been made under similar situations. Given these two types of training content, the phases of employee training can be as follows:

- **Phase 1 (Basic Training):** The trainee must gain familiarity with the new system or process through lessons. Depending on the complexity of the content and prior familiarity with the system or process, such lessons can be done through self-review of training content, computer-based interactive training, or classroom (virtual/physical) instructor-based training. This training should be done through integrated modules so that the student receives digestible chucks. The totality of the content should have a sequential and hierarchical organization so that students can track and control progression.
- **Phase 2 (Extended Training):** After basic training, the trainee must gain proficiency through hands-on training. Depending on the nature of a system or process, conducting hands-on training in live operational environments can have risks. Instead, it is better to let trainees work in an established systems-integration environment with trainee user accounts and test/demonstration data. Throughout the hands-on process, instructors must be there to observe the trainees and provide coach-based guidance. We first want trainees to be able to follow steps and then we want trainees to be able to implement their

workflows by simply using the training manuals. The latter endeavor will require initial coaching on best practice and identification/correction of poor habits.

- ■ **Phase 3 (Achieving Mastery):** In order for employees to become coaches and trainers of others, they must gain mastery of the system or process. Once a trainee is proficient and ready to apply his or her skills for day-to-day work, a growth period should be anticipated where his or her skills can continue to advance when given proper mentorship. The mentor should observe and study the trainee's challenges and unique capabilities to help each individual gain mastery in his or her own ways. Those who gain system and process mastery can then coach and mentor others.

In service contracts, the effectiveness of training is demonstrated through the meeting of performance metrics and deliverable quality as required in the PWS. With government-specified performance metrics, the offeror's training and performance evaluation process must be at a timing and fidelity that allows for corrective actions and prevents the failure to meet requirements. This could be through continuous monitoring, random sampling, gate reviews, testing in the training environment, statistical models, and pattern analysis. When the government's requirements are directed at the performance of the system to be developed, the offeror must formulate staff performance metrics to enable the management of development activities. These metrics must then be integrated with the training and evaluation process.

As noted, the evaluation process is associated with the retention process for rewarding high-performing employees. It is also associated with the management process in correcting or eliminating poorly performing employees. The range of functions in program management is explained in Appendix C. The next section focuses on how to use management techniques to correct personnel issues. The correction of process, architecture, and technology issues can be addressed based on approaches presented in Chapters 9, 10, and 11. Sometimes, process, architecture, and technology issues further impact personnel performance. This interrelationship between issues is also addressed below.

12.3 Organization and Management

When processes, architectures, and technologies are effective, then personnel with adequate capabilities complete the total solution. When an employee encounters a performance issue, the management team must first determine whether the issue is associated with the person or with the situation to which the person is assigned. We can increase training, reassign people, and increase reviews to address a continuing lack of employee capability. We can increase incentives, mentorship, and team activities to address a continuing lack of employee motivation. Finally, we can terminate the employee when the capability or motivation is simply inadequate. Before managers give up on individual employees, however, the performance of all employees should be studied to determine whether there are systematic issues such as stovepipe processes, excessive levels of oversight and reporting, illogical workflows, overwhelming quantities of information, excessively complex tools, and erroneous procedures.

As Figure 12.1 shows, the performance of employees should represent a bell curve distribution [1]. Through training, oversight, and mentorship, managers can decrease the deviation by concentrating more employees around the mean or shifting the mean to a higher point of performance. Decreasing the deviation is often desired when there are set performance expectations that are being satisfied by the mean. Shifting the mean is often desired when the overall performance can be improved. In either case, employees at the lower end of the curve might be pulled high enough on the performance spectrum to merit retention. Inversely, some companies brutally achieve performance increases by periodically eliminating the lowest employees on the curve. The bell curve, however, seeks a point of stability. When the curve cannot be compressed further or when the mean cannot be pushed further, continued employee eliminations will become a disincentive by crushing morale, adding stress, and increasing new hire challenges.

Figure 12.2 reveals greater performance challenges across the program or company. When multiple performance peaks appear in employee evaluations, then the staff has stratified into a category of personnel understanding performance expectations while others do not. The manager must quickly figure out what differences are causing the staff to divide and correct the process, architecture, technologies, or personnel elements causing the division. For example, employees who telework might have noticeably lower performances than those who work at company offices.

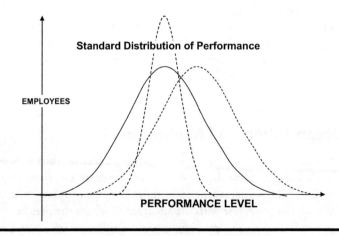

Figure 12.1 Adjusting performance in a standard employee population.

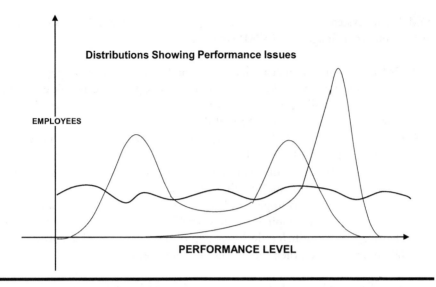

Figure 12.2 Correcting performance issues in an employee population.

Employees mentored by select people might not be as effective as those mentored by others. And, employees of a set age might encounter challenges with specific modern technologies that have been readily used by employees of a younger generation. Most of these problems are quite easily fixable, but they do have to be identified and quantified.

Figure 12.2 further identifies a randomly flat curve with no center of performance. This suggests that the communication of a common standard for expected performance has failed and employees are freely interpreting what they must do. Though rare, we might see this configuration for communities of siloed employees placed in assignments without clear instructions. Even if we allow the employees to communicate among themselves, they might compare experiences and self-normalize performance to yield a bell curve.

The last curve in Figure 12.2 is one in which high performance is sustained by an elite group. The performance rapidly drops off with the rest of the staff. The capabilities of the elite group in adapting to issues in processes, architectures, or technologies cover up the issues and allow the issues to proliferate. To truly fix the issues, people need to stop compensating and let issues manifest. Corrections are then made through controlled discovery. Once the corrections have been implemented, the bell curve should center around the position already held by the elite group.

We would be remiss in discussing the management of personnel without exploring the capabilities of knowledge management tools. Current knowledge management tools include document management/enterprise content management

(DM/ECM) systems, customer relationship management (CRM) systems, and business process management (BPM) systems.

- DM/ECM systems, such as SharePoint and Open Text, have very good content search functions with some workflow management capabilities. If the management challenges lie in utilizing high quantities of procedural knowledge, then these tools might be useful.
- CRM systems, such as Microsoft Dynamics and Salesforce, focus on activity tracking and internal/external collaboration with some documentation coordination capabilities. If the management challenges lie in utilizing situational knowledge, then these tools might be useful.
- BPM Systems, such as Appian and Pegasystems, provide/support frameworks and patterns for developing workflow-enabled solutions. If the management challenges lie in utilizing decision-support mechanisms and adaptive capabilities in processes, then these tools might be useful.

Many of the tools are platform systems where additional capabilities can be added on through configuration and development activities. Thus, these tools are often incorporated into service solutions for the government to add performance confidence, and these tools are sometimes acquired by the government with development support to become enterprise solutions within government agencies. All these tools, however, cannot replace the importance of leadership in elevating teams to their full potential. We have focused on management activities to increase staff capabilities and performance. Performance can also be increased through inspiration, loyalty, and motivation achieved through leadership. A leader inspires by working harder, showing more commitment, and having greater capabilities than his or her team. A leader garners loyalty by looking after the team and being willing to sacrifice for the team. A leader motivates by understanding and addressing individual needs and individual pain points. The power of leadership is a key component of all solutions.

Reference

1. Miller, T. 2016. *HR Analytics and Innovations in Workforce Planning* (Human Resource Management and Organizational Behavior Collection). New York: Business Expert Press.

Chapter 13

The Art of Proposing Solutions

When the business and solution development are complete, there remains the task of finishing a proposal to present the solution in the most positive light. The finishing process led by the proposal manager consists of:

- Conducting a compliance check between all RFP requirements and the proposal volumes.
- Reworking the diagrams created by the solutions architect/developer to have greater artistic appeal.
- Assessing the flow in the proposal volumes to validate that there are no breaks in logic.
- Testing the final gold draft of the proposal on new readers to improve comprehension.
- Checking the consistency of terms and quoted numbers between proposal volumes.
- Checking the alignment between the technical proposal and pricing.
- Ensuring that all language have a common voice.
- Refining headings to improve readers' understanding of proposal organization.
- Testing to see whether key topics can be found through keyword searches.

This stage of the proposal process is both rigorously mechanical and an art. The art lies in getting into the minds of the evaluators and leveraging business intelligence about competitors. This art starts at the beginning of the proposal process and is brought to completion in the submitted proposal. By studying who might be in the source selection groups and their technical backgrounds, the right balance between representing key concepts through graphics and words can be achieved. When the font size for table content can be smaller than the font size for normal proposal text, a decision needs to be made regarding how much additional content can be squeezed into tables. RFPs that impose a low page limit for complex PWS/ SOW/SOO create unique presentation challenges. In such situations, it is almost guaranteed that some potential offerors have engaged government customers prior to RFP release and received understanding about government priorities—the secret code.

When refining diagrams, the concepts can be expressed in the form of hierarchies, process flows with feedback loops, functional blocks with interfaces, categorized containers, groups with and without overlapping boundaries, node and link structures, schedule flows, bar and pie graphs, and graphical curves. Each form of expression can be fairly detailed as long as the approach is consistent. Mixing forms of expression in a single diagram can cause confusion and is risky in the proposal process. The solutions developer should be actively involved in making sure that all diagrams are conceptually effective before and after artistic endeavors. Ambitious artists can significantly change the content in diagrams. So, final review is merited. The following focal points will help keep the expression of concepts consistent for different forms of diagrams.

- Hierarchies: Focus on the consistent definition of each hierarchical layer and the balance between the branches of the hierarchy. Imbalanced tree structures might require compensation schemes when used for decision-making.
- Process Flows with Feedback Loops: Focus on the completeness and continuity of process with key control/decision points. Explain the purpose of each feedback loop and each branch of the process.
- Functional Blocks with Interfaces: Focus on the clear delineation of functions, boundaries, and interrelations. Explain what goes into each function and make sure that there is one strictly adhered to methodology for defining functions.
- Categorized Containers: Focus on clear methodology for defining categories that separate what goes into each container. Define scales for the quantity of items in each container.
- Groups with and without Overlapping Boundaries: Focus on boundary definitions and how boundaries can overlap. Explain the consequences of when items fall within two or more groups. Are integrated traits treated equally or does belonging to one group take priority over others?
- Node and Link Structures: Focus on standardizing definitions for nodes and links. Design structures based on configuration types such as tightly formed, stretched out, loosely formed, and shifting. Describe forces that are acting on the structures.
- Schedule Flows: Focus on presenting complex schedules from tools, such as Microsoft Project, in a visually understandable way that conforms to

graphical font size requirements. Display only summary levels of the schedule, key tasks, and key dependencies.
- Bar and Pie Graphs: Focus on the nature of the data and the best type of graph for representing it. Determine what the graph needs to communicate and design the graph for achieving the desired communication objectives.
- Graphical Curves: Focus on either the exact connectivity of data or approximate curves that best fit the data. Identify and explain inflection points, pattern changes, peaks, and low points. Explain the significance of the overall curve.

In reviewing the final draft of the proposal, compliance with the RFP is important. However, equally important is the commonsense test. The proposal should present a clear winning argument. If other offerors are likely to present different solutions, then the proposal should consider incorporating counterarguments against the competition. The strategy of "ghosting" competitors is to understand alternative solution approaches and being able to attack those approaches based on deep understanding. The metrics for comparing solutions can be performance, schedule, cost, and risks. When seeking a competitor's weaknesses in performance, the solutions developer can start with alternative workflows and alternative architectures plus technologies to question why others would select different paths. One reason for selecting a different path is that a competitor has traded off performance, schedule, cost, and risk differently than one's own solutions team. In such a case, the competitor's assessment must be fiercely discredited. Another reason for selecting a different path is that a competitor has existing experience, products, and processes that favor their path. In such a case, we must explain our path as the best path and their path as the compromise. Finally, it may be possible that a competitor's path is better, but we are not able to offer that path. In such a situation, it is good to remember that the competition for government contracts exists in multiple dimensions. If our solution is not the most attractive, then drastically lowering our price could make the combination of our solution and price the most attractive. If the better solution still has risks, then offering complete risk mitigation in our solution could appeal to more conservative evaluators.

The purpose of developing proposals is to win. Thus, good solutions must support the objective of winning. An elegant solution that is too complex for the evaluators is not a good solution. The perception of risks is very subjective. So, how a solution is written will influence the evaluation results. Good writing that turns complex concepts into simple language is a part of the art in proposal submission. The investment of time and resources in good editing is always worthwhile. Unfortunately, the process of editing is often curtailed when facing demanding proposal schedules. When a proposal reads well and the diagrams are clear and attractive, it is time to submit.

Once a proposal is submitted in accordance with the steps explained in Appendix B, the solutions development process continues once the proposal has passed competitive range and if the government has decided to initiate formal discussions. Every evaluation notice sent by the source selection evaluation team needs a timely and accurate response. Yet, the response must also be strategically shaped to support winning. Within government guidelines, solutions can be modified to better align with clarified government needs and prices can be reduced to increase competitiveness. Many proposals fail during the discussion phase because offerors are too proud to change solutions and decide to provide justifications in response to evaluation notices. Many proposals further fail during final proposal revision because offerors are overconfident about their prices. When the RFP asks for "realistic" pricing, any final price reduction must be well justified. However, when the RFP only requires "reasonable" pricing, almost any competition can evolve into a price war. At the end of the day, the most important question might be, "Are we hungry enough to win?"

Chapter 14

Winning Is Only the Beginning

This book concludes with a simple reminder that we started this journey with the objective of developing effective solutions for the government. Thus, winning the contract is our opportunity to prove that the proposed solution is effective. The solutions developer, upon contract award, must work with the transition team led by the PM to help the team understand what was bid. It is only by keeping promises to the government that a company will achieve long-range growth. In the ideal environment, each implementation of a solution is an opportunity to gather lessons learned and to refine the solution for future bids. This synergy between business development and company operations promotes growth.

The establishment of a robust solutions development capability can be transformative for a company. Key transformations include the following:

- Managers/company leaders committed to discovering customer pain points and owning the strategic approaches for resolving customer pain points.
- Technical proposals written by dedicated company solution architects and not serendipitously by staff during non-business hours.
- Creation of a proposal content database with easy access to past performance information, employee resumes, modifiable graphics, and basic company process language for key topics.
- Adoption of a CRM tool–supported process in which business intelligence is gathered from across the company to support strategic solutioning.

The balance that must be achieved in growing solutions development is that we want scalable capabilities and we want unique innovativeness in approaching every business opportunity. This can be done by growing solutions developers individually through apprenticeship and then mentorship.

Though simple in concept, companies that can develop great solutions for contract award and deliver great solutions in contract performance are still unique within the community of federal government contractors. Faith in business growth through relationships often causes companies to invest more in business consultants than solutions architects. Even when faith is lost, companies will often withdraw back to core business areas instead of charging forward with new ideas. Faith in performance due to incumbent experience often causes the government to set up source selections in favor of key incumbent contractors. Even when faith is lost, the government will more likely switch to name-brand companies to defer blame instead of trying new solutions. Overcoming these mutually enforcing patterns will require dedication. Avoiding not winnable RFP scenarios has been emphasized. However, there is sometimes a fine line between not winnable and a huge opportunity for radical innovation. Figuring out this fine line is a real test for BD and the solutions development team.

These are exciting and challenging times for solutions developers. Government pain points are increasing, effective solutions are lacking, years of LPTA competitions have degraded workforce capabilities, and some government customers are looking beyond traditional outcomes. The fundamentals presented in this book will hopefully be helpful in formulating and delivering many solutions in the years to come. Skillful solutions development requires practice, and there is no better way to practice than to bid and continue bidding. Learn from the losses, but do not get bothered by the losses. One great win erases the bad memory of many defeats. So, happy hunting and best wishes for many wins and many deliveries.

Appendix A:
A Brief History of the U.S. Department of Defense's Acquisition Process

The United States Department of Defense (DoD) is the world's largest buyer of system and service solutions. The way in which the DoD buys these solutions is known as the *defense acquisition process* [1]. This process, which includes the prioritization of what to buy, the budgets for specific solutions, the statutes and regulations governing procurement and development, and the policies that provide acquisition instructions, has been evolving for the past many decades. Therefore, studying the history of this process will help us connect the fundamentals of developing solutions to some of the most challenging real-world situations and demanding user communities.

The weapons, electronics, and IT products that the DoD has acquired are among the most complex systems ever developed, and the services that the DoD has acquired support millions of personnel with many in highly dangerous combat environments. Thus, the acquisition workforce within the DoD has gone through an incredible learning curve in delivering these systems and services. In fact, many of our fundamentals are shaped by the lessons learned from DoD acquisition history. We return to the roots of history and quickly re-experience the learning curve in this appendix. This experience will obviously help us to better develop and present solutions to the DoD. However, it will also help us to better prepare solutions for all federal government agencies.

To begin, the solutions within DoD are born from available funding, and funding is driven by times of great national need. In the United States, the Cold War and the Korean War, which served as a surrogate battlefield for the superpowers, drove defense funding to over 50 percent of the entire U.S. federal budget. As shown in Figure A.1, this high burden on the taxpayers was maintained through

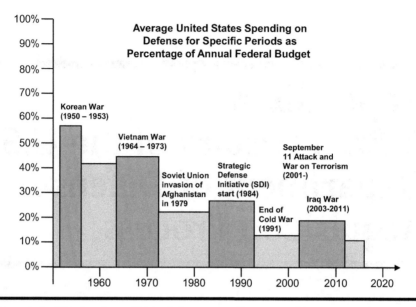

Figure A.1 The burden of U.S. defense spending upon the tax payer. (From the U.S. Department of Defense.)

the Vietnam War and then dramatically lowered in the later 1970s, until the Cold War continued to heat up with the Soviet Union's invasion of Afghanistan [2]. The U.S. maintained its spending through the final years of the Cold War and then lowered spending until the September 11, 2001, terrorist attacks on U.S. soil. Even though the Strategic Defense Initiative may have been the highlight of the Reagan-era Cold War investments, a remarkable array of advanced weapons was developed and deployed in the late 1980s that enabled the United States' overwhelming victory during the Persian Gulf. The War on Terrorism and the Iraq War initiated by the United States after 9/11 once again increased U.S. defense spending. Though the percentage of federal budget was not as high as during the Korean and Vietnam Wars, the actual post–9/11 spending was still higher in dollar value even when adjusting for inflation. In fact, as the DoD is continuously spending more money, the study of acquisition history should focus on what has been bought and whether the capabilities match the needs of strategic postures and global military engagements.

After the financial crisis of 2008 and a prolonged presence in Iraq, the United States drew down defense spending and reduced military commitments across world. This led to a defense budget of $583 billion in 2015, as shown in Figure A.2 [3]. This budget pays for military personnel, military health, civilian personnel, support contractors, acquisition of systems, building of infrastructure, research and development, supplies, spare parts, fuel, and other items. The balancing of these DoD expenditures as well as the balancing of defense spending with other major

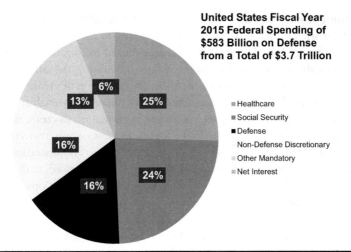

Figure A.2 **The recent relevance of defense compared to other national spending priorities. (Courtesy of the U.S. Congressional Budget Office.)**

federal commitments, such as healthcare and social security, determine to what degree the DoD is pursuing solutions as opposed to just sustaining operations. In sustaining operations, military missions are satisfied largely through the brilliance of command in leveraging existing trained forces and deployed systems. In pursuing solutions, military missions are further supported by new technologies, better systems, improved processes, and advanced training. In the pursuit of solutions, the Unified Combatant Commands represent users with operational needs and the military services (Army, Navy and Marine Corp, Air Force) utilize the defense acquisition process to address user needs through their role in training and equipping forces. The military services and combatant commands, as massive organizations, also have support needs that may further require solutions.

To understand how to present solutions to the U.S. DoD in the future, we need to understand how the United States has acquired solutions in the past. The defense acquisition process of the United States is in no way simple, and the amount of policies, regulations, and processes has been a barrier to many companies and to people without prior experience. What we learn from history is that none of these barriers emerged from randomness or irrationality. However, many of these barriers may need to be reduced to address the changing national security environment. As we look toward the future based on lessons from the past, the biggest overall question we need to ask is, how should the DoD balance between seeking innovative solutions to resolve problems and using increased operational intensity to resolve problems by brute force? History has always shown that innovation wins in the end.

The defense policies and priorities of the United States have been driven by each presidential administration and the appointed secretary of defense. Therefore, we will study history based on this structure. While military innovations in the United States stretch back to the Civil War and even to the Revolutionary War, we can suggest that the first time military thinkers started to consider the soldiers and machines as a single integrated complex system was during the administration of President John F. Kennedy. Before then, inventors were still creating ever more advanced weapons, but the weapons were viewed more as an enabler of warfare. Strategic processes were simpler, such as flying in formation to create mass attack, time the attack to create surprise, and moving faster to out-maneuver adversaries. This all changed with the conduct of systems analysis and operations research [4]. Suddenly, brilliance of command is augmented by advanced analysis of combat outcomes, simulations of military engagements, and projections of adversary behaviors. This coincided with advances in technology-based intelligence gathering and advances in computer modeling. The net result is greater sophistication in requirements for systems, processes, and training as well as greater demand for the development of solutions. From this starting point, history takes us to the modern defense acquisition process with thousands of military, civilian, and support contractor personnel dedicated to the art of buying solutions, and even more contractor personnel dedicated to providing solutions. So, let us begin the summary of history with the administration of President John F. Kennedy. Instead of providing references for every detail of history, the following summary is based on a combination of the author's personal notes over three decades in Washington, DC, and a list of key reference documents [5–16].

A.1 The Administration of President John F. Kennedy (1961–1963)

The Kennedy administration was marked by a dramatic increase in tension between the United States and the Soviet Union. This tension reached its peak during October 16–28, 1962, with the Cuban Missile Crisis. Although First Secretary Khrushchev withdrew the nuclear missiles from Cuba after the U.S. blockade and after negotiations, the need for the United States to stay ahead of the arms race became clear. The Soviet Union had already taken the lead in the space race in 1957 with the launch of Sputnik.

A.1.1 The Appointment of Secretary of Defense Robert McNamara (1961–1967)

Secretary McNamara's priorities were quite clear given the start of the arms race. First, there had to be centralized DoD policies to govern the acquisition of new weapons technology. Second, acquisition of weapons had to be accelerated. Third, the discipline of systems analysis was initiated to better align development and planned performance.

The following events and items were established to implement new acquisition priorities:

- Draft presidential memorandum, which calls for the development of Issue Papers to quickly brief leadership.
- Five year defense plan (FYDP) process, which functionally breaks down phases of the systems development life cycle.
- Planning, programming, budgeting system (PPBS), which establishes funding based on requirements.
- Total package procurement process, which seeks to control cost by fixing price for systems development.
- Cost reduction program, which has aggressive cost policies that fight against a traditional culture of the military services fulfilling wish lists.
- Office of Economic Adjustment created (1961) within DoD to assist communities impacted by base closures and other defense investment changes.

During this starting period for the arms race, the United States deployed its first ballistic missile submarine—*George Washington* class (1959–1960) and the Minuteman I ballistic missile (1962).

A.2 The Administration of President Lyndon B. Johnson (1963–1969)

The Johnson Administration's defense priorities were dominated by the Vietnam War (1964–1973). At the same time, the rise of the Space Age yielded opportunities for new defense-related satellite systems. Secretary of Defense McNamara remained after President Kennedy's assassination to continue the policies of the Cold War, and the nuclear arsenals of the United States and Soviet Union grew under the doctrine of Mutually Assured Destruction (MAD).

A.2.1 The Appointment of Secretary of Defense Clark Clifford (1968–1969)

Secretary Clifford maintained the defense acquisition approach of Secretary McNamara.

The following entities and items were established to enhance the acquisition approach:

- Defense Systems Acquisition Review Council (DSARC) (1969) established centralized oversight on how acquisition efforts conform to policy.
- Readiness, information, and control tables were used as detailed presentations of systems development status.

- Development concept papers were used to summarize defense system technologies, performance, risks, and capabilities.
- PERT/COST method was used to track contractor performance and cost. This process evolved to earned value management (EVM) in the late 1980s.

During this period of war, the F-111 fighter/bomber was deployed (1964). And, the United States launched the first Defense Support Program (DSP) satellites (1966) to detect Soviet Intercontinental Ballistic Missile (ICBM) launches and provide early warning.

A.3 The Administration of President Richard M. Nixon (1969–1974)

The Nixon Administration focused on drawing down defense from the commitments of the Vietnam War. The toll of the war, which included an unpopular draft and nearly 60,000 military personnel killed in action, led to a strong anti-military posture by the American people. Therefore, defense spending was cut, and the DoD had to operate under severe financial limitations. The nuclear arms race, however, continued to intensify with the introduction of the first multiple independently targetable reentry vehicle (MIRV) ICBM, Minuteman III, in 1970.

A.3.1 The Appointment Secretary of Defense Melvin Laird (1969–1973)

Faced with the new defense climate, Secretary Laird decentralized the execution of the acquisition process within the services, called for the Joint Chiefs of Staff (JCS) to be key drivers in defense acquisition planning, and created PPBS ceilings for each of the military services.

The following events and items drove DoD process changes and established the process changes:

- Fitzhugh Commission (1970) concluded that technology difficulties cannot be foreseen. Therefore, DoD was encouraged to adopt flexible acquisitions with periodic operational evaluations.
- Packard Policy Memo (1970) called for decentralized execution of defense acquisitions, streamlined management, and appropriate contract mechanisms.
- First Issue of DoD Directive 5000.1 (1971) established the decentralizing of authority, accountable program managers, minimize reporting burdens to PM, decision points at initiation/full scale development/production/deployment, early testing and evaluation, and program characterization.

A.3.2 The Appointment of Secretary of Defense
James R. Schlesinger (1973–1975)

After the post–Vietnam War budget cuts, Secretary Schlesinger focused on stabilizing the declining DoD budget and mitigating the impact of budget cuts.

The following organization helped to bring back stability:

- Office of Federal Procurement (1974) established as White House Office of Management and Budget (OMB) organization for centralized U.S. acquisition policy.

Despite the challenging acquisition environment of the 1970s, the DoD still fielded an impressive collection of modern weapon systems, including the F-14 Navy Fighter deployed (1970), F-15 Air Force Fighter deployed (1972), and F-16 Air Force Fighter deployed (1974). These systems marked a significant capabilities increase from Vietnam War–era systems.

A.4 The Administration of President Gerald Ford (1974–1977)

The Ford Administration had to deal with the aftermath of Watergate and President Nixon's resignation as well as the aftermath of the Arab Oil Embargo in response to the United States supporting Israel with weapons during the 1973 Yom Kippur War. Secretary Schlesinger continued to run the DoD until the appointment of Donald Rumsfeld.

A.4.1 The Appointment of Secretary of Defense Donald Rumsfeld (1975–1977)

Secretary Rumsfeld focused on maintaining a strategic and conventional force balance with the Soviet Union. Further, the defense acquisition process continued to advance with the reissuance of DoDD 5000.1 along with DoD Instruction 5000.2 (1975). The instructions provided specific process execution guidance to include guidance on the Decision Coordination Paper and DSARC process.

A.5 The Administration of President Jimmy Carter (1977–1981)

President Carter inherited the issue of the United States backing an unpopular regime in Iran. The overthrow of the Shah of Iran in the Islamic Revolution of

1979 led to the Iran hostage crisis as well as Iraqi and Soviet concerns over the rise of Shia Islamic political authority in surrounding regions. The bloody Iraq–Iran War occurred (1980–1988), and the Soviet invasion of Afghanistan occurred (1979–1989) under fear of Afghanistan's collapsing secular government.

A.5.1 The Appointment of Secretary of Defense Harold Brown (1977–1981)

Secretary Brown dealt with specific system development issues in a climate of reducing the defense budget and then increasing the budget as wars raged in the Middle East.

The following programs and events brought about acquisition reform:

- Defense Economic Adjustment Program (1978) established by Executive Order 12788 absorbed the Office of Economic Adjustment as a field office and focused on resolving the impact of defense program cuts. Solutions such as dual use for military technologies and military use of COTS technologies were introduced.
- Defense Acquisition Improvement Program (1981) implemented 33 acquisition reform initiatives including appropriate contract type, funding flexibility, defense acquisition executive, thresholds for milestone reviews, preplanned product improvements, budget to most likely cost and for risk, source selection and contractor incentives, design to cost and increased competition, visibility of logistics/support, and fast track programs.
- Reissuance of DoDD 5000.1 and DoDI 5000.2 (1980) to provide guidance on reducing cycle time and improving the interaction between the acquisition process and budgeting process. DoDI 5000.2 expanded with more detailed descriptions, Integrated Program Summary, and dedicated executive for DSARC.

Major systems fielded during these years included the *Ohio*-class Trident submarine (1981) and the first launch of global positioning satellites (GPS) (1978).

A.6 The Administration of President Ronald Reagan (1981–1989)

The Reagan Administration came at the height of the Cold War with thousands of nuclear warheads ready to launch from land-based silos, strategic bombers, ballistic missile submarines, and mobile launchers. While the Strategic Arms Limitation Talks (SALT) I and II efforts of the 1970s provided some constraints, each side protected the advancement of their most sophisticated nuclear systems. As a new round of discussions with the Soviet Union in 1982 to achieve a Strategic Arms Reduction Treaty (START) was being proposed, President Reagan adopted a posture of strength and increased defense investments. A part of this investment went to the Strategic Defense Initiative (1984) in an effort to counter the Soviet nuclear threat and move the United States away from MAD. The U.S. investments were matched by Soviet investments, which ultimately contributed to its economic collapse.

A.6.1 The Appointment of Secretary of Defense Caspar Weinberger (1981–1987)

Secretary Weinberger managed large DoD budget increases for enhancing readiness, sustainability, and systems modernization. Meanwhile, Congress expanded its attention to the effectiveness of the defense acquisition process.

The following items reflected the increased oversight of Congress and the DoD response to new statutes, regulations, and guidance:

- The Nunn McCurdy Amendment (NDAA FY82) limited cost growth for major weapon programs. Selected Acquisition Report required in 10 U.S.C. Chapter 144.
- Reissuance of DoDD 5000.1 (1982) with Mission Element Need Statement (MENS) replaced by Justification for a Major Systems New Start (JMSNS). JMSNS must be submitted with the Program Objective Memorandum (POM), which explains planned resource allocation.
- DoD Director, Operational Test and Evaluation (DOT&E) position/office created by Congress (1983) to address DoD responsiveness to technology issues.
- Senior procurement executive must be designated for each agency (1983), Public Law 98-191.
- Grace Commission (1984) became the President's Private Sector Survey to cut waste and inefficiencies in government.
- The Competition in Contracting Act (1984) established common standards in federal contracting. Led to combined DoD and civil agency regulations in the Federal Acquisition Regulations operated by the General Services Administration.
- Reissuance of DoDD 5000.1 (1985) in response to acquisition horror stories— designated the deputy secretary as defense acquisition executive.
- Packard Commission (1986) found that the DoD acquisition system was too encumbered with no clear line of authority leading to cost overruns and delays. Recommended organizational change.
- The Goldwater–Nichols Act (1986) executed Packard Commission recommendations by (1) shifting acquisition authority from services to USD/

Acquisition and Technology, (2) establishing service acquisition executives (SAE) and program executive officers (PEO), (3) placing program managers in tiered oversight, (4) making the vice chairman JCS head of Joint Requirement Oversight Council (JROC), (5) requiring interoperability between services, and (6) requiring joint assignments for military promotions.

■ DoD requests moratorium on further reform legislation (1986) because it could not keep pace with changes.

A.6.2 The Appointment of Secretary of Defense Frank Carlucci (1987–1989)

With massive growth in the defense industry, Secretary Carlucci focused on acquisition reform, stronger "revolving door" laws, appointing a special inspector general for procurement fraud, and establishing quality controls.

Events that shaped this period include the following:

■ Ill Wind Procurement Fraud (1988), which was a scandal involving bribery within the DoD acquisition process.
■ President's DoD Management Review (1989) assessed the implementation of Goldwater–Nichols Act and compelled Services to make SAEs and PEOs dedicated acquisition positions.
■ USD (AT&L) assumed EVM Oversight (1989).
■ Adoption of a total quality management (TQM) approach to acquisition.
■ Preplanned Product Improvements (P3I).
■ Reissuance of DoDD 5000.1 (1987), which implemented Packard Commission recommendations: (1) establish system of committees (three on program matters and seven on policy matters) to support the Defense Acquisition Board (DAB) which replaced the DSARC, (2) establish committees replacing the 100-plus councils and boards that previously served the function, (3) hold Milestone IV review 1–2 years after development initiation to assure operational readiness, (4) hold Milestone V review 5–10 years after development initiation to assure effectiveness and need for major upgrades, and (5) establish rigorous lifecycle focus in acquisition process.
■ Issue DoDD 5200.28 Security Requirements for Automated Information Systems (1988).
■ Create Acquisition Professional Development Program (1989 timeframe) to train and establish an acquisition workforce for the new Goldwater–Nichols system. DoD 5000.52M certification for series 1102 professionals.

During the Reagan Administration, the number of major DoD programs identified as ACAT I increased to more than 40 and the federal acquisition workforce reached 500,000 in 1985. The M1A1 tank, which is still the army's primary battle weapon, was deployed in 1985, and the B-2 stealth bomber was deployed in 1989. Other systems deployed during this period include the M2/M3 Bradley fighting vehicle, Stinger surface-to-air missile, Patriot short-range ballistic missile interceptor, SH-60 Seahawk helicopter, *Iowa*-class battleship, *Kidd*-class destroyer, F/A-18 Hornet, Tomahawk cruise missile, AV-8B Harrier jet, F117 stealth fighter, B1-B bomber, AWACS early warning and control aircraft, KC-10 refueling tanker, Defense Meteorological Satellite Program (DMSP), Defense Satellite Communications System (DSCS), and MX ICBM.

The start of the information age also brought about software systems dedicated to the needs of the DoD. One such system was the Composite Health Care System (CHCS), initiated in 1988, which handled the electronic health records of military personnel, retirees, and their dependents. Even before then, computers have for many years been used within military intelligence and as components of major weapon systems.

The hallmark weapon system of the Reagan Administration was, however, never fully built. SDI was conceptually formulated as a system of many systems to include space sensors for ICBM boost phase and warhead midcourse detection, space-based directed and kinetic energy weapons for boost vehicle and warhead kills, and terminal phase interceptors. Years of heavy research investments eventually led to some systems such as the Terminal High Altitude Area Defense (THAAD), deployed in 2008, and the Airborne Laser, which was successfully tested and then canceled in 2010. Most of the SDI programs, however, were either canceled during development or down-scoped after the Cold War and inherited by the Missile Defense Agency.

A.7 The Administration of President George H.W. Bush (1989–1993)

The Bush Administration saw the economic collapse of the Soviet Union, which led to the end of the Cold War (1991). The Strategic Arms Reduction Treaty was signed in 1991 and approximately 80 percent of the world's nuclear weapons were decommissioned by 2001. The failure of Iraq in the Iraq–Iran War promoted the Iraqi invasion of Kuwait. This resulted in the Persian Gulf War (1990–1991), where the modern weapons of the United States overwhelmingly defeated the substantial Iraqi army with Soviet-supplied weapons in Operation Desert Storm. U.S. victory in the Persian Gulf marked the height of U.S. hegemony. Afterwards, the United States went through another cycle of defense budget cuts.

A.7.1 The Appointment of Secretary of Defense Dick Cheney (1989–1993)

Secretary Cheney focused on controlling the downsizing of the DoD budget and shifting the defense posture from the Cold War to handling regional conflicts.

With a massive number of programs coming from the Reagan era, the strategy was to both eliminate programs and build systems faster/better/cheaper. Mechanisms such as integrated product teams (IPTs) were used to improve the efficiency and effectiveness of acquisitions.

The following events governed the policy shifts after the Cold War:

- A-12 Avenger II canceled (1991) because the EVM process detected performance issues.
- Base Force review (1991) for JCS to establish a force structure baseline that emphasized readiness for major regional conflicts.
- Reissuance of DoDD 5000.1 (1991): (1) responded to the 1989 Defense Management Review, (2) consolidated acquisition policy at the OSD level, (3) canceled 50-plus other related DoD acquisition policy directives, and (4) established ACAT categories. DoDI 5000.2 grew to hundreds of pages.
- Defense Acquisition University (DAU) created (1991) to standardize acquisition workforce training.
- Cost Analysis Improvement Group (CAIG) (1992) established by DoDD 5000.4 for cost assessment at milestones.
- DoDD 5000.4-M issued for cost analysis guidance and procedures (1992).
- Bottom-up review (1993) shifted defense architecture away from monolithic threat to two major regional conflicts strategy.
- National Performance Review (1993) used a business best practice baseline. Shifted DoD acquisition reform from the rigid control-based approach.
- Section 800 Panel (1993) emphasized use of commercial capabilities.
- Government Performance and Results Act (1993) required agency strategic plans, annual performance plans, pilots, and accountability for performance.

By the early 1990s, the number of ACAT I Programs had soared to more than 100, and the new systems that entered into service included *Arleigh Burke*–class destroyer, F/A E/F Super Hornet, CH-60 Seahawk helicopter, C-130 Hercules transport aircraft, Joint Direct Attack Munition (JDAM), C-17 Globemaster transport aircraft, Joint Surveillance Target Attack Radar System (JSTARS) aircraft, and the Milstar communications satellite.

A.8 The Administration of President Bill Clinton (1993–2001)

The Clinton Administration faced the rise of Al-Qaeda, formed from the Mujahedeen fighters of Afghanistan, and the first bombing of the World Trade Center in 1993. The concept of terrorism spread from the Middle East to match the global mobility and cash flow that came after the Cold War. As borders weakened, ethnic conflicts emerged, such as between the peoples of Bosnia and Herzegovina, that required a U.S.-led bombing campaign in 1995 to help end further human atrocities. Despite many areas of tension across the world, the United States' use of military force was tempered. Instead, the focus turned to expansion of global trade with the establishment of the European Union in 1993, North American Free Trade Agreement (NAFTA) in 1994, and World Trade Organization (WTO) in 1995.

A.8.1 The Appointment of Secretary of Defense Les Aspen (1993–1994)

Secretary Aspen managed the reduction of the force structure while still organizing to fight and win two major regional campaigns. Developing systems faster and simpler remained a high priority.

The following few events reflected the priorities of the period:

■ DoD Advanced Concept Technology Demonstration (ACTD) programs (1994) were first used to test the utility of mature technologies prior to the formal acquisition process.
■ Federal Acquisition Streamlining Act (1994) required the reduction of unique purchasing, increased use of simplified acquisition, and delivery of goods/services faster and cheaper.
■ Under Secretary of Defense/Acquisition and Technology (USD/A&T) changes to the Acquisition Professional Development Program (APDP) (1994) modified the certification process for acquisition professionals in compliance with Defense Acquisition Workforce Improvement Act (DAWIA).

A.8.2 The Appointment of Secretary of Defense William Perry (1994–1997)

The DoD under Secretary Perry focused on maximum reliance on COTS, using cost as an independent variable (CAIV), conforming military contracts/bidding/accounting/other business procedures, and eliminating outdated regulations. Many military base closures and realignments occurred to save costs.

The following are some key events during this period:

■ Commission on Roles and Mission of the Armed Forces (1995) concluded that the military services prematurely endorsed weapon systems.
■ JCS Joint Vision 2010 (1995 timeframe) required military solutions to support dominant maneuver, precision engagement, full dimensional protection, focused logistics, and information superiority.

- The paper Reduction Act (1995) required agencies to be accountable for reductions in paperwork.
- The Federal Acquisition Reform Act (1996) called for single process initiatives, integrated product teams, and CAIV.
- The Clinger–Cohen Act (1996) abolished the 1946 Brooks Act, which meant that the GSA was no longer the single acquirer of IT.
- Quadrennial Defense Review (1997) emphasized Joint Vision 2010, command/control/communications/computer/intelligence/surveillance/reconnaissance (C4ISR) as a community, reviving revolution in military affairs and ability to respond to small-scale contingencies.
- Defense Management Council (1997) established a senior board of directors to cause change in the acquisition community.
- Defense Reform Initiative Office (1997) defined Revolution in Business Affairs (RBA) to parallel RMA.
- Deputy under Secretary of Defense (DUSD) for Acquisition Reform (1995–1997) called for process action teams, integrated product teams, and capture of lessons learned.
- Commission on Roles and Missions of the Armed Forces (1995) emphasized outsourcing and privatization.

The Defense Authorization Acts of FY96, FY97, and FY98 cut the acquisition workforce, which had reached approximately 270,000 in 1997, by 25 percent as the year 2000 approached. At the same time, tens of thousands of students from the acquisition workforce received formal training. The number of ongoing ACAT I programs dropped to around 70, and the systems that were deployed include the Predator drone aircraft (1995) and Paladin mobile artillery (1994).

A.8.3 The Appointment of Secretary of Defense William Cohen (1997–2001)

Secretary Cohen focused on aligning U.S. forces against chemical and biological weapons, electronic attacks, and other unconventional warfare methods. Price-based acquisition in understanding best value evolved into the Earned Value Management System (EVMS).

The following events and organizations reflected the priorities of this period:

- Federal Procurement Executives Council established (1999) with priorities on creating (1) interagency groups to monitor and improve the Federal Acquisition Regulations, (2) mission-focused leaders, (3) technology as a key enabler, (4) collaboration for business results, (5) integrated socioeconomic programs, and (6) transforming the system.
- JCS Joint Vision 2020 (2000) developed based on the concept of full-spectrum dominance.

- Quadrennial Defense Review (2001) focused on a capabilities-based approach, transformational capabilities, and business process modernization.
- Commission to Assess U.S. National Security Space Management and Organization (2001) addressed future priorities in space investments and recommended that the Air Force become the DoD executive agent for space.
- OSD Product Support Reengineering Team (1998) responded to 1998 Defense Authorization Act direction to restructure weapon system sustainment.
- Joint Simulation Based Acquisition Task Force (1998) established a roadmap for simulations capability in acquisition process.
- USD/AT&L Road Ahead Document (1999) continued to emphasize building systems faster and cheaper. Systems Integration should be solely on the contractors, and the government should assume more performance risks.
- Office of Acquisition Initiatives established (2001) to champion acquisition reform.

A.9 The Administration of President George W. Bush (2001–2009)

The most devastating terrorist attack upon the United States occurred on September 11, 2001. The activities of the Bush Administration were then dominated by the response to this attack by Al-Qaeda. The War in Afghanistan immediately followed 9/11, with Operation Enduring Freedom to topple the Taliban government and capture Osama bin Laden. Then, in 2003, the United States invaded Iraq based on concerns that Iraq was stockpiling weapons of mass destruction. After initial military victories, the U.S. occupation forces in Iraq and Afghanistan faced years of insurgency. This demand on resources and the continued global War on Terror dominated defense spending.

A.9.1 The Appointment of Secretary of Defense Donald Rumsfeld (2001–2006)

Secretary Rumsfeld, in his second time leading the DoD, focused on managing multiple campaigns, commercial outsourcing, quality of the acquisition workforce, and streamlining development. Because of the complexity and evolving nature of threats, the DoD transitioned from threat-based requirements to capability-based requirements.

The following activities reflect the effort to shift to new threats and new needs:

- National Security Strategy of the United States (2002) made the case for preemptive war.
- PPBS changed to planning, programming, budget, and execution (PPBE) process (2003) with performance metrics to be established in execution phase.

- SecDef Transition Planning Guidance (2003) emphasized adaptive planning, capabilities-based allocation, and accelerated acquisition.
- New 5000 Series Guidance (2003) called for streamlining, increased flexibility, enhanced business practices, evolutionary acquisition, and integrated acquisition business model with new requirements generation process (Joint Capabilities Integration Development System [JCIDS]).
- OMB Circular A-76 Performance of Commercial Activities (1983, revised 2003) presented new requirements for public-to-private competition.
- USD (AT&L) Memo EVM (2005) established contract thresholds and types for performance, schedule, and cost reporting.
- USD (AT&L) Memo Acquisition of Service (2006) established categories of IT/non-IT services, reporting requirements, and decision authority.
- Performance-based acquisition (2006), Part of FAR 37.6, revised 2006, defined the responsibilities of program management.
- Quadrennial Defense Review (2006) focused on agility against asymmetric challenges and uncertainty, and argued for enterprise-wide change.
- DoDD 4630.5 Interoperability and Supportability of IT and National Security Systems (2002/updated 2007) supported by DoDI 4630.8 (2004).

The period of the early 2000s was marked by major advancements in computer and network technologies. In response, the DoD began investing in information technology systems that support entire organizations and mission areas. These so-called enterprise solutions became increasingly complex both in the structure of requirements and in the integrated software components. While the DoD still deployed physical systems such as the F-22 fighter (2002), tools and techniques for other regimes of conflict began to gain importance. The DoD began to study information warfare and information operations in the late 1990s, but it was the technical advancements in the following decades that yielded new threats and opportunities. By 2009, the United States would create the Cyber Command, located with the National Security Agency (NSA) at Fort Meade, Maryland, as a force dedicated to fighting in the information realm.

The acquisition workforce, with more than 100,000 students receiving certifications, had to adapt to many statutory, regulatory, and policy changes in the 21st century. Despite these changes, program delays and failures persisted.

A.9.2 The Appointment of Secretary of Defense Robert Gates (2006–2011)

Secretary Gates focused on changing tactics in Iraq after years of insurgency, and he kept his position into President Obama's administration.

The following items tried to increase control during a chaotic period of multiple ongoing global operations:

- USD (AT&L) Memo—Configuration Steering Board (2007) to conduct reviews to prevent requirements creep.
- USD (AT&L) Memo—Prototype and Competition (2007) required competitive prototypes in technology development.
- DPAP Memo—Peer Review of Contracts for Supplies and Services (2008) required ways to ensure proper implementation of contracting policies and regulations.
- Reissuance of DoDI 5000.02 (2008) with new language on Materiel Development Decision, updates to match new policies, and extension of requirements to lower level programs.
- Weapon System Acquisition Reform Act (2009) called for (1) Cost Assessment and Program Evaluation office to replace PA&E, (2) disbanding of the Cost Analysis Improvement Group, (3) Joint Requirements Oversight Council to seek Combatant Command inputs, (4) programs modified under Nunn–McCurdy to have additional milestone approval, (5) new director of developmental T&E and system engineering, and (6) competitive prototyping.
- DepSecDef In-Sourcing Guidance (2009) transitioned 10,000 contractor acquisition positions to federal civilian positions.
- 10 U.S.C. Chapter 144A (FY07 NDAA, revised FY09 NDAA) established new congressional reporting process for Major Automated Information System (MAIS) programs.

By the end of the Bush Administration, the United States was facing the Great Recession and the ability to sustain global operations became a major question.

A.10 The Administration of President Barack Obama (2009–2016)

The Obama Administration came after the start of Great Recession in 2008. Therefore, economic considerations became a key component of defense planning. The War on Terror continued and reached a major benchmark with the killing of Osama Bin Laden in 2011. The United States maintained its troop strength of more than 80,000 in Afghanistan until mid-2012, and then reduced the number of troops to less than 10,000 by 2015. In Iraq, the administration began to immediately withdraw troops from more than 150,000 in 2008 to a nearly complete withdraw by 2011.

The wars in Afghanistan and Iraq were marked by high survival rates from insurgent attacks due to advances in military medicine. This, however, dramatically increased the number of soldiers and veterans with disabilities that require permanent care and injuries that require extensive recovery time. So, the demand for the modernization of the DoD's electronic health record system and the integration of this system with the Department of Veterans Affairs' EHR system continued. DoD management of the consequences of war dominated investment demands.

A.10.1 Continuation of Secretary of Defense Robert Gates (2009–2011)

As Secretary Gates continued to lead the DoD, the organization faced several failures in developing major IT systems. Defense Integrated Military Human Resources System (DIMHRS) managed by the Business Transformation Agency (BTA) failed to develop a personnel management system that is the enterprise solution for the Army, Navy, and Air Force. Assistant Secretary of Defense for Networks and Information Integration (ASD/NII) struggled with on-time development of major enterprise systems. For example, the billion-dollar–level Net-Enabled Command and Control (NECC) System was canceled in 2011 as design efforts dragged on and risks in meeting user needs emerged.

The following activities reflect the priorities of the period:

- DoD Efficiency Initiates (2010): (1) 10 percent annual reduction in service support contractors FY 2011–2013, (2) government billet freeze and zero baseline review, (3) reduce senior level positions, (4) simplify reporting, (5) reduce studies and boards, (6) eliminate ASD/NII organization, (7) eliminate BTA Organization, (8) recommend closure of United States Joint Forces Command (JFCOM), and (9) required cost estimate for program and policy proposals.
- USD (AT&L) Better Buying Power (2010): (1) guidance for obtaining greater efficiency and productivity in defense spending, (2) target affordability and control cost growth, (3) mandate affordability as a requirement, (4) incentivize productivity and innovation in industry, (5) promote real competition, (6) improve tradecraft in services acquisition, and (7) reduce non-productive processes and bureaucracy.
- National Security Strategy of the United States (2010): Tied national security with the economy and referenced terrorism as a general threat to avoid the term of *Islamic extremism*.

A.10.2 The Appointment of Secretary of Defense Leon Panetta (2011–2013)

Secretary Panetta took control of the DoD as Arab Spring started and uprisings spread from Tunisia across social media into Libya, Egypt, Yemen, Syria, and other

Arab states. As a part of the chaos and under U.S. hesitation to commit protective military force, a series of coordinated attacks were launched upon the U.S. embassy in Benghazi, Libya, that led to the death of U.S. Ambassador J. Christopher Stevens and three other U.S. personnel.

- BTA and ASD(NII) disestablished (2011). BTA core functions integrated with Deputy Chief Management Officer (DCMO) and ASD(NII) retained role as DoD Chief Information Officer (CIO).
- SECDEF Report to Congress on Delivering IT Capabilities (2011) emphasized short duration projects, flexible/tailored processes, stakeholder engagements, rationalized requirements, iterative development, and early and incremental delivery.
- USD (AT&L) Memo—Should Cost and Affordability (2011) required affordability for pre-MS B planning, Should Cost for post-MS B control.
- Joint DoD and Department of Veterans Affairs Integrated Electronic Health Records (iEHR) program initiated to replace current systems that grew from 1980s.

A.10.3 The Appointment of Secretary of Defense Chuck Hagel (2013–2015)

Secretary Hagel took over leadership of the DoD when the DoD was hit by massive funding cuts due to the 2013 Congressional Budget Sequestration. His disagreements with the administration led to resignation within two years. Prior to his resignation, the Islamic State of Iraq and Syria (ISIS) started to rapidly gain territorial control across Syria and Iraq in 2014, officially declared itself as the caliphate, and used social media to recruit fighters from across the world. The U.S. military resisted committing forces to Iraq, and the U.S. people watched as captured citizens were beheaded.

The following events reflect some of the conflicting priorities for the DoD:

- SecDef Strategic Choices and Management Review (2013) presented option of reducing U.S. Aircraft Carrier groups from 11 down to 8.
- The iEHR program is canceled (2013) and the DoD and VA began pursuing independent system modernization strategies.
- National Security Strategy of the United States (2015) argued for the establishment of a rules-based international order sustained by American leadership.
- New DoD Healthcare Management System Modernization (DHMSM) program awarded the EHR system replacement contract to the Leidos/Cerner Team (2015).
- Reissuance of DoDI 5000.02 emphasized flexible acquisition processes and soft transition across phases when adopting Agile development.

A.10.4 The Appointment of Secretary of Defense Ashton Carter (2015–2016)

Secretary Carter ordered the DoD to open all military positions to women and to allow transgender individuals to openly join the military. Defense Innovation Unit Experimental (DIUx) was established in Silicon Valley (2015) to leverage technologies from companies that have not typically worked with the DoD in the past.

A.11 The Administration of President Donald Trump (2017–)

The Trump Administration started with major changes in foreign policy and increased tensions with North Korea. The first President's budget contained more than $50 billion increase for defense.

A.11.1 The Appointment of Secretary of Defense James N. Mattis (2017–)

Secretary Mattis is focusing on increasing force readiness, procuring systems for the future, and maintaining worldwide operations.

A.12 The DoD Acquisition Organizations of Today

As history shows, the acquisition process of the U.S. Department of Defense is adapting continuously to budgetary environments, national security priorities, and technology opportunities. For decades, government leaders guiding the process and analysts endeavoring to support the process have struggled with the balance between the unique needs of defense and the capabilities already being sold in the commercial world. Because of the unique needs of defense, a substantial collection of policies has been written to add to the complexities within statutes and the FAR. The requirements for many systems and services have grown to such magnitudes that some acquisition programs could not escape severe schedule delays and cost overruns. As the pendulum swung toward accepting commercial products, particularly in the area of software systems, the incompatibility of commercial products to DoD operational demands have led to some program failures. This oscillating acquisition emphasis will continue to haunt the development of solutions for the DoD.

We explored DoD acquisition history from the highest level across presidential administrations and appointed secretaries of defense. Further, we noted some of the largest systems that were developed under Acquisition Category Level 1 (ACAT I) programs. Within the DoD, the oversight of the acquisition process is vested in the Under Secretary of Defense (Acquisition, Technology, and Logistics) and the Defense Acquisition Executive (DAE). This authority is then either retained for specific programs, retained with the head of a military service or DoD agency designated to act on behalf of USD (AT&L), or completely delegated to the Component Acquisition Executive (CAE) of a service or agency for specific categories of acquisitions. The head of a military service or DoD agency can redelegate his or her authority to the CAE but no further. USD (AT&L) must then report to the Secretary of Defense, the President of the United States, and Congress, as shown in Figure A.3. Congress has levied specific reporting requirements for MDAP and MAIS programs within statutes, such as the annual National Defense Authorization Act (NDAA), and may further require testimonies and reports on specific acquisition efforts or groups of acquisitions.

The secretaries of the military departments and heads of agencies designate their CAEs, who then report to them on budgets, expenditures, and portfolios of programs, and report to USD (AT&L) on acquisition activities for major programs to which he or she has authority. In the military departments, the officials designated as CAEs are, respectively, the Assistant Secretary of the Army for Acquisition, Logistics, and Technology (ASA[AL&T]); the Assistant Secretary of the Navy

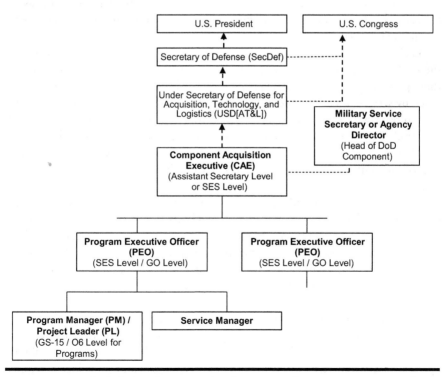

Figure A.3 Typical chain of command and reporting for DoD acquisition efforts.

for Research, Development, and Acquisition (ASN[RD&A]); and the Assistant Secretary of the Air Force for Acquisition (SAF/AQ). Each CAE then typically designates program executive officers, military or civilian officials with responsibility for directing programs within specific portfolios of systems and services. Each program will have a program manager who is the designated individual with responsibility for accomplishing program objectives for design, development, production, and sustainment to meet operational needs. The PMs will be accountable for cost, schedule, performance, risk reporting to the Milestone Decision Authority (MDA), and must maintain execution within set threshold and objective parameters.

In accordance with DoDI 5000.02, all programs must be executed based on a structured lifecycle with phases as explained in the instructions and milestone reviews where the MDA will approve the progression of program activities into the next phase. The phases of the DoD systems acquisition life cycle are Materiel Solution Analysis, Technology Maturation and Risk Reduction, Engineering and Manufacturing Development, Production and Deployment, and Operations and Support. With programs that are applying Agile software development methodologies and rapid prototyping, the transition across phases can be gradated so that the milestones are not barriers to advancement. With programs that are using mature technologies and products, both the Materiel Solution Analysis and Technology Maturation and Risk Reduction phases can be greatly shortened or even bypassed to accelerate the schedule toward operational testing and achieving initial operational capability (IOC).

Each military service and DoD agency has many acquisition programs below the ACAT I level, and some programs are so small and non-mission critical that they do not require an official acquisition categorization. These programs are governed by service or agency internal policies and are typically identified as projects. Each project will have a decision authority, who is a senior official, and a project lead (PL). Unlike PMs, who must receive DAU certifications in accordance with the Defense Acquisition Workforce Improvement Act, PLs merely need to have the acquisition skills and experience consistent with the size, complexity, scope, and risk of his or her project.

Each military service and agency also has many contracts for services. The oversight of these efforts is also based on size standards and categorizations. Each service procurement will have a decision authority and a service manager (SM). The SM could be the PM for a large operational system. However, as SM, he or she will manage service contract activities for functions such as maintenance, operations, program office support, testing, and post-deployment system updates and upgrades.

To explain how the DoD categorized the acquisition of systems, Figure A.4 shows that the first division is between combat systems and information systems. Combat systems include all weapons and other hardware supporting military operations, and they will naturally have IT components and imbedded software. However, they are largely physical systems that enable conflict on land, in the air,

COMBAT SYSTEMS	INFORMATION SYSTEMS
ACAT I Major Defense Acquisition Program (MDAP) • Greater than $480M in FY 2014 constant dollars for research, development, and test and evaluation • Greater than $2.79B in FY 2014 constant dollars for procurement • Designation by Milestone Decision Authority as MDAP or Special Interest	**ACAT IA Major Automated Information System (MAIS)** • Greater than $40M in FY 2014 for definition, design, development, deployment, and sustainment in one fiscal year • Greater than $165M in FY 2014 constant dollars for definition, design, development, deployment • Greater than $520M in FY 2014 constant dollars for all increments • Designation by Milestone Decision Authority as MAIS or Special Interest
ACAT II Acquisition Program • Less than ACAT I and greater than $85M in FY 2014 constant dollars for research, development, and test and evaluation • Less than ACAT I and greater than $835M in FY 2014 constant dollars for procurement • Designation by Milestone Decision Authority	
ACAT III Acquisition Program • Less than ACAT II and greater than threshold established by Component Acquisition Executive (CAE) • Designation by Milestone Decision Authority	**ACAT III Automated Information System (AIS)** • Less than ACAT IA and greater than threshold established by Component Acquisition Executive • Designation by Milestone Decision Authority
Project • Less than ACAT III threshold established by Component Acquisition Executive	**IT Project** • Less than ACAT III threshold established by Component Acquisition Executive
Simplified Acquisition Threshold (Less than $150 K)	**Simplified Acquisition Threshold** (Less than $150 K)

Figure A.4   DoD 5000.02 categorization approach for programs and projects.

in space, and over/under the sea. In contrast, information systems are independent computer hardware, network, and software systems that support operations in the information domain. Information systems can enable combat in the information domain, but they are still categorized as information systems for acquisition. For each class of systems, the acquisition category is based on the dollar value of the acquisition program and the MDA decision on program mission criticality. For any program regardless of dollar value, the MDA can designate it as being at a specific ACAT level because it merits higher visibility and oversight. The MDA can also declare that a program is at the ACAT I or ACAT IA level in oversight without the program being a MDAP or MAIS. In some cases where the dollar value does not reflect the extremely high importance of the effort, the program is simply designated as Special Interest.

USD (AT&L) either retains MDA status for MDAPs or delegates a Head of Component or the Component's CAE as the MDA when the program is categorized as ACAT IC. Also, USD (AT&L) either retains MDA status for MAIS or delegates a Head of Component or the Component's CAE as the MDA when the program is categorized as ACAT IAC. The CAEs of DoD Components then automatically have MDA status for all programs below ACAT I and IA. This MDA status can further be delegated by the CAE to PEOs or other officials with appropriate acquisition training and certifications.

In DoD policy, there is no set lower limit for ACAT III programs. Instead, the line between programs and projects is determined by each CAE for the DoD

Component or for specific programs. At the project level, the acquisition process is determined by the policies of each military service and DoD agency. For projects costing less than $150,000, the awarding of contracts and execution of activities can all be done rapidly and unencumbered by standard regulations and oversight. Like other federal departments, the DoD further has an active Small Business Innovation Research (SBIR) program that funds emerging technologies at the project level. The DoD will also establish Joint Concept Technology Demonstrations (JCTD) to rapidly prototype technical capabilities that can either be inserted into programs or be the foundation for new programs.

References

1. Fox, J.R. 2011. *Defense Acquisition Reform, 1960–2009. An Elusive Goal.* Arlington, VA: Historical Office—Office of the Secretary of Defense.
2. Greenberg, M.R. 2014. *Trends in U.S. Military Spending.* Washington, DC: Council of Foreign Relations.
3. *Fiscal Year 2015 Budget.* Washington, DC: United States Office of Management and Budget.
4. Quade, E.S. 1963. *Military Systems Analysis.* Santa Monica, CA: Rand Corp.
5. Baker, D. 2004. *Jane's Space Directory 2004–2005.* London, UK: Jane's Information Group.
6. Brown, S.A. 2005. *Providing the Means of War—Historical Perspectives on Defense Acquisition, 1945–2000.* Arlington, VA: Historical Office—Office of the Secretary of Defense.
7. Lassman, T.C. 2008. *Sources of Weapon Systems Innovation in the Department of Defense—The Role of In-House Research and Development, 1945–2000.* Arlington, VA: Historical Office—Office of the Secretary of Defense.
8. Boyne, W.J. 2007. *Beyond the Wild Blue: A History of the U.S. Air Force, 1947–2007,* 2nd ed. New York: Thomas Dunne Books.
9. Rearden, S.L. 1984. *History of the Office of the Secretary of Defense: Vol. 1: The Formative Years, 1947–1950.* Arlington, VA: Historical Office—Office of the Secretary of Defense.
10. Condit, D.M. 1988. *History of the Office of the Secretary of Defense: Vol 2: The Test of War, 1950–1953.* Arlington, VA: Historical Office—Office of the Secretary of Defense.
11. Leighton, R.M. 2001. *History of the Office of the Secretary of Defense: Vol 3: Strategy, Money, and the New Look, 1953–1956.* Arlington, VA: Historical Office—Office of the Secretary of Defense.
12. Watson, R.J. 1997. *History of the Office of the Secretary of Defense: Vol 4: Into the Missile Age, 1956–1960.* Arlington, VA: Historical Office—Office of the Secretary of Defense.
13. Kaplan, L.S., Landa, R.D., and Drea, E.J. 2006. *History of the Office of the Secretary of Defense: Vol 5: The McNamara Ascendancy, 1961–1965.* Arlington, VA: Historical Office—Office of the Secretary of Defense.

14. Drea, E.J. 2011. *History of the Office of the Secretary of Defense: Vol 6: McNamara, Clifford, and the Burdens of Vietnam, 1965–1969.* Arlington, VA: Historical Office—Office of the Secretary of Defense.
15. Hunt, R.A. 2015. *History of the Office of the Secretary of Defense: Vol 7: Melvin Laird and the Foundation of the Post-Vietnam Military.* Arlington, VA: Historical Office—Office of the Secretary of Defense.
16. Keefer, E.C. 2017. *History of the Office of the Secretary of Defense: Vol 9: Harold Brown: Offsetting the Soviet Military Challenge, 1977–1981.* Arlington, VA: Historical Office—Office of the Secretary of Defense.

Appendix B: More Details on the U.S. Federal Source Selection Process

Many contractors react to the U.S. federal source selection process without fully understanding the government activities behind the process. They respond to RFIs, comment on draft PWS/SOW/SOO, develop proposals for RFPs, and change proposals based on evaluation notices (ENs) and items for negotiation (IFNs). However, their lack understanding limits their ability to be proactive as discussed in Chapters 4 and 5. Seeking to understand the government end of source selections is not an easy endeavor because (1) the process is governed by countless pages of FAR, (2) those in federal government who implement the process represent a fraternity with no vested interest to simply explain the process, and (3) the process is further tailored by different departments and agencies. As our objective is to increase understanding and not to turn everyone into government contracting officers, a simplified approach to explaining the source selection process can be taken that avoids FAR references, agency-specific details, and extensive study of the *Defense Acquisition Guidebook* [1]. This conceptual explanation is represented in Figure B.1 through four phases. In these phases, the source selection process is a component of the overall acquisition process implemented by the program office. The program office would initiate the process through requirements definition, gaining funding, conducting market research, and completing acquisition planning. Then, the program office will work with each department or agency's procurement organization to execute the source selection. A contracting officer is assigned, and the acquisition team will step back after completing the procurement package as the source selection takes over.

This appendix is organized based on the phases presented in Figure B.1, and the basic methodology for conducting each task is explained. Given the vast number of source selections executed by the government, the quality and rigorousness of events will vary. The following explanations therefore further support decisions by contractors to protest the rules of a source selection as well as the conduct of a source selection that led to unfair results.

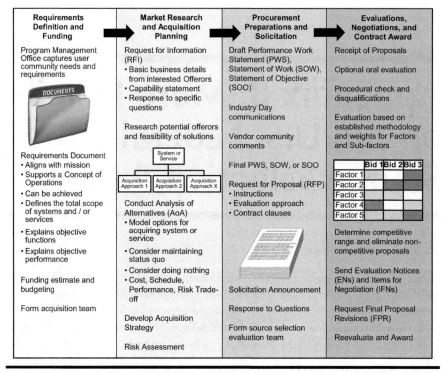

Figure B.1   General workflow for federal source selections.

B.1 Requirements Definition and Funding

Some might consider that this phase is not really a part of the source selection process as the decision to proceed with a source selection is far from this point. However, we need to start at this point because so many contracts for solutions have failed at the point of requirements definition and funding. In other words, the misalignment of requirements, funding, and schedule have created many no-win scenarios, and yet contractors reacting to opportunities have often marched off cliffs under the promise of financial profit. Contractors offering solutions may not always be able to get involved in shaping government expectations in this phase. However, it is useful to understand what is or should be occurring.

B.1.1 Program Management Office Captures User Community Needs and Requirements

Federal programs and projects are generally formed based on defined needs, and a need can be simply a strategic statement about the new system or service that should be established. The intended community of users for the system or service could have already developed a detailed set of requirements, or it is the program office's responsibility to further define the requirements for the acquisition process. If an initial set of requirements already exists, the program might start with funding from the user community. Otherwise, the program might have to start with initial funding and develop a budget to complete the acquisition process.

Regardless of which group starts requirements gathering, an effective identification of requirements must start with current operational states and anticipated changes if new systems or services are not applied. From this perspective, the systems or services are parts of overall operational solutions. The goal of applying new systems or services is to stably change the operational states to match user needs and desired outcomes. So, if the requirements are for building a new jet fighter, these requirements should connect with projected future conflict environments, dynamics of combat, strategic deployment options, tactical scenarios, and methods of sustainment (inspections, repairs, refueling, pilot training, basing, etc.). Equally, if the requirements are for staffing a government organization, these requirements should connect with the mission of the organization, specific products the staff must develop, specific tasks the staff must perform, and organizational outcomes that must be achieved. This outcome- and purpose-driven approach to establishing requirements helps to prevent requirements from being a wish list mentality; many users want to maximum capabilities under a belief of value regardless of whether they address operational objectives.

The captured requirements typically either define functions for the system or service, performance parameters, or operational characteristics. For example, in capturing the requirements for an IT system, we will document all the things the system must do within the operational workflow of its intended deployment environment; performance standards such as for reliability, accessibility, and security; and deployment characteristics such as the system must operate from a government cloud. If the user community is very large with diverse subgroups, then the art of requirements capture is to converge requirements in such a way that users can all accept the compromises. Many times, similar requirements can be combined into one requirement if users are willing to compromise. Other times, requirements may be conflicting, and a decision-maker must sacrifice one set of requirements for the greater good of getting new capabilities.

Given the complexity of modern operational environments and the breadth of the associated user community, it is common for users to specify hundreds and even thousands of requirements. Therefore, the operational process analyst needs to be prepared to use a common tool for documenting and managing the requirements. The first step in managing requirements is not consolidation but organization. Requirements need to be organized by groups and hierarchies so that the analyst can understand scope and comprehensiveness. Once requirements are grouped by a standard for association across the program, one might realize that some requirements are at higher levels of description than others. This supports the establishment of hierarchies where some requirements are subrequirements for a broader requirement. Based on the hierarchy, several tasks should be taken to complete the requirements set.

- Task 1: Eliminate requirements that reflect the users' attempt to dictate a technical solution as these requirements can prematurely limit innovation without analytical justification. However, these technical specifications can be provided to winning contractors to further define user expectations.
- Task 2: Identify gaps in requirements based on what is needed under each higher-level grouping. Reengage users to help fill gaps. Propose new requirements for validation by users as necessary.
- Task 3: Consolidate requirements that are similar to reduce the complexity of the acquisition process. The consolidated requirement can capture all the characteristics of source requirements, the intersect/common characteristics of source requirements, or a combination of common and unique characteristics.
- Task 4: Identify requirements that are either stating opposing characteristics for the same function or performance parameter, creating operational incompatibilities in dependent functions, or yielding different than desired operational results. Resolve requirement conflicts through operational analysis, decision-making, and negotiation with users.

Once a structured set of requirements has undergone these refinement tasks, a draft requirements document can be produced for the process of review, validation, further refinement, and approval.

In modern software development, the modularity of software architectures and the ease in which solutions can be modified have encouraged the use of the Agile development process to accelerate production. Agile development hinges on the concept that users initially do not have to set defined rigid requirements. Instead, flexible requirements are captured in the form of user stories that go into a product backlog. Developers then build the software product from the backlog in rapid sprints, and the users quickly see capabilities continuously emerging through demonstrations and tests associated with each sprint. As the users gain a better understanding of how the product is forming, they then provide feedback on how to modify requirements/user stories to shape the end-state product. For large systems development, a scaled Agile methodology can be used in which user stories are organized into architectural epics and the development is done through release trains.

If Agile development is adopted for the program, then the requirements-gathering process shifts to capturing user stories. The tasks for refining user stories are still appropriate. However, we do not need to go through a formal cycle of approvals to initiate development. The flexibility of software development creates two requirements-based risks in source selection and contract execution. The first risk is that users might want to create massive systems with many integrated modules so that the system can be all things to all users. The enthusiasm spawned by high-capacity global networks has led to several high-profile program failures where the requirements have grown to be too complex. In response, some agencies have chopped requirements apart into such small projects that their coordination and integration became a concern. Achieving the right balance for software systems that serve enterprise-wide users remains a challenge. The second risk is that users might want to continuously change requirements because Agile development allows for change. In developing physical systems, such as a jet fighter, a change in requirements immediately impacts the design of the systems and the schedules for completion. In modular software systems, requirements change is often expected. However, the abuse of this capability can lead to poor code quality due to constant shifts, prolonged schedules, and external integration issues as architectural flexibility may not be as great as software component flexibility.

The risks in requirements capture must be continuously managed by the PMO. Unfortunately, many PMOs take the position that they are acting on behalf of the users and therefore allow user-created risks in requirements to migrate into the solutions delivery process. An effective PMO must be the bridge between solutions formulation, development, and requirements. It must push for optimal performance and affordability by those delivering products and services in response to requirements. However, it must also understand when requirements have gone beyond feasible expectations as dictated by budget, schedule, available technologies, and contractor capabilities. Even when the first set of requirements came well-organized from users, the PMO must evaluate its effectiveness for guiding the creation of implementable solutions.

In the current financial environment, contractors are hungry or greedy enough that someone will always bid regardless of whether government demands are reasonable. However, if the PMO allows those demands to yield a condition of probable failure, then it will not be serving the best interest of users. Thus, once the PMO has captured the first set of requirements from the user community, it must take the lead in shaping those requirements to be effective in both expressing user needs and enabling the delivery of solutions for meeting user needs.

B.1.2 Requirements Document

The documenting of requirements merits special discussion because communications is important in achieving agreement across the user community and in helping the developers formulate operational solutions. Requirements in their raw form from the users are seldom effective in comprehensive communications. After the captured requirements have been grouped, organized, and deconflicted, the language of the requirements must be fine-tuned for communications. The first coordination step for a requirements document is typically with the user community, to validate that the requirements as a whole are aligned with the mission of the user agency and that an end-state concept of operations based on the requirements will meet user needs and operational objectives. This coordination step may take several rounds of draft revisions, and the tracking of reviewers' feedback must be done in a rigorous auditable way. This tracking will be used when or if the requirements must be cut back due to funding cuts or acceleration of schedule.

Once an initial requirements document has been approved by users, it is advisable that the document be forwarded to contractors who can respond to the requirements for feedback. If no group of contractors feel that they can develop a solution to meet the requirements, then this reality must be discovered and assessed early in the process. As an alternative to early contractor community engagement, the PMO can elect to employ support contractors who have high familiarity with capabilities from commercial communities. These support contractors are prevented from developing the solution due to OCI. Thus, as noted in Chapter 3, they are expected to provide objective analysis to help optimize the requirements document for solutions development.

If a solution calls for the development of a product/system with advanced technologies, then the requirements document might have to be refined after each phase of technology maturation. In the Agile development process, the requirements can be modified based on development results after each sprint. In waterfall development, the requirements can be modified in preparation for advancing to the next acquisition phase. In each case, the refinement should be based on what has been learned about limitations and potentials through technology development.

For a larger of set of requirements that calls for a complex solution, the priority in reviewing the requirements by both users and developers is that the set comprehensively addresses the total scope of the system or service. Despite proper organization, it is very possible for a key requirement to be missing to cause functional or performance deficiencies in the objective state workflow. To ensure comprehensiveness, a reviewer of the requirements document should be able to identify all the required functions, how functions interconnect, and key performance metrics for the objective state workflow. Some performance metrics could be associated with the new functions and other performance metrics could be associated with characteristics of the total system or people being provided. For example, a requirement for provided staff to have security clearances and technology certifications does not directly connect to the tasks to be completed by the staff. However, they are still metrics that govern whether the staff is eligible to complete the tasks and the risks associated with the staff assigned to the tasks. In the case of systems, requirements such as reliability, accessibility, and ease of maintenance are non-functional because they describe how the system should be instead of what the system must do.

Finally, very technology-aware users and PMO analysts might want to place design characteristics and solution features into the requirements set. Although these constraints can be viewed as risk and outcomes management, they could potentially restrict innovation. If promoting innovation is desired, then the placing of design specifics into a requirements document should be limited to those aspects of design that must be a specific way to enable integration with current and future systems. For IT services, this would be application programming interface standards, data taxonomy conventions, specific data fields, operational cycles, and hosting environment specifications for software applications to be developed.

B.1.3 Funding Estimate and Budgeting

Once a user need has been validated and an associated new set of requirements has been determined, the search for funding begins with the decision to satisfy requirements. Funding to satisfy requirements within U.S. federal agencies typically are appropriated by the U.S. Congress for each fiscal year, as shown in Figure B.2. This appropriation is based on the President's submitted budget and must follow the enactment of the authorization bill. The authorization act grants agencies and programs the authority to execute and spend money. Guidance is typically provided on what must be done. The appropriations act then funds the agencies, programs, and required activities. The funding comes as different colors/categories of money for specific types of expenditures, which have set periods for when the money must be spent. Appropriated money for operations, to include pay for military and civilian personnel, typically must be spent in one year and reappropriated for the next year.

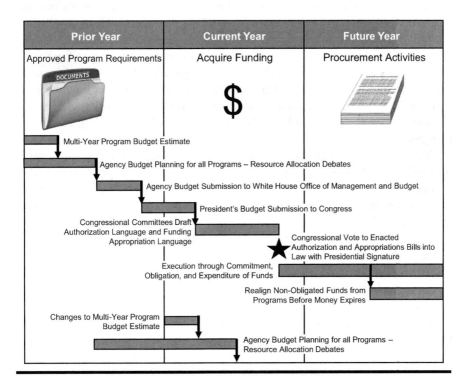

Figure B.2   Summary of U.S. federal agency and program funding process.

In contrast, money for research, production, and construction can be spent over the course of multiple years.

The way a federal agency spends congressionally appropriated money for addressing requirements is to commit the funds to program activities based on legislative guidance and to obligate the funds through award of contracts. When a contractor has been paid, the funds are expended. Committed funds that have not been obligated can be moved to fund other programs. The moving of funds between programs all under one congressional funding line is at the discretion of the agency. In contrast, moving funds between congressional funding lines requires congressional reporting after set limits. In most agencies, oversight organizations start to look in late summer for funds that might not be obligated by the end of the fiscal year on September 30 and will expire. These funds from programs that are behind schedule can then be used for other projects and programs through rapid procurement.

As the process of getting funding bills passed by the Senate and House of Representatives to be signed by the President can be long, programs that do not want to wait a year and a half for funding can take money from other programs either immediately or as non-obligated (fallout) money in the summer timeframe. Some agencies might also have working capital funds that allow an agency to operate like a commercial business where fund money is used for investments that are recuperated in the future years. These funds might also be available to rapidly initiate programs. If the program will provide a service or product that is consistent with user community operational funding, then that program might further be able to tax the user community operational funding lines. All these alternative ways of getting federal funds rely on other organizations to go through the congressional authorization and appropriations process. Thus, many requirements will remain unfunded if every program solely waits for others to fight for funding in front of Congress.

Returning to the primary process of getting funding, a rough order magnitude (ROM) budget needs to be established for the approved requirements. If this estimate is for a multiple-year program, the budget can be adjusted annually as more understanding of the solution is gained. For large programs, Congress will accept a period of research and development. However, once a system is ready for production, more precise requirements and modeling of costs to build the system are necessary. To prevent cost escalation, a program manager will be held accountable to manage threshold and objective metrics in cost, schedule, and performance. Program cost buildouts might include an estimated number of personnel (expressed in labor category rates and hours for each labor category), price of raw materials, price of components, product licenses, facility expenses, and price of consumed fuels.

For each agency, all the program cost estimates are integrated into a master plan that projects the ideal agency's budget for several years. Since we do not live in an idealized world, a resource allocation group will debate this budget, cut lower priority programs and reduce the scope of other programs to meet anticipated availability of funds. During the fall of every year, each agency will submit their budget for integration into the President's budget to Congress. The White House Office of Management and Budget (OMB) can make further adjustments to the budget based on directions from the President. Then, the President's budget is submitted to Congress typically in the first week of February. Congressional authorization and appropriation committees in the Senate and House of Representatives review and adjust the budget over the summer months and hold conference committees to resolve differences. After further adjustments to the budget and development of instructions to the agencies, the authorization and appropriation bills are approved by vote. The President can then sign/enact the bill into law (statute) or veto the process. If Congress cannot reach agreement on the budget or if the President will not sign by September 30, then the government will not have funds for the next fiscal year. Facing a government shutdown, Congress can pass a continuing resolution to run the government and agency plus programs at a percentage of the prior fiscal year's funding based on a formula.

B.1.4 Form Acquisition Team

To manage the acquisition process and source selection activities, the designated government program or project manager typically forms a team. This can start with requirements gathering, if a great deal of user community engagement is required. But, the team will have to be formed with borrowed resources until program funding has been acquired. With program funding, federal acquisition teams are typically formed with civilian personnel, military personnel if the program is in the Department of Defense, and contractors. Team members will include staff who understand the requirements areas, technology opportunities, contractor markets, and relevant statutes/regulations/policies, as well as staff who can analyze options, develop schedules, build cost models, and develop procedure documents.

The work of the acquisition team is to first establish procurements to meet requirements and program objectives and then to manage the awarded contracts for on-time and within-cost delivery of specified products or services [2]. Because the work of this team affects competition during procurement, all documents are safeguarded until they are approved to be shared with industry contractors. Documents that are directly tied to the source selection process are generally marked as "source selection sensitive" and must be securely handled to prevent a violation of the FAR. Other documents, such as for requirements and strategic plans, are often marked as FOUO until a draft or final version can be shared. Early dialogue with potential solution providers from the industry is encouraged in the acquisition process so that the acquisition team can identify the best path toward satisfying requirements.

Members of the acquisition team are typically asked to sign non-disclosure agreements to protect acquisition information. Further, companies receiving contracts to provide personnel for the acquisition team must (1) prove that they do not have a real or perceived OCI in doing the work, and (2) accept the restrictions on their future bidding activities to prevent new OCI concerns. OCI, according to Federal Acquisition Regulations Subpart 9.5, can be due to bias, impaired judgment, and unfair access in the source selection process. Bias can occur when a contractor is preparing specifications or work statements to which its own company is seeking a contract to satisfy. Therefore, OCI exists because the company's acquisition team personnel are motivated to develop the specifications or work statements in favor of themselves. Impaired judgment can occur when a contractor is supporting the evaluation of proposals to which another business unit in the company has submitted a bid. Therefore, OCI exists because the company's acquisition team personnel may not be able to objectively evaluate all proposals. Finally, unfair access can occur when a contractor is working in a program office where there is no sure way to shield their personnel from acquisition-sensitive information. Therefore, OCI exists because the company's program office support personnel could obtain information that gives the contractor unfair advantage in bids. To prevent acquisition process support contractors from creating future OCI issues, most contracts for program office support will have language that forbids the contractor from bidding on source selections related to their area of acquisition support.

The OCI divide has created two commercial company communities in support of federal government needs. It has also promoted the breakup of companies that tried to pursue both acquisition support contracts and systems development contracts. Nevertheless, developing solutions for the federal government involves efforts from both sides. The discussion of the remaining phases in the federal source selection process is largely about the endeavors of the acquisition support team.

B.2 Market Research and Acquisition Planning

Once requirements have been approved and funding has been acquired, the next phase is for the acquisition team to develop a plan for getting an affordable solution to satisfy requirements (FAR Part 7). While this plan does not have to result in a source selection, the planning is an important part of the source selection process. The way to conduct planning is to first understand the capabilities in the marketplace and then to select a solution path to control outcomes. Programs that seek innovation may want the requirements to be a high level and the range of possible solutions to be very wide. However, specific and detailed requirements will demand a narrowing-down of approaches before asking commercial contractors to bid and propose a solution. Otherwise, the proposals will come in all shapes and sizes, making comparative evaluation extremely challenging.

The purpose of market research is stated as arriving at the most suitable approach to acquiring, distributing, and supporting supplies and services (FAR 10.000). Market research determines applicable business practices, what is available commercially, and industry inputs on requirements and acquisition strategies. Members of the acquisition team are encouraged to both conduct passive research on companies plus technologies and actively talk to contractors and product vendors to discuss what is needed. Site visits to see technology demonstrations, inspecting production capabilities, and gaging company operations will improve the accuracy of assessing commercial capabilities. All collected data should be well documented to support an analysis of alternatives on how to achieve desired solutions.

Even for considering alternatives, the analysis of the market should answer the following questions:

- Are there capabilities in the marketplace for satisfying the government's requirements?
- Are there COTS technologies (non-development items) that can be used in part as components or in whole as a system to address the requirements?
- If COTS components must be reconfigured or customized to be effective in addressing requirements, what is the nature and magnitude of this effort?
- Determine the nature and level of development that is needed if the requirements must be satisfied with a system.
- If COTS components can be used, what is the business process of acquiring the components (type of contract, terms of warranties, buyer financing options, etc.)?
- If COTS components can be used, what is the logistical process of delivering and sustaining components (producers, distributors, supporting commercial items, maintenance, packaging, etc.)?
- How can the use of recycled materials and conservation of energy strategies be incorporated into solutions?
- Does the set of requirements have to be bundled or can the requirements be satisfied through multiple contracts of sizes that favor small business participation?
- How can small business participation criteria, as stated in FAR 19, be addressed?
- Do the market capabilities justify the procurement being a small business set aside competition or even a sole source (noncompetitive) award to a disadvantaged small business, such as a service-disabled veteran-owned small business (SDVOSB) or a HUBZone small business?

If the preliminary results of market research are not favorable for satisfying the requirements, then the acquisition team should consider returning to the requirements definition and funding phase to adjust the framework of the acquisition. If additional funding could yield a successful solution, then other sources of funding need to be identified. If reducing the more challenging requirements could yield a solution, then the user community should be reengaged to see if a reduced solution can still address mission needs. After such adjustments, the acquisition planning would then resume until an acquisition strategy has been developed.

B.2.1 Request for Information

A primary instrument for conducting interactive market research is the RFI. RFIs have no specific format and are basically public announcements that a PMO is seeking information to support its acquisition planning. The RFI will pose a set of questions for the contractor community and can include draft acquisition documents for the community to provide comments. Although the announcement may set a page limit and a due date, there are no regulations regarding what the government can do. As there are no contractual mechanisms linked with the RFI, it is up to the acquisition team to determine what extra material and late material they wish to evaluate.

Contractors responding to an RFI will generally include their company capability statements and answers to questions that attempt to steer the acquisition approach in their favor. Small disadvantaged companies will try to convince the government that they have enough capabilities to make the source selection a set-aside. Large businesses may try to convince the acquisition team to put language in the final RFP that favors their capabilities. The acquisition team must understand such motivations from the contractor community in designing RFI questions and in evaluating RFI responses.

As the RFI data should support an AoA, the acquisition team needs to pose questions that are traceable to key decisions and ask for answers that are verifiable. As many contractors will have limited resources to respond to an RFI, the questions should also be lean and focused on the most important matters.

B.2.2 Research Potential Contractors and Feasibility of Solutions

The acquisition team needs to recognize that an RFI is only the beginning of researching contractors and potential solutions. Based on the responses to the RFI, the acquisition team should refine the concept of operations, formulate objective state workflows, identify key features if systems are required, and identify key skill sets if the solution involves services. While perception of fairness must be maintained, the acquisition team can further engage contractors based on RFI results to investigate options. The acquisition team should also seek independent sources that can validate contractor claims of capability.

Based on such analysis, groups of requirements can start to be described in terms of work that must be done and metrics for performance. If there is still great uncertainty regarding what contractors could produce when given proper incentives, then the market research could lead to the conclusion that a SOO should be used for the procurement. SOOs challenge the innovativeness of contractors and should be evaluated based on innovation. As performance metrics are not specified for the SOO, contractors should be incentivized to produce anticipated outcomes. SOOs represent a high-risk but potentially high-reward approach to acquisitions and should never be used as a substitute for poor quality market research.

If tasks in satisfying requirements can be determined, then an SOW can be defined to drive the procurement process. SOWs manage risks by requiring the winning contractor to accomplish specific tasks. However, the contractors are still given great flexibility on how they will perform the tasks. The flexibility allows proposals to present solutions that could yield unanticipated high performance and to accept tasks where the contractor and government jointly manages uncertainties in performance.

Finally, for requirements that can be satisfied by a set of well-defined tasks and subtasks, a PWS can be developed. PWS is a powerful instrument for service-type work because metrics and quality control mechanisms can be established for each task as a part of the procurement process. For long tasks, incremental measures can be used to control the work based on the government's understanding of anticipated performance at the time of contract award. In fact, incentives and penalties can be established based on performance metrics as a part of contract award.

The acquisition team should start to develop pieces of draft documents to support the source selection as soon as possible and refine those pieces through more research and iterative analysis. At some point, the viable approaches for achieving requirements will manifest. Then, a rigorous analysis should be conducted to select and defend the best approach. Even when the best approach appears to be obvious, an AoA should still be conducted to validate that no driving factors and hidden consequences are overlooked.

B.2.3 Conduct Analysis of Alternatives

The purpose of the AoA is to identify all the acquisition approaches based on market research and to select the best approach through comparative analysis. For all AoA efforts, both the approaches of "doing nothing" and "maintaining status quo" should be considered to enable comprehensive evaluations. For doing nothing, the analyst evaluates the consequences of letting requirements go unsatisfied, contracts expire, and funds be reprogrammed for other purposes. After considering what systems or services can be achieved based on capabilities in the market, user communities might realize through trade-off that they can live without their requirements so that other users can benefit from the extra funding. For maintaining status quo, the analyst evaluates extending current contracts for services, continuing research and development activities for systems, or delaying competitive procurement. In cases where market capabilities are changing rapidly, delaying critical decisions on how to move forward with systems development or acquiring new services can lead to significant technical advantages or cost savings for the government. For example, market research might reveal that specific commercial technical breakthroughs are only a year away or that prices will drop on specific components.

Beyond the alternatives of doing nothing and maintaining status quo, the other alternatives are specific to the type of acquisition and nature of each requirements set. The first level of alternatives for acquiring services tend to be considering the use of commercial contractors, government staff, FFRDCs, or not-for-profit institutions to perform the service. Hybrid teams of these types of service providers can further be considered as additional alternatives. If the trade-off between cost, schedule, performance, and risks for these alternatives reveals that acquiring commercial contractors is the best alternative, then the second level of alternatives can be types of commercial procurements approaches such as single-award contract, multiple-award contract, and task order on specific IDIQ contracts. Alternatives can also address whether the competition should be full and open, small business set aside, limited to a disadvantaged small business type, or even sole source. However, such decisions are often governed by federal regulations, Small Business Administration (SBA) guidelines, and agency-specific policies.

Alternatives for acquiring systems should focus on competing technologies and design methodologies. The goal is not to select a specific contractor but to narrow the range of competition based on available data so that the actual source selection can have metrics that evaluate detailed offerings. In some cases, the data does not support a narrowing-down of technologies and methodologies. Then, the acquisition path might have to be burdened so that the technology down-select is made through the source selection process and involves detailed proposals.

In comparing alternatives, the cost comparison between vastly different approaches may require conversions to common cost elements. For example, there are formulas for converting government civilian pay to commercial equivalent salary, and there are models for computing total life cycle cost of government-developed systems relative to COTS systems. The performance comparison between vastly different approaches may require process models for alternative ways to deliver services and concept of operations for competing types of systems. With these process and operational models, we can then identify common performance metrics and use the models to produce projected values for the metrics. Finally, the schedule comparison can be achieved by identifying common major milestones, which include IOC of systems and task completion for services. There is a level of risk in the ability to achieve projected cost, performance, and schedule for each of the alternatives. Also, there is a margin of error in making cost, performance, and schedule projections. This margin of error relates to the metrics and scales used for comparative analysis. Scales that are too precise will incur higher error if the available data cannot support such precision. Scales that are too high-level will lead to more subjectivity in the comparison of alternatives. This complexity suggests that AoAs must be conducted by experienced systems and operations research analysts. Further, the AoA can often be considered the first step in the solutions development process. Mistakes in this step can cause opportunities to be overlooked and downstream failures to be set in motion. On the other hand, choosing the correct alternative/acquisition approach can yield great savings and optimized schedules.

B.2.4 Develop Acquisition Strategy

The acquisition strategy document is the master plan for the entire acquisition, and the approval of the acquisition strategy by the decision authority initiates the source selection process. This document has many sections, as shown in the description of contents below. However, the most important feature of the acquisition strategy is that it must present a logical and analytically defended approach for spending resources to achieve a solution that satisfies requirements. This approach must be supported by mature technologies and capabilities from the commercial market and a way to manage the risks in systems development or performance of services. With the acquisition strategy, the acquisition team can start to prepare the source selection package. The process then moves from market research to procurement planning and solicitation.

B.2.4.1 Example of Acquisition Strategy Contents

1. Bottom Line Up Front
   a. Decisions Requested
   b. Concerns
2. Program Overview
   a. Description: Business process improvements, concept of operations, configuration management approach, program organization and management, program plan, data management, analysis of cost and operational effectiveness, deficiency correction, use of simulations/models in acquisition, cyber security, statutory/regulatory/policy compliance, systems integration if relevant, deployment process for systems, sustainment process for systems, technology and capability maturity, system architecture, testing approach.
   b. Requirements documentation: High-level description, explanation of collection process and organization, identification of source documents, degree of requirements completion, requirements for Agile development, connectivity with operational concepts, currency of requirements, capabilities to be established year by year, translation to performance metrics if appropriate, linkage with technical specifications.
   c. Identified decision authority for the source selection process.
   d. Current contract summary (if appropriate): Performing contractor, period of performance, major milestones, quality of performance.
3. Program Funding
   a. Program funding status presented by fiscal year and color of money acquired.
   b. Identify additional funds needed based on government cost estimate.
   c. Present plan to resolve shortfalls in necessary funding.

4. Program Risks
   a. Identify risks in program schedule, required resources, technology maturity, integration with other systems or processes, migration from legacy capabilities, program execution, and deliverable quality. Recommend mitigation approaches.
   b. Identify risks in the acquisition process and contracting. Recommend solutions such as modular contracting (distribute risk), evolutionary acquisition (increment acquiring of capability), earned value management system application (rigorous contract performance reporting), post-award oversight (performance analysis), performance-based contracting (performance metrics establishment), and so on.
5. Analysis of Acquisition Strategies
   a. Present AoA summary results and trade-off methodology.
   b. Explain the specific acquisition approach selected.
6. Proposed Acquisition Strategy
   a. Present the overall purpose and objectives of the acquisition approach and explain alignment with agency strategic plans.
   b. Explain the details of the acquisition strategy and implementation steps from funding, source selection, and contracting to performance, testing, and post-delivery support.
   c. Identify the delivery blocks for evolutionary acquisition and components for modular contracting.
   d. Explain the risk analysis and factors used to select the proposed acquisition strategy and how this strategy will support the overall objectives.
   e. Explain how the acquisition strategy is tailored for the program to yield a lean cost-effective process.
   f. Identify process improvement and streamlining initiatives and opportunities.
7. Source Selection Organization
   a. Present the organization of the proposed source selection team to include positions, responsibilities, assigned personnel, and supporting organizations.
   b. Identify approach for completing the source selection team if not already complete.
   c. Show the training that will be provided to the team and how the qualifications and capabilities of the source selection team members will be validated.
   d. Explain how inherently governmental functions will be performed, contractor support (if any) is kept to appropriate tasks, and source selection sensitive information will be protected to fully comply with Procurement Integrity Act.

8. Business Considerations
   a. Explain the market research process to include data collection mechanisms, evaluation methodologies, results, and confidence in market capability to satisfy acquisition strategy.
   b. Identify the target sources from the market that justify either full and open competition, small business set aside, small disadvantaged business set aside, or sole source award.
   c. Explain how management, technical approach, past performance, cost or price, and other factors should be evaluated and present top-level evaluation criteria.
   d. Explain best form of contracting with contract parameters such as firm fixed price, cost plus, time and material, and so on.
   e. Present the proposed contract incentives, such as award fee, performance penalties, and delivery-based payments, and explain how these incentives are tied to risk mitigation.
   f. Present special provisions such as government furnished information (GFI), government-furnished equipment (GFE), contractor furnished equipment, contractor-provided technology platforms, and so on.
9. Milestone Schedule
   a. Identify all major milestones such as presolicitation decisions, reviews, RFP release, competitive range, final proposal revision receipt, and final decision briefing, and so on.
10. Post-Award Management Plan
   a. Present post-award contract management concept, administrative processes, oversight structure, decision-makers, metrics for contract performance, risk mitigation approach, and so on.
   b. Identify contracting officer representative (COR) from program office to oversee technical performance.
   c. Explain process for ensuring quality in contract performance and discuss involvement of agency contracting organizations.
11. Recommendation
   a. Present recommended decision for the acquisition.

B.2.5 Risk Assessment

The final component of market research and the completion of the acquisition strategy is the risk assessment. In the acquisition process, risk is defined as uncertainties in the program's ability to achieve its purpose and objectives in the future. Risk lies in the ability to maintain cost and schedule, and the ability to achieve planned system and service performance specifications. Risk is typically defined as relative to adverse potential outcomes, and each outcome is assessed to have a probability of occurrence and level of impact. Each risk item should be traceable to the ability to satisfy requirements and should be described in a way that criteria for determining levels of risk are established. Figure B.3 shows a standard scale for measuring the level of risk in an acquisition, and the combination of probability of occurrence and level of impact will determine whether a risk is low, moderate, and high.

All moderate and high risks need to be addressed by the acquisition team, first in terms of consequences and then in terms of mitigation approach. Industry inputs for mitigating risks should be welcomed and the RFP should have ways to get contractors to present verifiable risk mitigation approaches in their proposals. Some risks are well-understood enough that constraints can be placed in the RFP for limiting risks in the awarded contract. Other risks can be managed during contract execution with appropriate benchmarks, reporting, performance metrics, and corrective mechanisms. As risks evolve over time, risks in the acquisition process should be continuously reassessed as the program progresses. This assessment should determine the effectiveness of prior risk-mitigation steps, formulate improvements to risk-mitigation approaches, identify new risks, and formulate new risk mitigation. The risk mitigation plan is a key component of the acquisition strategy and must be approved with it.

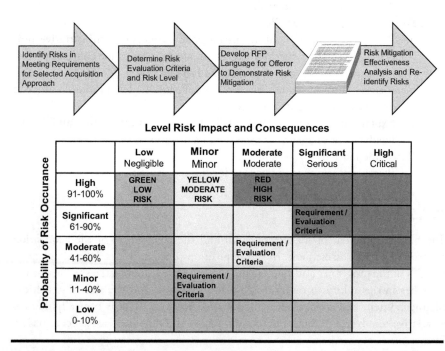

Figure B.3   Standard federal risk evaluation matrix.

B.3 Procurement Preparations and Solicitation

After the approval of the acquisition strategy, the acquisition team establishes a schedule and proceeds to prepare the source selection package that culminates into an RFP. Once an RFP is officially released, all communication with industry must be formal to ensure fair competition. A source selection package has documents that are presented to the potential offerors through the RFP and documents that are presented to the source selection team to establish a consistent evaluation methodology. The RFP package will be further explained, and the responsibilities of the source selection team will also be presented. To support the source selection team's evaluation of proposals submitted based on RFP, the evaluation methodology, scoring standards, and cost estimates should be established prior to receipt of proposals and ideally prior to release of RFP. This includes government internal evaluation metrics. Without a well-defined methodology, proposal teams will be vulnerable to losing objectivity in the evaluation process.

The development of these source selection documents can be an iterative process where there is at least one round of engagement with industry to validate that the source selection is not totally off track and multiple rounds of internal reviews prior to and after industry engagement. A document component checklist for agency internal reviewers is presented below.

Checklist for Reviewing Acquisition Documents

- Is the content in alignment with agency policy and strategy?
- Does the document contain all the parts required to support the source selection evaluation process and contract award?
- Are all stakeholder issues and required actions addressed?
- Has the document been properly coordinated and approved?
- Has the document been reviewed by external subject matter experts to validate accuracy and effectiveness?
- Is the document compliant with statutes/regulations/policies?
- Is the document content consistent with data sources?
- Does the document connect with other key documents?
- Has the document been properly safeguarded from disclosure?
- Are all the government tasks associated with this document ready to proceed?
- Are all the stakeholders identified and aware of the acquisition status?
- Has the agency acquisition executive been properly briefed?

B.3.1 Draft Performance Work Statement (PWS), Statement of Work (SOW), Statement of Objective (SOO)

The essence of the source selection process is effectively communicating with industry on what the government needs and having industry (product vendors and government contractors) provide compelling proposals. A way to enhance this communication is to provide industry with the draft PWS/SOW/SOO to gain feedback. The feedback will help the government acquisition team determine whether contractors fully understand the requirements translated into objectives, tasks, and performance metrics. Also, it will give the government a glimpse into the possible number and types of responses they will receive.

Draft documents also allow potential offerors to make bid or no-bid decisions, start to craft solutions, build teams, and identify proposal development resources. However, the government must be clear that it is not bound by the condition of the draft documents and there is no obligation to even award a contract.

Contractor profiles can help the government develop or refine evaluation methodologies and modify the language of the PWS/SOW/SOO to get better or more responses. In special cases where the market has suddenly changed so that there will not be any good bids based on the PWS/SOW/SOO as written in the draft, the acquisition team should return to the requirements analysis and market research process.

B.3.2 Industry Day Communications

For large procurement efforts that demand complex teams, the government will typically host industry day events to directly promote communications. Industry day allows potential contractors to meet and build teams, directly ask government questions, and size up the competition. Industry days can also be held at the agency level where the status of multiple acquisitions is presented together.

At industry day, the government will typically introduce the program management office organization and how the program fits within the agency's strategic roadmap. Then, the highlights of the draft PWS/SOW/SOO will be discussed and the government's tentative schedule for completing the source selection will be presented. Though the government is not obligated to pursue the approach presented at industry day, it can reveal whether the RFP is for a small or small disadvantaged business set aside and whether the contract will be of a specific type.

Contract types are discussed in detail under FAR Part 16. A summary of the contract types and their advantages is presented below.

B.3.2.1 Fixed-Price Contracts

When a fair price can be negotiated between the government and the offeror, establishing a fixed-price contract places the burden of cost control on the winning contractor. As the contractor will be paid based on a set price, it is inherently encouraged to meet contract deliverable requirements in the most efficient and expedited manner. Sometimes, fixed price can only be established on set conditions and set periods, thus there are variations to the fixed-price concept, as shown below. Other times, the fixed priced must be anchored to some conditions or be incentivized to reduce the governments risks. For example, anchoring the price to specific positions will reduce the risk of a contractor severely understaffing for fear of breach of contract. Also, if the contractor might be able to minimally comply with the contract, additional incentives for better performance might prevent such a contractor strategy. These variants of the contract type are also presented below.

- Firm Fixed-Price Contracts: Government price will not change as along as terms of the contract are met.
- Fixed-Price Contracts with Economic Price Adjustment: Price adjustment provisions are added into the contract that will be triggered by economic conditions.
- Fixed-Price Incentive Contracts: Incentive is added based on contract performance.
- Fixed-Price Contracts with Prospective Price Redetermination: Mechanism added in contract to trigger or allow price adjustment because fair price can only be established for initial period.
- Fixed-Ceiling–Price Contracts with Retroactive Price Redetermination: Used for R&D low-dollar value contracts where initial price cannot be established.
- Firm Fixed-Price, Level-of-Effort Term Contracts: Price linked to proposed labor categories and hours in proposal.

B.3.2.2 Cost-Reimbursement Contracts

When the nature of work is so dynamic that fair price cannot be established upon award, then a contract that reimburses the cost of work to the contractor can be used. The least risk to the contractor is when the fee is set at the beginning of contract, and some protection from contractor cost overruns can be achieved if an award-fee structure is established. These variants are presented below. To further control cost, the government can have the contractor share in the cost, but the contractor must understand the gains if they are to make company investments. Typically, intellectual property ownership is a primary commercial motivation in accepting a sharing of cost. Without sharing cost, the contract can also connect incentives to directly reducing cost. However, the incentives must yield greater profitability for companies if it is to work.

- Cost-Sharing Contracts: Reimbursement for only a portion of the allowable cost.
- Cost-Plus-Incentive-Fee Contracts: Incentive fee is based on formula between allowable cost and target cost.
- Cost-Plus-Award-Fee Contracts: Award fee is preset based on specific criteria in contract.
- Cost-Plus-Fixed-Fee Contracts: Fixed fee is negotiated at the beginning of the contract and does not change unless the terms of the contract are breached.

B.3.2.3 Indefinite-Delivery Indefinite Quantity (IDIQ) Contracts

Contracts can also be issued to preselected contractors for pending work issued in the form of task orders. This preselection can be down to a list of evaluated contractors or it can even be down to a single contractor. Either way, the contractors who won an award on the IDIQ contract would have demonstrated their capabilities and past performance and agreed upon a list of labor categories, definition of staff qualifications, and labor rates. Then, RFP for task orders can be issued with specific requirements and award periods. Task order competitions, which are more solution-focused, can be very quick with proposals sometimes due within 10 days and winner selection within weeks.

Each IDIQ contract will typically have a total contract value ceiling which can be on the level of billions of dollars. If the contract is for small business competition, then IDIQ contract holders that have graduated from the small business status or lost their disadvantaged status might either need to be removed from the contract or be barred from bidding on the follow-on contract. Disadvantaged small business categories include veteran-owned small business (VOSB), service-disabled veteran-owned small business (SDVOSB), women-owned small business (WOSB), economically disadvantaged women-owned small business (EDWOSB), small disadvantaged business (SDB), and HUBZone small business. Further, disadvantaged small businesses can qualify for the Small Business Administration (SBA) 8(a) program, which has dedicated set aside competitions. Also, Alaskan native corporations (ANCs) have special advantages in participation in federal contracting. In general, most IDIQ contracts require at least 30 percent participation by small business on full and open competition contracts and further has specific components of the IDIQ or specific task orders dedicated for award to small business.

Blanket purchasing agreements (BPAs) work similarly to IDIQs but are intended for repetitive purchases of a particular type of goods or services. BPAs are competed through leveraging a rate schedule such as from the General Services Administration and the one or few winners would then compete for task orders under the BPA.

B.3.2.4 Time and Materials, Labor-Hour, and Letter Contracts

If a fair price for the total scope of work cannot be negotiated in advance because of uncertainties, then it may be to the government's benefit to issue a time and material (T&M) contract. Such contracts have agreed-upon labor categories and rates as well as agreed-upon unit goods. Then, the final price becomes how many hours were delivered and how many units where used to meet PWS/SOW/SOO requirements. The trade-off between T&M and firm fixed price is that offerors will sometimes manage their risks on FFP contracts by artificially justifying a higher price. If the government is uncertain about the advantages of fixed-price contracts or if the government anticipates an increase in level effort, then T&M contracts are preferred.

A labor-hour contract is simply a T&M contract without material pricing requirements. Finally, a letter contract is a mechanism that allows a contractor to start work immediately even though total cost is not well-understood.

B.3.3 Contractor Community Comments

Potential offerors will recommend document language changes that maximize their ability to win and to provide the most effective solution to the government [3]. Sometimes, the contractor's winning strategy will conflict with providing the best solutions. Other times, the contractor's determination of the best solution is biased by a false understanding of its own capabilities. The government acquisition team receiving contractor community comments must see past these agendas, collect nuggets of insight, and identify the real issues in the acquisition documents.

If multiple contractors/potential offerors are recommending the same changes, then those changes should receive greater consideration. If key contractors are prohibited from bidding unless changes are made, then the ability to acquire the best solution without such contractors must be reassessed. Contractors might also identify valid problems in statutory/regulatory/policy compliance as well as inconsistency between different parts of the RFP package. Finally, even when potential offerors are recommending the wrong changes, their mistakes could indicate areas where the RFP package is unclear or vulnerable to different interpretations. The acquisition team must make corrections not only to get the best proposal but also to avoid protest on the ground rules of evaluation prior to proposal submission or the evaluation results after award announcement.

B.3.4 Final PWS, SOW, or SOO

The completion of the final PWS, SOW, or SOO should be accompanied by a complete set of instructions for offerors on how to respond. Further, a methodology for evaluating the proposal responses should be established prior to the issuance of RFP. Parts of the evaluation methodology can be disclosed to all potential offerors to establish a consistency across the proposals. Other parts of the methodology can be kept hidden from the potential offerors to discover their depth of understanding. The critical fact is that the evaluation methodology must be applied equally for all proposals without bias. If the evaluation methodology is established or modified after receiving the proposals, then an inherent potential for bias will exist and the proposal evaluation process can be protested.

As the final PWS, SOW, or SOO is the document upon which all proposals will be based, its release to the public as a part of the RFP package must be strictly controlled to enable fair competition. Once released, the potential offerors will be given a timeframe for developing and submitting proposals. So, the RFP package must be rigorously reviewed and approved before being declared as final.

This review includes validating the relationship between PWS, SOW, or SOO with user requirements and legally making sure that the RFP is not vulnerable to protest.

In select cases where the nature of work in the PWS does not require an offeror-defined technical solution, the RFP might only require the submission of the proposal past performance and cost volumes. In other cases where past performance is not a good indicator of future performance, the RFP might only require the submission of the proposed technical and cost volumes.

B.3.5 Request for Proposal (RFP)

The RFP generally contains elements listed under the uniform contract format as shown below. For developing solutions in response to the RFP, the most important sections are Section C, which presents the PWS, SOW, or SOO; Section L, which presents the instructions such as page count, format, and required content; and Section M, which explains enough of how the proposals will be evaluated to achieve consistency in response. The government does not have to disclose the entire evaluation methodology, but the methodology must be defined and rigorously applied to all submitted proposals.

The RFP can also have appendices/attachments that provide details, such as requirements documents, current user community workflows, legacy system architectures, government policies, assets lists, and other information that will help offerors develop the most effective solutions. This component of the RFP is often overlooked by the government when there has been dialogue and working relationships with a set of potential offerors because there is a belief that the offerors already understand the user situation. Such omissions in the RFP are not OCI issues as long as no offeror is given access to source selection sensitive information and program office internal FOUO information. However, poor attachments do make it difficult for offerors without government organizational understanding to develop effective solutions.

B.3.5.1 Uniform Contract Format

- Part I: The Schedule
  - Section A: Solicitation/contract form
  - Section B: Supplies or services and prices/costs
  - Section C: Description/specifications/statement of work
  - Section D: Packaging and marking
  - Section E: Inspection and acceptance
  - Section F: Deliveries or performance
  - Section G: Contract administration data
  - Section H: Special contract requirements

- Part II: Contract Clauses
  - Section I: Contract clauses
- Part III: List of Documents, Exhibits, and Other Attachments
  - Section J: List of attachments
- Part IV: Representations and Instructions
  - Section K: Representations, certifications, and other statements of offerors or respondents
  - Section L: Instructions, conditions, and notices to offerors or respondents
  - Section M: Evaluation factors for award

B.3.6 Solicitation Announcement

RFPs open for competitions by all companies or a category of companies must be announced to the general public. The federal government website (http://www.fedbizopps.gov) presents such announcements, which includes the RFP package, competition summary, contracting officer contact information, and a history of official changes in the form of amendments.

For RFPs connected with already-awarded IDIQ contracts, the government is only required to make the announcement to IDIQ contract holders. Such RFPs for the awarding of task orders may have reduced content requirements because of prior evaluation. In some cases, the page count for the technical proposal might be further limited or past performance exhibits might not be required. In conjunction, the potential offerors will be given less time to respond and the evaluation time will be faster. Select IDIQ contracts might also have clauses that prohibit losing offerors from protesting an award unless the dollar value is above a certain level. This provides a higher assurance of task order start date.

B.3.7 Response to Questions

Potential offerors can still ask questions upon reviewing the final RFP package. These questions will be handled by the contracting officer so that official responses to all potential offerors are made. Questions can generate clarification responses by the government, amendments to the RFP, or no response at all. Potential offerors can also directly request a change to the RFP, such as the extension of a due date, addition of user community or system information, modification of page count limitations, or even adjustment of evaluation methodology.

If the RFP presents a methodology that reveals unfair competition, potential offerors can protest the rules of the RFP. This protest must be submitted prior to receipt of proposals and start of the evaluation process.

B.3.8 Form Source Selection Evaluation Team (SSET)

As the source selection is a dedicated process strictly governed by the FAR and the agency's contracting/procurement organization, the formation of the source selection evaluation team, typically with only government personnel, to execute the process is essential. The acquisition team will transition responsibilities to the source selection team on or before receipt of proposals. Government members of the acquisition team can be selected to be on the source selection team, but the change in responsibilities will be specific.

As shown in Figure B.4, the source selection team will typically have the technical assessment group that reads the technical proposals and scores the technical and management factors, the performance confidence assessment group (PCAG) that determines the relevance of submitted past performances and scores the confidence in each offeror performing proposed work, and the cost/price assessment group that determines the realism of cost based on independent government cost estimate (IGCE) and the competitiveness of cost. These groups will form the SSET, and the chairperson of the SSET will coordinate activities and manage the integration of scores for presentation to the Source Selection Authority (SSA).

For large source selections, members of the program office, user community offices, and contracting organization picked to be on the SSET often must take a temporary leave of absence from their normal jobs to conduct the evaluation. This evaluation of dozens of proposals, each hundreds of pages long, could take

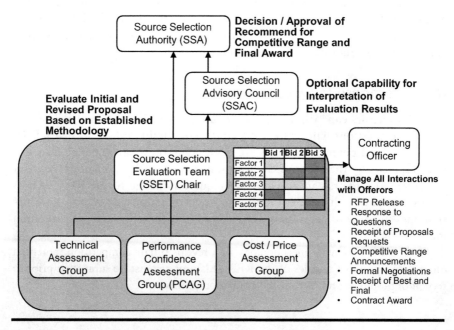

Figure B.4   General organization of a source selection team.

several months. To further interpret the results of the SSET, the SSA may establish a Source Selection Advisory Council (SSAC). The responsibilities of the SSAC chairperson, SSA, and SSET chairperson are further explained below.

B.3.8.1 Source Selection Authority Responsibilities

The SSA is accountable for the efficient and FAR-compliant conduct of the source selection. He or she will appoint the SSET and SSAC chairpersons, establish the SSET and SSAC teams, and ensure team membership remains consistent for the duration of the selection process. The SSA will get commitments from supporting organizations to provide dedicated resources and ensure that leaders have specific responsibilities.

The SSA must make sure that the source selection is executed based on quality and outcome instead of just schedule. He or she must also make sure that all team members understand Subsection 27(a) of the Office of Federal Procurement Policy Act (41 USC Sec. 423 and FAR 3.104) regarding unauthorized disclosure of source selection information. Members may be asked to sign nondisclosure agreements.

B.3.8.2 Source Selection Advisory Council Chairperson Responsibilities

The SSAC chairperson guides the SSAC in reviewing the Source Selection Plan (SSP) which outlines the conduct of the source selection. Once the SSA approves the SSP, the SSAC convenes again at the request of the SSA and typically evaluates the findings of the SSET. The SSAC will provide recommendations and interpretations to the SSA as requested. Typically, the SSAC will validate accuracy, consistency, and defensibility of the evaluation results.

B.3.8.3 SSET Chairperson Responsibilities

The SSET chairperson ensures that members of the SSET in each group are aware of their responsibilities and have the knowledge to meet their responsibilities. He or she must lead the preparation of the SSP and guide SSET group leads on following SSP. He or she must facilitate appropriate coordination and communications.

The SSET chairperson is accountable for the evaluation by following approved methodology and criteria that are stated in the SSP and whatever is presented in Section M of the RFP. He or she coordinates with the contracting officer (CO) on communications with offerors while remaining compliant with all contracting procedures. The SSET chairperson will approve evaluation notices and items for negotiation as a part of the evaluation process and will present evaluation results either to the SSAC or directly to the SSA. ENs is a broader term, which can represent a range of communications between the source selection team and an offeror. Identified inconsistencies in the proposal and points in need of further clarification can all be required corrections in ENs. IFNs are more focused communication messages that address specific terms in which the government wishes to gain more favorable offers.

B.3.8.4 Contracting Officer Responsibilities

The CO manages all business aspects of the acquisition and source selection. This includes coordinating all approvals, applying appropriate contract clauses, safeguarding source selection information, and maintaining source selection records. The CO advises the SSA on FAR compliance and is the single point of contact (POC) for potential offerors/prospective offerors. The CO will control offeror engagements to include clarifications, IFNs, competitive range announcements, final proposal revision (FPR) requests, and award announcements. The CO will manage the debriefing of unsuccessful offerors and manage the signing of the contract and kick-off of contract activities.

The CO has the authority to review all evaluation results and can provide recommendations on competitive range and awards. In some cases, a CO can independently interpret evaluation results based on established evaluation methodology and reverse the recommendation of SSET or even the SSA. If an award is made by the CO to a different offeror than the one the SSET has selected, the CO needs to make sure that he or she is not conducting some rogue reevaluation and that policies are strictly adhered to.

B.4 Evaluations, Negotiations, and Contract Award

Once the RFP has been issued and all the question responses and amendments have been released, the SSET prepares for the evaluation of proposals. The evaluation typically has two stages. First, proposals with scores that do not exceed the threshold competitive range are eliminated from further considerations. Then, the remaining proposals are further evaluated to select those that will receive an award [4]. The RFP will specify whether the contract will be for single or multiple awards.

After the competitive range assessment, the government may elect to negotiate with the remaining offerors. After negotiations, the offerors may be given a chance to provide best and final proposals to complete the competition.

B.4.1 Receipt of Proposals

In the receipt of proposal process, the CO can receive proposals by email, physical hard copy and CD delivery, or web-based upload. The submission instructions must be a part of the RFP announcement, and the receipt mechanism should be able to handle the file sizes of the proposals to be received. Upon documentation of receipt, the proposal elements are stored in a secure document management system as competition-sensitive and proprietary information for the SSET. Proposals received after the due date and time are automatically disqualified.

B.4.2 Optional Oral Evaluation

The solicitation might also call for the use of oral presentations as a filter to stream-line the evaluation process or technology demonstrations to reduce acquisition risks. These evaluation methods must be declared in the RFP announcement with instructions provided.

In oral presentations to filter offers, the government establishes a high-level methodology to evaluate the offeror's description of their solution. During the presentation, the government evaluator may ask predesignated questions to help clarify understanding, but the questions should not unfairly lead select presenters to better outcomes. Upon selecting a group of solution concepts that are most likely to succeed, the government would then request detailed proposals.

In risk reduction technology demonstrations, the government first evaluates the written proposals and then selects solutions that are most likely to succeed. However, an award must depend on the resolution technology risks, which are a part of the final evaluation factor/metric. Demonstrations are then held to assess the risks and validate claimed capabilities. Such demonstrations can be simply showing the current state of products and technology. However, the government may also allow the offerors to invest in modifying their products and technologies to show integration with other federal systems, how new features can be developed, or how the objective workflows can be achieved. The key is that such investments by offerors are not meant to create finished products but only to confirm that there is a viable path forward.

B.4.3 Procedural Check and Disqualifications

Written proposals are typically reviewed by the CO to see whether offerors have properly followed instructions. Major structural mistakes, such as missing volumes, missing data, and incorrect format, might call for the disqualification of a proposal. Minor errors such as the exceeding of page count could be resolved by eliminating the extra pages from the evaluation process. The objective of the procedural check is to ensure fair competition. However, in competitions where dozens of proposals are received, the CO may be incentivized to disqualify proposals early to reduce the evaluation burdens.

B.4.4 Evaluation Based on Established Methodology and Weights for Factors and Subfactors

Technically, the SSET with the approval of the SSA can follow a very tailored evaluation methodology. The primary requirement is that the methodology addresses a set scope associated with the PWS/SOW/SOO and that the methodology cannot unfairly penalize a class of offerors or any single offeror. Additional material submitted by offerors beyond the scope of the RFP can be evaluated, and missing material not asked for in the RFP cannot be scored as deficiency. The SSET can, however, reopen an RFP for offeror changes and resubmission if it is discovered that another amendment is needed. Regarding unfairness, the SSET cannot in full and open competitions automatically show prejudice against the size and business characteristics of offerors unless those features can be directly connected with the capability to perform or risks in performance. Equally, the SSET cannot favor a specific small disadvantaged business category unless a set-aside competition has been intentionally established or select small business participation levels have been identified as metrics.

Given the flexibility provided to the SSET, the FAR does present baseline evaluation processes. These processes, as discussed below, look at the importance of technical and management evaluation factors, price factor, and past performance factor under different RFP scenarios and create streamlined approaches when full evaluation is not required.

B.4.4.1 Lowest Price Technically Acceptable (LPTA) Process

This evaluation process can be used if the government will get the best value by selecting the lowest evaluated price proposal from those proposals that have been evaluated as meeting or exceeding minimum requirements for the technical and management factors and subfactors. Evaluation of past performance is not required in this process and further trade-offs in technical evaluations beyond technically acceptable is not allowed. RFP Sections L and M must clearly state that this approach is being used.

The challenge in developing a LPTA methodology is determining the threshold for technical acceptability. Above this threshold, the government then does not care about performance as long as it is getting the lowest price. If this threshold can be accurately determined, then an example evaluation scale might be as follows.

Technical Evaluation

- Acceptable: Meets specified minimum performance or capability requirements. A proposal must have no deficiencies to receive an acceptable rating, but may have weaknesses that are correctable through negotiations.
- Unacceptable: Fails to meet specified minimum performance or capability requirements. The proposal has one or more deficiencies and is thus not awardable.

Price Evaluation

- Lowest Price: Proposal price is reasonable based on analysis against government estimates and is the lowest price.

Performance Price Trade-off (PPT) Process

This evaluation process can be used if the government will get the best value by only doing a trade-off between past performance and price. Proposals that meet or exceed minimum requirements for the technical and management factors and subfactors are scored as "acceptable" and further trade-offs in technical evaluations beyond "technically acceptable" is not allowed. RFP Sections L and M must clearly state that this approach is being used.

In evaluating past performance, an offeror's past performance exhibits are first rated as very relevant, relevant, somewhat relevant, or not relevant. Relevancy of past contracts should be based on similarity, complexity, contract type, contract dollar value, program phase, division of company, major or critical subcontractors, teaming partners, and joint ventures. However, the past contract does not have to be the same as the contract to be awarded through the RFP. Then, the evaluation team should engage government COs on prior contracts, review CPARS data, and look for other sources of data to determine an accurate assessment of the quality of past work. The combination of relevancy and quality then yields a level of confidence in whether the offeror can perform against the RFP.

An example evaluation scale might be as follows.

Technical Evaluation

- Acceptable: Meets specified minimum performance or capability requirements. A proposal must have no deficiencies to receive an acceptable rating but may have weaknesses that are correctable through negotiations.
- Unacceptable: Fails to meet specified minimum performance or capability requirements. The proposal has one or more deficiencies and is thus not awardable.

Past Performance Evaluations

- Substantial Confidence: The government has a high expectation that the offeror will successfully perform the required effort.
- Satisfactory Confidence: The government has an expectation that the offeror will successfully perform the required effort.
- Limited Confidence: The government has a low expectation that the offeror will successfully perform the required effort.
- No Confidence: The government has no expectation that the offeror will be able to successfully perform the required effort.
- Unknown Confidence: The government has no expectation that the offeror will be able to successfully perform the required effort.

Price Evaluation

- Price Ranking: Proposals with reasonable prices are ranked and traded off against past performance.

B.4.4.2 Full Trade-Off (FTO) Process

The FTO process is the standard process for determining the best value for the government. If it is not to the government's benefit to award a contract to the lowest price or to the highest technically rated proposal, then a complete trade-off of all the factor scores is merited. The factors can still be weighted in this trade-off to place emphasis on price or cost, technical, or past performance. The key consideration is whether a better-than-acceptable technical proposal justifies the additional cost.

In the technical evaluations, the terms of *strength, weakness, significant weakness,* and *deficiency* are typically used to describe the proposal. Strength is a significant aspect of a proposal that exceeds specified performance or capability requirements in a way that is advantageous to the government. Weakness is a flaw in the proposal that increases the risk of unsuccessful performance on contract. Significant weakness is a flaw that substantially increases the risk of unsuccessful performance on contract. Finally, deficiency is a combination of significant weaknesses that escalates the risk of unsuccessful performance on contract beyond acceptable levels. In addition to such evaluations, the SSET can further assign risk ratings to technical and cost factors to reflect the offeror's likelihood of achieving a proposed solution and cost. Thus, a technical proposal can be exceptional in that there are strengths and no identified deficiencies or weaknesses. However, situational conditions can still make the proposed solution a moderate, high, or even unacceptable risk. Likewise, the cost can be realistic based on models, but may still be moderate or high-risk based on conditions.

An example evaluation scale for FTO might be as follows. However, some SSETs have raised the bar for acceptability to green instead of yellow.

Technical Evaluation

- Exceptional (Blue): Exceeds specified minimum performance or capability requirements in a way that is beneficial to the government. A proposal must have one or more strengths and no deficiencies or weaknesses.
- Good (Green): Meets specified minimum performance or capability requirements. A proposal must have no deficiencies, few weaknesses, and identified strengths to receive a good rating.
- Acceptable (Yellow): Meets specified minimum performance or capability requirements. A proposal must have no deficiencies to receive an acceptable rating but may have weaknesses that are correctable through negotiations.
- Unacceptable (Red): Fails to meet specified minimum performance or capability requirements. The proposal has one or more deficiencies and is thus not awardable.

Past Performance Evaluations

- Substantial Confidence: The government has a high expectation that the offeror will successfully perform the required effort.

- Satisfactory Confidence: The government has an expectation that the offeror will successfully perform the required effort.
- Limited Confidence: The government has a low expectation that the offeror will successfully perform the required effort.
- No Confidence: The government has no expectation that the offeror will be able to successfully perform the required effort.
- Unknown Confidence: The government has no expectation that the offeror will be able to successfully perform the required effort.

Price/Cost Evaluation

- Price: Determine reasonableness based on market price analysis and rank proposed prices.
- Cost: Determine realism based on cost buildout and comparison with government cost estimates and rank proposed costs.

B.4.5 Determine Competitive Range and Eliminate Non-Competitive Proposals

Typically, competitive range is established as proposals with acceptable technical volume and limited or high confidence in past performance. Reasonable price or realistic cost may also be a threshold for competitive range. Offerors with proposals that are not above competitive range are notified and no further evaluation of their proposals will be conducted.

The concept of competitive range is that it filters out proposals that cannot win through the refinement process of negotiations. If the SSET will not conduct negotiations, then competitive range filters out proposals that clearly cannot win even under deeper evaluation. In the latter case, competitive range evaluation of proposals can be at a high level to examine key concepts, technologies, processes, and personnel. If deficiencies can be determined at such levels, then further trade-offs are not required.

B.4.6 Send Evaluation Notices and Items for Negotiations

After establishing competitive range, the government can ask for additional clarifications/corrections and initiate official negotiations with offerors to gain best value. This process will be done through documented IFNs that identify the weaknesses in each offeror's proposal. The offerors are then given a limited time to respond to the weaknesses and increase their competitiveness. Response to weaknesses may include explanations that become an official part of the proposal or modifications of the original proposal. However, such modifications should be directly traceable to each IFN.

The government can hold multiple rounds of negotiations. However, the government negotiations language should not be leading specific offerors to winning changes or revealing the strengths of other proposals. Instead, strict objectivity must be maintained while allowing offerors to correct weaknesses.

B.4.7 Request Final Proposal Revisions

After negotiations are complete, the government asks for final proposal revisions. This proposal should capture all the changes submitted during the negotiation process and may include other changes that increase the proposal's chances of winning unless the process prohibits additional changes. This is then the best and final offer for the government to make a source selection decision.

Most offerors will reconsider proposed price or cost and may provide further discounts if allowed. The key when providing proposal changes beyond negotiated items is that those changes must be clearly justified. If there is further reduced cost while the technical proposal has remained the same, then where is this reduction coming from? An offeror can cut fee and reduce some overhead contributions, but at what point will the realism be lost and the risk of achieving the proposed cost be too high? Many government agencies have lowered the bar on cost realism in the modern budget-constrained environments. This has unfortunately led to performance issues and contracts that had to be modified with added funds after award.

B.4.8 Reevaluate and Award

The end of the source selection occurs with the evaluation of EN/IFN responses and reevaluation of the best and final proposal. Changes from the original factor and subfactor scores are identified and documented. If there are no discovered inconsistencies, the SSET chairperson or SSAC chairperson can then present the results to the SSA for an award decision. The winning proposal and selection process is placed under legal review and then awarded by the contracting officer. The CO will make sure that all terms and conditions (T&C) and contract clauses are included in the awarded contract. The losing offerors are typically notified slightly before the award announcement.

The losing offerors may request individual debriefings of the evaluation results, and they may launch protests, unless prohibited by the IDIQ, to either the awarding agency or to the GAO. If no protests are filed, then the process is complete and contract execution begins. How the government handles protests is legally complex and situation specific. Therefore, this introductory text will not attempt to explain what could happen when the source selection process breaks down.

References

1. Defense Acquisition University. 2015. *21st Century Military Defense Acquisition and Doing Business with DoD: Complete Defense Acquisition Guidebook (DAG)—Decision Systems, Program Strategies, Estimates, Logistics, Test and Evaluation.* Cleveland, OH: Progressive Management.
2. Parvey, M. and Alston, D. 2010. *The Definitive Guide to Government Contracts: Everything You Need to Apply for and Win Federal and GSA Schedule Contracts (Winning Government Contracts),* 1st ed. Wayne, NJ: Career Press.
3. Amtower, M. 2010. *Selling to the Government: What It Takes to Compete and Win in the World's Largest Market.* Hoboken, NJ: Wiley.
4. Hamper, R.J. and Baugh, L.S. 2010. *Handbook for Writing Proposals,* 2nd ed. New York: McGraw-Hill Education.

Appendix C: Government Oversight Processes for Solutions Implementation

In this appendix, we will review some of the priorities in federal government oversight to ensure that the development and implementation of solutions are successful after contract awards. As the government's role is to review, approve, and take corrective actions, the burden of enabling government reviews falls largely upon the contractor/solutions provider. Poor organization and poor communication of program status to the government can derail contract performance evaluations even when the capability to achieve a proposed deliverable is still present. Therefore, the business end of delivering solutions to the government is equally as important as the technical end of establishing solutions.

While the specific processes of government oversight will vary from agency to agency, most oversight of contract execution tends to care about (1) the contractor's methodology for organizing and managing the program, (2) the contractor's methodology for developing the products that are associated with the solution, and (3) the contractor's methodology for executing the day-to-day activities that meet the plans established under program management. The following sections describe some of the key processes, instruments, and data that the government wants to see in each of the three methodological areas identified above. For each government organization, there may be unique presentation formats, reporting timelines, and approval criteria. However, the nature of the content will not vary too much and the principles are largely the same.

C.1 Program Management Methodology

In approving the methodology for program management, the government tends to care about organization and control, resourcing, reporting, and oversight. Program management connects contract execution with the government evaluation of contract performance metrics. While the government will care about the processes of execution to achieve baselines, control points, corrections, and preventive actions, program management presentations to the government should be focused on progress and results. Assessment of execution methodology becomes a concern when program management benchmarks cannot be reached. Given this perspective, we can lastly discuss what the government typically wants to see as a part of oversight.

C.1.1 Program Organization

Given a set of requirements and the PWS/SOW/SOO, the expectation in proposals and after contract award is that the winning contractor understands the work well enough that a work breakdown structure (WBS) can be established. A contractor might not have had the opportunity to engage the user and stakeholder communities regarding solution needs prior to the release of the RFP. If so, then that engagement needs to occur after contract award. With a well-defined WBS that will lead to the proposed solution, a contractor program management structure can be established and a schedule for completing the work can be developed. A notional high-level WBS for systems development is presented in Figure C.1.

A WBS-based program management structure establishes staff groups and leaders based on WBS sections, defines required staff qualifications directly associated with the nature of work, and provides staff and leadership responsibilities. In the development and delivery of a system solution, both the WBS and the program management structure are connected with the concept of operations and system architecture. In the development and delivery of a service solution, the WBS and the program management structure are connected with performance objectives and anticipated service outcomes.

The first step in using the WBS to create a schedule for completing the proposed work is to understand the agency's policy requirements for organizing the work. For example, DoD Instruction 5000.02 as discussed in Appendix A provides a phased approach for systems development. Each phase, as shown in Figure C.2, is meant for a series of tasks with results captured in key documents. The results are evaluated through a milestone review and the milestone decision authority approves the progression of the systems acquisition effort into the next phase. While a singular contractor can support a program across all phases, contracts are many times competed for again at the start of engineering and development and at the start of production and deployment. The rationale is that the contractor who refined the technologies may not be the best one to build the system. Also, the contractor who built the system may not be the best one to maintain the system through its operational life.

If a contractor is working across multiple phases, this high-level program life cycle must be the top-level framework of the integrated master schedule (IMS). Based on this framework, the WBS then specifies tasks and subtasks for each of

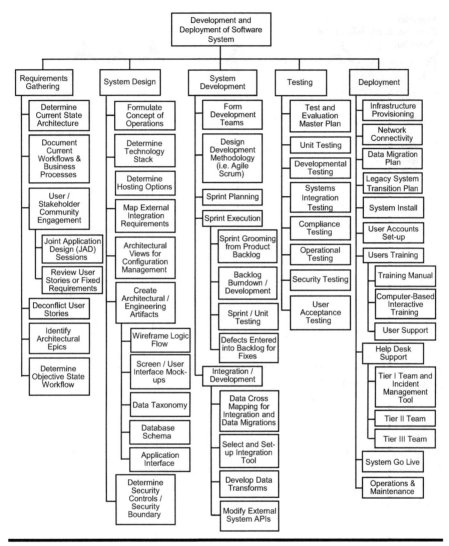

Figure C.1 **Notional high-level WBS for software systems development.**

the phases. By studying how each task and subtask is to be completed, a protection of task and subtask durations can be established. Also, the dependencies between tasks can be determined as a part of such studies. Some tasks can only be started after other tasks are complete. Some tasks must start in conjunction with other tasks. And, some tasks must finish in conjunction with other tasks. Modern scheduling software, such as Microsoft Project, allows the scheduler to create these relationships in a hierarchical schedule of task and subtasks. In fact,

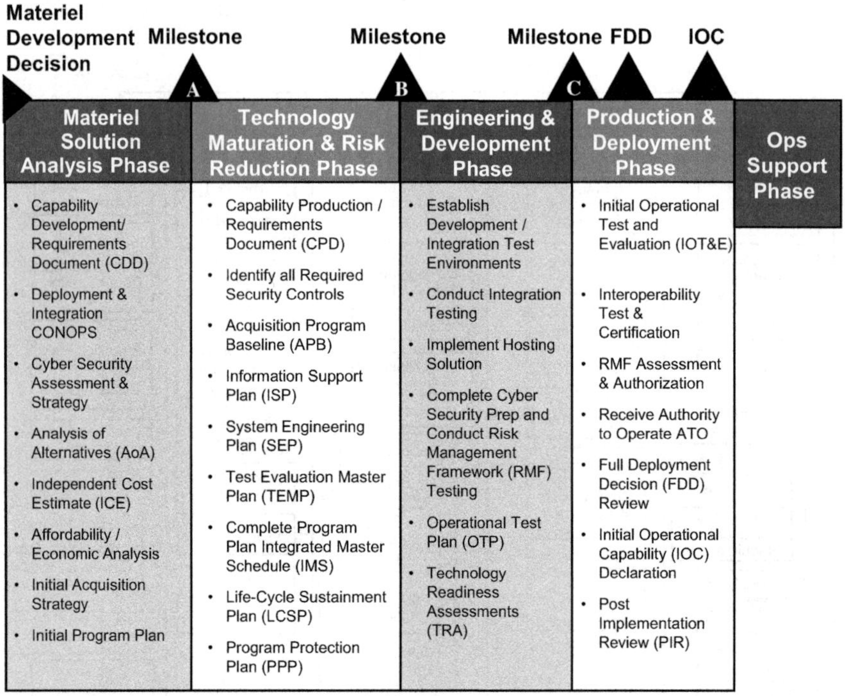

Materiel Development Decision	Milestone A	Milestone B	Milestone C	FDD	IOC
Materiel Solution Analysis Phase	**Technology Maturation & Risk Reduction Phase**	**Engineering & Development Phase**	**Production & Deployment Phase**	**Ops Support Phase**	
• Capability Development/ Requirements Document (CDD) • Deployment & Integration CONOPS • Cyber Security Assessment & Strategy • Analysis of Alternatives (AoA) • Independent Cost Estimate (ICE) • Affordability / Economic Analysis • Initial Acquisition Strategy • Initial Program Plan	• Capability Production / Requirements Document (CPD) • Identify all Required Security Controls • Acquisition Program Baseline (APB) • Information Support Plan (ISP) • System Engineering Plan (SEP) • Test Evaluation Master Plan (TEMP) • Complete Program Plan Integrated Master Schedule (IMS) • Life-Cycle Sustainment Plan (LCSP) • Program Protection Plan (PPP)	• Establish Development / Integration Test Environments • Conduct Integration Testing • Implement Hosting Solution • Complete Cyber Security Prep and Conduct Risk Management Framework (RMF) Testing • Operational Test Plan (OTP) • Technology Readiness Assessments (TRA)	• Initial Operational Test and Evaluation (IOT&E) • Interoperability Test & Certification • RMF Assessment & Authorization • Receive Authority to Operate ATO • Full Deployment Decision (FDD) Review • Initial Operational Capability (IOC) Declaration • Post Implementation Review (PIR)		

Figure C.2   Basic DoD systems acquisition life cycle.

a large program can have thousands of specific tasks at the point of execution. These lower-level tasks are then treated as subtasks to higher-level parent tasks. There could then be several levels of parent tasks to organize a program schedule. As the government reviews the IMS, they will validate that the following design features have been satisfied [1]:

■ The IMS has a clear structure with tasks at each hierarchical level defined to be appropriate for that level.
■ The IMS has a critical path that leads to the delivery of the solution as proposed in the contract.
■ The critical path has enough built-in slack time to manage the risk of delayed completion for tasks.
■ The tasks cover the totality of work that must be done.
■ All task dependencies are properly established (linked) and the schedule is allowed to slide based on dependencies.
■ All task dependencies have a clear flow that connects to the critical path.
■ There is a governance plan for how the IMS is to be baselined and updated in accordance with actual task performance results.

■ There are no regions in the IMS where the number of simultaneous tasks is so dense that they pose completion risks.

■ There are no specific tasks where the number of dependencies is so high and complex that any delay in completing those tasks will cause massive program disruption.

At oversight reviews, the government may elect to use the IMS to test downstream outcomes when given different scenarios for schedule slips. This exercise can also be conducted by the program manager to internally assess execution risks. In cases where delays in completing such tasks will cause a massive ripple effect in the schedule, mitigation strategies can be formulated for when delays appear unavoidable. These mitigation approaches include restructuring task dependencies, establishing backup tasks, redesigning task execution to avoid delays, and adding more resources to avoid delays.

C.1.2 Program Resourcing

The allocation of resources to produce contract deliverables and achieve performance criteria is another area of government oversight concern. This concern varies depending on whether the contract is firm fixed price, time and material, or cost-plus fixed fee. Regardless, the contractor should have a clear understanding of resource needs and resource allocation. Resources are divided into personnel, software products, equipment, material supplies, and facilities. They enable the completion of IMS tasks, and the IMS tasks help us to estimate the resource requirements. The total amount of resources required to complete the program is the summation of resources allocated to each task over the span of the IMS.

The most challenging resource to allocate is perhaps personnel. Despite the validated credentials of staff, staff performance can vary greatly to yield a margin of error in all staffing-level estimates. Also, staff is easier to allocate to contracts as full-time dedicated resources. When people are expected to work on multiple contracts, they often lose focus. Multiple assignments are therefore better reserved for high-end subject matter experts whose availability is limited. Programs with steady staffing demands and low staff turnover rates are typically the most stable. Programs with vast fluctuations in staffing needs over the life of the contract create staffing challenges. When faced with these challenges, we can (1) over-staff to account for surge demands, (2) maintain a pool of reach-back part-time staff for surge support, (3) adjust the IMS to avoid sudden surges in demand, or (4) allow existing staff to work extra hours.

Once a staffing profile has been established for the life of the contract, the actual staffing needs can be defined in terms of position descriptions for staff to complete specific sets of tasks, labor category descriptions for required staff qualifications, and current year plus out year labor rates for each labor category. A single labor category, if defined broadly enough, can be used to satisfy a range of positions. Also, large, complex tasks may require many personnel to fill one type or multiple types of positions. Estimated hours for completing tasks are then formulated based on positions and mapped labor categories and rates to yield a complete cost estimate for labor. Other direct costs (ODCs), such as software licenses, equipment purchases, travel expenses, and supply purchases, can be added to the labor cost to create a complete program cost estimate.

For firm fixed-price contracts, the contractor assumes the risk for cost overruns and must manage staff performance to stay within the proposed cost. For time and material as well as cost-plus–type contracts, the government will monitor and evaluate the need to go beyond the originally estimated cost. Once the labor categories and hours are firmly established, staff is recruited and aligned with assigned labor categories and positions. Resumes are used to validate that the proposed staff/candidate employee's education, certifications, and experience meet labor category and position requirements. Upon employment, a process for staff training can be used to ensure rapid transition into assigned positions. While the government cannot tell contractors who to hire, it can validate that hired staff satisfies agreed-upon qualifications.

Beyond personnel resources, the acquisition of software licenses depends on the size of the user community, number of daily transactions, and level of data involved. These factors help to determine which licensing structure is most advantageous to the government user organizations. The allocation of facility resources to staff not working at government offices is calculated as an added overhead expense that increases the associated labor rate for the staff. The determination of whether staff should work at government locations or contractor offices is typically specified in the RFP. If not specified in the RFP, then the location of staff is a part of the proposed solution. Driving factors include the need to work in close collaboration with government staff, the availability of government space, the cost of different commercial locations, and the connectivity of infrastructures.

C.1.3 Program Reporting

The purpose of reporting by the contractor to the government is to help the government (1) understand the state of performance on the contract, (2) prepare for the receipt of deliverables, and (3) take actions that support program success. Although the government will take punitive actions when they see poor contract performance, it is bad practice for contractors to wait for government response instead of recognizing performance issues and starting corrective actions prior to government presentations. All problems reported by the contractor should be accompanied by proposed corrective solutions or mitigation approaches.

The high-level metrics in tracking program progress and contract performance are execution cost relative to allocated budget, current schedule relative to IMS baseline, current performance relative to planned thresholds, and execution risks based on probability of occurrence and level of potential impact. These high-level metrics can be presented in a briefing quad chart or through a program management dashboard that tracks status on a weekly and monthly level. While dashboards are great in analyzing program and contract dynamics, the program managers and project leaders must be committed to providing up-to-date information aligned with dashboard metrics. For large-value contracts, federal regulations and agency policies may demand that the contract is managed through an EVM system. EVM systems track cost, schedule, and technical performance details for the contract as integrated parameters and report these metrics for oversight analysis.

While the government program office will want comprehensive reporting, risk tracking, and weekly explanations of open-action items, decision-makers tend to focus on reports that provide a macro understanding of the program and contract activities. These reports are reviewed at multiple levels and approved for submission to the decision authority. For some programs, such as DoD programs at the ACAT I and ACAT IA levels, extracts of the reports are further submitted to Congress to satisfy statutory requirements. Some key reports for system development efforts using DoD terminology include the following:

■ Acquisition program baseline (APB): Provides a schedule, cost, and performance baseline for the program with threshold and objective values for key parameters. The inability to meet threshold values will generally constitute a baseline breech. Breeches then initiate reporting and corrective action requirements.

■ Analysis of alternatives (AoA): Presents all the solution options considered for the program and the decision process in which the best solution path was determined. The selected best solution path then governs the development of the acquisition strategy.

■ Integrated master schedule (IMS): Presents the entire structure of activities needed to complete the program and satisfy the contract. Shows current state of progress as measured against schedule baselines, and enables the analysis of downstream program risks.

■ Independent cost estimate (ICE): Government estimate of total cost to complete a development program and total cost for product ownership after deployment. This estimate can be used for budget planning and assessing the cost realism of proposals.

■ Cyber security assessment and strategy: Summary of the information assurance (IA) approach that includes an understanding of threats and the nature of specific security controls as specifically determined in the system security plan (SSP).

■ Systems engineering plan (SEP): Summary of the design for the system to include key components and functionalities, technologies applied, information flow, infrastructure, and other elements of the architecture. The technical solution is clearly explained through this document.

■ Test evaluation master plan (TEMP): An integrated view of testing with specified testing activities, testing approach, schedule, and test result assessment methods. Provides a comprehensive understanding of how all the tests will combine to yield a high-performance product.

- Life cycle sustainment plan (LCSP): Presents the approach for the operations and maintenance of the developed and deployed system that ensures the system reaches plan operational life and stays within the projected total cost of ownership.

For large service contracts, the reporting must focus on cost of services, whether key tasks are performed on schedule, and whether the quality of service is acceptable. The key difference between services and systems development contracts is that the tasks and deliverables in services contracts do not have to integrate into a single testable product. Therefore, services contracts must be measured across their swim lanes and the points of measurement are more incremental than specific milestones. The way to measure services is based on the quality control approach as explained in Section C.3 on Program Execution. Quality metrics should be designed to quickly detect service performance issues and isolate root causes for corrective actions. As the quality of services is often hard to quantify, reporting sometimes defaults to measuring whether (1) staffing levels are sustained, (2) the qualifications of staff and replacement staff meet threshold standards, (3) completion time for tasks, and (4) percentage of tasks that needs rework.

C.1.4 Program Oversight

The important fact about program oversight is that oversight is not the same as program management. Program management by the contractor focuses on task execution to fulfill PWS/SOW/SOO requirements. Program management by the government program office focuses on coordinating government responsibilities such as defining requirements, establishing processes, and integrating operations with contractor activities. While the government program manager has oversight responsibilities, his or her role really should be to collaborate with the contractor and guide the contractor based on insights about government needs and processes that the contractor does not have. If the collaboration between the government program office and the contractor breaks down and both sides are guarded against one another, then the program is generally in trouble.

Government oversight, on the other hand, should be the forcing function that keeps people who are most knowledgeable about the program and most able to execute program tasks committed to the correct path. Thus, oversight is about benchmarks and acceptable variances in performance. The decision-maker conducting the oversight does not have to have complete program knowledge. However, he or she must have strong professional experience in detecting when reports are not right, issues simmer beneath the data, and managers have lost control of their program and contract activities. The mechanism for enforcing oversight is often punitive. The decision authority may decide to block program advancement until problems are fixed, replace key government staff, leverage contract performance penalties, or even cancel the program.

The ultimate oversight for all federal programs is the White House and Congress. The White House can control funding to all programs through the annual President's budget and guide the use of funding. Congress controls the allocation of funding to programs and can establish statutory language for how program funds must be used. In fact, Congress can create all manner of statutes, as shown in the history of the U.S. defense acquisition process presented in Appendix A, to structure acquisition organizations, designate key acquisition positions, create acquisition processes, and demand specific acquisition reporting. The President can equally make such changes through regulations and policies.

C.2 Solutions Development Methodology

If the government is investing in the development of a system, then it will care deeply about the development methodology. The failure to select the correct methodology or the mistakes in implementing the selected methodology have led to major program failures. Thus, some agencies have developed extensive policies and procedures on how to develop systems. These government documents tend to adapt standard methodologies and include more agency specific oversight requirements. The goal of this appendix is not to review polices but to provide an operational understanding of the methodologies most commonly used to develop systems for the government and the situations in which each methodology is advantageous. Contractors will typically either have to follow the methodology specified by the RFP or propose a methodology that is most suitable for the presented requirements. Either way, understanding the principles of development is key to successful systems development and oversight reporting.

For systems that are leveraging completed commercial products or proposed investments to be made by the offering company, the risk of development is not upon the government. Therefore, the government typically only cares about the negotiated prices and delivery dates. In the case of commercial investments, companies might still wish to adopt methodologies that are familiar to the government to enable transparency and ensure that the end product meets government expectations.

During the 1990s and early 2000s, the government methodologies focused on the development and delivery of physical systems. As dedicated software-based systems started to increase, attempts were made to adapt the existing systems development life cycles to software development. Then, federal software projects began to increase, and commercial software development techniques also continued to advance. In response, the government started to place software projects on dedicated oversight paths that have the flexibility and adaptiveness to leverage the nature of modern software languages/coding. This transition varies from agency to agency, and some agencies still prefer the rigor of set schedules and oversight gate reviews. The following development methodologies include those appropriate for both software and physical systems and those only appropriate for software.

C.2.1 Rapid Prototyping

Given a set of requirements for either a software or physical system, a rapid prototype can be developed for the user community. The reason for rapid prototyping is to (1) get some level of usable capability to users because of urgency of need, (2) allow users to see the application of technologies to reduce risks before further investments are made, or (3) demonstrate multiple technology paths to support selection of the final solution. During more economically prosperous times, the government invested in competing systems, such as different jet fighter designs, because the complexity of the systems made prototyping the only reliable means of validating design effectiveness. Even slight decreases in actual performance relative to designs can have significant operational impact, particularly when large quantities of the system are purchased. These days, the purpose of prototyping is more for seizing technology opportunities or early control of technology risks. Thus, the term rapid prototyping has placed emphasis on speed.

As Figure C.3 shows, the first step in adopting a rapid prototyping methodology is to understand the relationship between requirements and technology well enough that the requirements can be broken apart into sets that can immediately be satisfied by a rapid prototype, sets that can be achieved through refining the prototype into a fieldable system, and sets that should be addressed as system enhancements. If the purpose of the prototype is to get capabilities to users quickly, then the refinement cycle should have a limited schedule. If the purpose is to manage technology risks, then we need to get the prototype quickly and have a robust refinement cycle to better satisfy requirements.

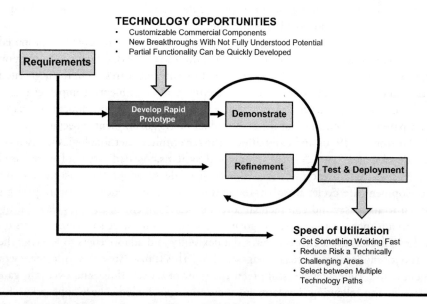

Figure C.3   Conceptual explanation of rapid prototyping.

The development of the prototype depends greatly on technology opportunities. In software development, some commercial products can be quickly customized with limited new coding or tailored configurations to get a prototype. If a modular architecture is adopted, then commercial platform as a service (PaaS) and software as a service (SaaS) offerings can serve as foundations for the prototype. Open source software and components with Apache 2.0 licenses can be included in the architecture. The challenge of integrating components into a prototype is not necessarily development but achieving component compatibility through API standards such as representational state transfer (RESTful) for web services, data taxonomy standards, and database schema standards. If database schemas are different between parts of the system, then transform functions will have to be utilized in component integration.

In physical systems, new scientific breakthroughs might offer technical opportunities that can only be realized through testing a prototype. As hidden potentials in the new scientific breakthrough are discovered, the prototype can be refined into a fieldable system. The prototype can alternatively be abandoned after it has achieved its purpose so that follow-on systems can start with technical understanding but with fresh designs. The decision on the scope of both software and physical system prototypes ultimately comes down to how fast and what partial functionalities are useful.

Rapid prototyping is a methodology that can work in conjunction with other methodologies. First, any other methodology can be used to complete the system after the testing of the prototype. So, the rapid prototype can even be in the early phases of a traditional waterfall development life cycle with a single linear timeline, set milestones, and limited feedback loops. To accelerate the development of software prototypes, the Agile development methodology can be applied in the rapid prototyping process.

This methodology does have risks, and they include the wasting of time in getting to a not-very-useful prototype when the time could have been better spent developing a more complete system. The user community might not understand the utility of a rapid prototype and have unreasonable expectations. And, the components used for the prototype might be poorly evaluated and selected because of a hasty schedule. In many cases, these risks are associated with poor implementation and a lack of understanding of the principles for this methodology. However, there are situations where rapid is not desired if it means that trade-off studies are minimized and where prototypes are not desired if they are too much of a drain on cost and schedule.

C.2.2 Agile Software Development

Agile development is a methodology that capitalizes on the modularity of modern software codes. Thus, a software solution can be developed by a team or multiple teams that work in short sprints (one to four weeks) to produce chucks of code that add functionalities to the overall system. At its heart, Agile is a time-to-market approach for software development and a government agency that adopts Agile as its software development methodology must understand this fact [2]. What time to market means is that user requirements are captured with enough flexibility to allow the developers to respond with speed and innovation. Typically, contractor business analysts seek to understand user beginning state and objective state workflows and then capture requirements in the form of user stories that describe aspects of the objective state. User stories need to be (1) prioritizable as independent requirements, (2) flexible enough to support negotiations between developer and user/product owner, (3) relatable to the objective state, (4) small enough to be addressed in one or a few sprints, and (5) measurable during testing. These user stories then form a product backlog as shown in Figure C.4.

For a very large and complex enterprise system, its software solution can be designed as an interdependent collection of Agile projects based on an advancing architecture. This approach is called the Scaled Agile Framework [3]. The overall solution takes form through a series of architectural epics where each epic governs

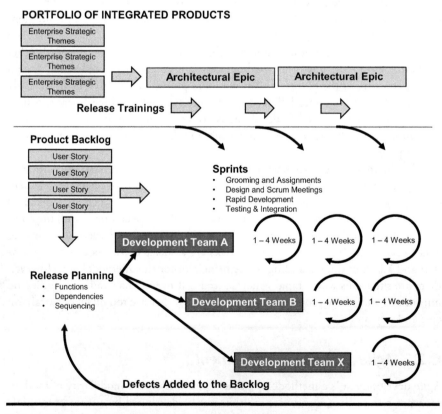

Figure C.4   Conceptual explanation of Agile development.

release trains for a portion of the complex system. Within the release trains, there are specific product backlogs to which the Agile development methodology is applied. For smaller projects and less interconnected applications, a single product backlog can be used to drive the development sprints and product releases.

In conducting the Agile sprints, the teams can adopt a Scrum-based approach or a Kanban approach. Kanban is a set of lean logistics principles, and it leverages a planning board to determine the sequence of software builds. In contrast, Scrum is slightly more structured in its process-driven release planning, sprint grooming, and daily Scrum meeting sessions to coordinate development activities. From a government oversight perspective, the Scrum approach is slightly easier to present development progress. In the release planning process, the solutions architect studies what functionalities will be developed from the user stories and the dependencies between the functionalities to determine the best organization of Agile development to create major and minor releases. The solutions architect also figures out the best technology stack for the product, the teams that will be needed to achieve the product releases, and the sequencing of team activities. Once the Agile teams begin to work, the sprints will proceed with a grooming session before the start of each sprint. In the grooming session, the Scrum master for the team will determine the portions of the product backlog to be addressed by the sprint and which developer is assigned to each set of user stories. The initial Scrum meeting might also discuss solution approaches, integration strategies, and sprint level testing. The solutions architect may further contribute enterprise roadmaps, architectural diagrams, product mockups, and database schemas to help guide the course of product development. Then, the team will hold daily Scrum meetings to coordinate development and advance the solution.

The change from waterfall to Agile development is a major transition for software developers. Thus, it is critical that contractors demonstrate an Agile culture that places team health as a key metric along with sprint velocity as measured by backlog burndown (user story satisfaction) rate. Agile development is best done in multiple environments where developers work on individual components, push their components into a systems integration environment for continuous integration and testing, and push fully tested components into the production environment. This creates a development and operations (DevOps)–linked culture that requires the commitment of the total team to have collective ownership of the code base. In DevOps and in Agile as a whole, testing as a part of sprints is the key to success. The test scripts and testing process should be developed along with the components and functionalities, and the user community should participate in sprint testing to help shape the interpretation of the user stories. Defects and requirement changes identified during sprint testing are reentered into the product backlog and prioritized appropriately. In test-driven development (TDD), the team approaches the completion of a release with clear understanding of product functionalities and quality. However, the great challenge in such level of user participation is agreement on when a product is done. The opportunity to adjust requirements can be misused, particularly when an agency is still in the midst of business transformation. As a result, the product becomes trapped in extended cycles of refinement sprints when it is better to first deploy and then do post-deployment upgrades.

As the Agile development process iteratively refines the product toward deployment, the iterations are also periods for opportunistic refactoring of the code. As the code is being evolved, developers can further clean up the code by eliminating redundant code segments, correcting nonstandard coding practices, deleting old code pieces, and integrating codes into more efficient forms. This clean-up should be done without affecting the behavior of the software product. The completed software components should go through functional testing with user story traceability, performance testing under all operational loads, integration and data migration testing, security testing, and compliance testing such as Section 508 compliant displays for the disabled. Then, the components are ready for the releases as planned.

As Agile development permits many releases, the releases should be designed to quickly offer capabilities to the user community without causing operational disruptions and other adverse impacts. Minor releases can be defined as functional upgrades, security patches, and performance enhancements that do not require user training and preparation. Thus, minor releases can often be done as soon as they are ready or during times of low operational activities. In contrast, major releases change the workflow and will require user training as well as added help desk support. Such releases should be well coordinated with the user training process and not be so frequent that there is user resistance.

Agile development does have limitations. Software that must be developed as a monolithic code set is not well suited for Agile. Customers who have rigorous requirements that are not open to developer interpretation should probably not use Agile. They might be better served by turning those requirements directly into system features/specifications and adopting a rigorous waterfall development methodology. A complex solution that require extensive design of the entire system prior to development is not well-suited for Agile. Then, there is the risk of Agile development iterations hitting design dead ends, and customers who demand extensive documentation will slow down the Agile process. The success of Agile requires understanding of the principles and commitment of the teams.

C.2.3 Incremental Development

The main risk of a massive waterfall (linear) development effort for both software and physical systems is that mistakes are not discovered until late in the process with investments lost and schedules delayed. The methodology to reduce this risk is to develop the system in fieldable increments. Each increment addresses a subset of the requirements and goes through its own waterfall life cycle. Then, multiple increments are established as sequential to one another or as tiers. Sequential increments allow for fast initial delivery but drags out the completion of the final system. Its benefit is that the users see a complete product, and the developers gain full lessons learned before commitment to additional development. Tiered increments decouple the schedules so that the delay of one increment does not automatically cause schedule slips across the broader development effort. Instead, integration points and strategies can be adjusted to keep the total effort on track.

As Figure C.5 shows, the key to incremental development is the ability to break down the requirements into useful modules and manageable schedules. The totality of increments may require more resources than if the system had been developed along a single linear schedule, but this methodology is about risk management. Some risks are associated with the maturity of technologies in the market, and so the increments might be organized in a way that higher-risk technologies are assigned to later increments. Some risks are related to the uncertainty of available resources. If so, then expending adequate resources to get a useable product from the first increment is better than being stuck with a half-completed product that faces a funding shortfall.

Given the purpose of incremental development, most increments are designed to get fielded products within one to two years. As each increment is a mini-waterfall life cycle, the methodology retains the rigorousness of the waterfall process and the inflexibility of the process. As each increment will have its own documentation requirements, milestones, and gate reviews for crossing phases, the accumulation of documents across the increments can be quite severe.

Poorly designed increments yield new risks such as separating requirements that should be naturally addressed together, creating stovepipes that block natural developmental synergies, and misaligning capability deliveries with user operational

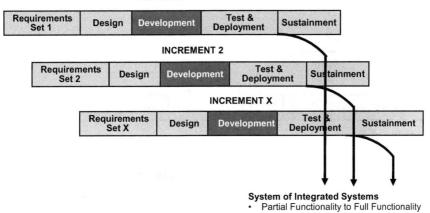

Figure C.5   Conceptual explanation of incremental development.

needs. So, the organization of the increments is critical to success as there are no iterations for refining the product as in rapid prototyping and Agile development.

C.2.4 Spiral Software Development

In a waterfall software development life cycle, the development activities after the requirements-gathering and design phases do not have to be linear. When the requirements are complex and the solution is uncertain, a series of development spirals can be established to build quickly, test what has been built, and apply greater system understanding to follow-on spirals [4]. The organization of spirals should naturally focus on development schedule and testing. However, enough time between spirals should also be allotted for studying test results and learning from the past spirals. As Figure C.6 shows, spirals are not like Agile development sprints and should follow a more defined process of analyzing requirements, establishing development approach, conducting development, and testing. Spirals are typically longer than Agile sprints, but spirals should still take weeks and not months.

Spirals are not like development increments because each spiral does not bring developed items to deployment. However, spirals can be within the development phase of an increment. The process of building, testing, and building some more is good for development that requires rigor but also has a learning curve. Design issues can be discovered early through testing. Product refinements are incorporated into the builds. And, risks can be better understood with analysis of test results. The pitfalls of spiral development include setting the spirals to be too small with cycles upon cycles that offer no advantage and setting the spirals to be too big with one or two spirals basically completing all development. An understanding

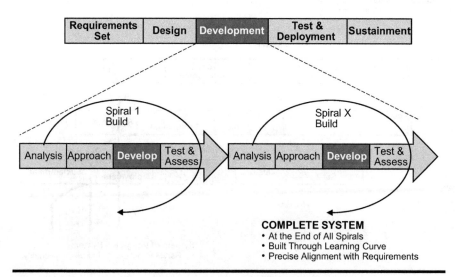

Figure C.6 Conceptual explanation of spiral development.

of the set requirements and how to estimate time and resources needed to meet requirements will help avoid these pitfalls.

C.3 Program Execution Methodology

As explained earlier, program execution is a subset of program management. However, while program management tends to focus on organization, resourcing, reporting, and oversight, execution is more concerned with baselining, control, corrections, and preventive actions. The results of execution support program management reporting and oversight. Also, lessons learned from execution may lead to organizational changes and resource adjustments. The results of organizational activities will sometimes dictate overarching processes. However, it is at the execution level where processes become translated into program-specific procedures and adoption of industry best practices. It is also at the execution level that continuous process improvements are made.

To gain confidence in a contractor's ability to execute a solution, the government sometimes looks for validation of established execution processes. One body that appraises a company's information technology processes is the Capability Maturity Model Integration (CMMI) Institute that started at Carnegie Mellon University. Another body that certifies a company's processes is the International Organization for Standardization (ISO). Further, a company that uses Six Sigma Black Belt–certified individuals to improve processes will add an additional level of confidence for the government. Also, a company that employs staff with Information Technology Infrastructure Library (ITIL) certifications and certifications for specific technologies to manage the delivery of IT services will increase government confidence.

While certifications are useful for demonstrating capabilities in proposals, they are no substitute for understanding the principles of program execution. It is only through understanding the forces and effects that a contractor team can tailor processes for the specific needs of a program. This tailoring should be a part of the solution provided to the government. We will thus explore execution principles for areas associated with baselining, control, corrections, and preventive actions.

C.3.1 Configuration Management (CM)

CM is the process for establishing and maintaining the system baseline throughout development and deployment. While CM is relevant to both software and physical systems, its role in physical systems development is limited to those with a high degree of variability. For example, the hardware for networks and data centers can be set up and rearranged in a variety of manners to enable an IT system infrastructure. Thus, it is easy for technicians to deviate the actual system from an approved architecture if a CM process has not been implemented and enforced. In contrast, a plane or ship has specific configurations to which all hardware must fit. Thus,

CM concerns are more with using wrong generation or brand of parts or with calibrating parts incorrectly during installation. These concerns are important but can often be resolved through standard operation procedures instead of a full CM process.

In the CM process, the first and most critical step is establishing the definitive architectural baseline. In software, the architecture can be captured in the 4 + 1 view model.

- Development view: Displays the system with components that align with development activities. Requires understanding of the technologies used, interface standards, taxonomy standards, data architectures, and modular software architecture.
- Logical view: Displays the functionalities of the system as seen by the users. This includes functional flow diagrams, task organizations, and system states.
- Physical view: Displays how the system is to be deployed by engineers from the infrastructure to the applications. This requires the identification of physical asset locations and configurations, software and firmware deployments, and network configurations.
- Process view: Displays how the system will operate, such as access, computations, and data flow. Performance standards and behavior characteristics are identified.
- Scenarios: The first four views enable the presentation of scenarios or use cases for system application. This integration validates the effectiveness of the four views.

To establish the architectural baseline, the program team might have to conduct site visits if the new system is to be deployed into an existing infrastructure or if the solution involves advancing existing (legacy) systems and infrastructure. Baselining the architecture does not mean that the architecture can no longer be changed. In fact, it is during periods of change that our understanding of the system must precisely align with the actual state of the system. For systems that have grown through poorly documented advancement steps, the architecture may have to be updated after system completion through operations analysis. Either way, the CM plan can be developed with the authoritative architecture.

The CM plan typical incorporates agency-specific policies and procedures on how changes can be made to the production/operational architecture. The industry best practice for CM is explained in ANSI/EIA 649 National Consensus Standard for Configuration Management. In summary, the configuration of the architecture is controlled through the identification of configuration items (CIs) that are monitored through a change control board (CCB). When the architecture is to be advanced through solutioning and development, change requests (CRs) are submitted to the CCB for approval. The CCB ensures that the CRs will not disrupt systems operations, adversely impact performance, and compromise security controls.

The security controls are an important aspect of the architecture, and they should be established as a part of development and documented as an integrated solution through the SSP. The government uses the Risk Management Framework (RMF) from the National Institute of Standard and Technology (NIST) to assess and authorize IT systems as a part of granting ATOs. Any change in the system that might alter the effectiveness of the security controls will require reassessment based on the RMF. The SSP and specific procedures for securing the system as presented in the Security Technical Implementation Guides (STIGs) will have to be adjusted to maintain the integrity of the configuration.

In complex systems with extensive architectural documents and CIs, the management of the configuration and the processing of CRs will require the use of a repository and change management tool. This tool would then provide complete traceability from one baseline state to the next baseline state. To validate the effectiveness of the CM process, audits of the system should be periodically performed. Audits can validate the system setup, components inventory, and performance. Security assessments can be done through vulnerability tests. And compliance with regulations and policies, such as the safeguarding of privacy information (compliance with Privacy Act of 1974, 5 U.S.C. § 552a) and access for the disabled (compliance with Section 508 amendment to the Rehabilitation Act of 1973), can be done through checklists and dedicated evaluation tools.

C.3.2 Quality Control (QC)

While CM is focused on aligning our understanding of the system with the real state of the system, QC is about achieving or maintaining objective performance for the system. As the performance of human systems can also be measured, QC can further be applied to services. QC for systems builds upon CM by defining objective system performance states, creating metrics for tasks needed to create objective states, and defining roles and responsibilities for achieving metrics. These roles and responsibilities include that of the program manager who takes actions to correct quality issues, the quality control lead who develops the QC plan and identifies quality issues, and the staff who will follow procedures to maintain QC.

QC extends the concept of program oversight gate reviews to metrics that the program managers and his or her teams can track on a day-to-day level to steer the course of design, development, testing, and operations. For services, these metrics become staffing level, staff qualifications, and staff completion of tasks. The approach of QC should not be major corrective actions after testing or inspections. Instead, the best QC should be a series of small-course corrections through the program life cycle so that major corrective actions are avoided. There are two strategies for conducting QC over the work being provided. The first strategy is to build metrics around the incremental outputs of work. For example, in component production, metrics might include units produced during overtime, defect rate, variation around specifications, and stability of production rate. In systems integration, metrics such as functional performance, operational reliability, and user accessibility might be appropriate. Each of these metrics could have threshold values where QC becomes an issue if thresholds cannot be achieved. After achieving threshold, then QC becomes a process improvement opportunity in striving for objective values. The second strategy in QC is to build metrics around the process of work. If work outputs cannot be seen for some time, then metrics, such as maintaining staffing level, getting staff certifications, adherence to standard operating procedures, and knowledge transfer, might be appropriate. These metrics can also have threshold and objective values for QC planning.

A component of QC planning is the Quality Assurance Surveillance Plan (QASP). This document creates an agreement between the contractor and the government on what will be measured, how the performance measurements will be done, who will be conducting the measures, and the presentation of results. The QASP can evolve over the life of the program as greater understanding between metrics and actual performance is gained, but this transition must be coordinated with the work being measured. Further, there must be traceability from one report to the next report. While reporting parameters in cost, schedule, and performance are a part of QC, QC is about finding and monitoring those specific metrics/key performance indicators (KPIs) that show if the program is off course or heading off course. These metrics could be specific elements of cost, schedule, and performance, or they could be computed as metadata from raw data in cost, schedule, and performance. The simplest approach for QC is to correct if cost, schedule, and performance cannot meet thresholds. However, even before falling below thresholds, metrics that are based on patterns and behaviors can yield QC concerns and opportunities for preventive actions.

A danger in QC planning is that the team spends more time measuring than doing the work. Thus, the timing and frequency of measurements as well as the scope of measurements need to be assessed as to not have adverse impact. Another danger in QC is to not understand the natural dynamics of performance cycles, such as certain work can only be done during specific seasons or under specific global conditions. In such a case, trying to force-fit steady-state performance instead of optimizing the existing performance cycles would be detrimental to the program.

As the QC plan establishes roles and responsibilities, there is an assumption that all QC issues will be resolved through situation-specific leadership and program-specific expertise. There are, however, some strategies for resolving QC issues to help guide decisions. A program manager can change the quantity and capability of personnel, advance the process and associated standard operating procedures, restructure the schedule to recover from delays, increase the frequency or fidelity of testing/inspections, or conduct cost-cutting assessments. Improving staff is typically done by gaining access to the greater pool of talent, such as from a different division in the company or a partner company, or adding training and supervision for current staff.

Improving process is achieved by applying operations research analysis, and Six Sigma is merely a formalized technique within operations research. Restructuring a schedule is a trade-off between maintaining schedule and assuming more risks if the stakeholders are unwilling to reduce the level of requirements or add resources. Schedule dependencies can be shifted to later points to enable more paralleled activities, and validation tasks can be reduced. For increasing testing, we have noted the concern of too many QC activities. However, increasing checkpoints and immediately implementing corrections can be a QC solution. Other times, prior tests might not have been looking for the correct indicators. Finally, cost-cutting is another trade-off with the government assuming more risks if the stakeholders are unwilling to reduce requirements. The simplest way for contractors to reduce cost is to sacrifice fee and lower overhead contributions. Beyond these limits, cost can only really be cut by hiring lower-salaried staff while trying to match capabilities and reducing staff levels on fixed-price contracts while trying to maintain productivity through process efficiencies. In the end, a key lesson on QC is the correct expectations by the user/stakeholder communities. If the government expectations are unreasonable, then no amount of corrective actions will achieve satisfactory results, and the consequences of QC might be worse than the original path with all things considered.

C.3.3 Testing Methodology

Testing is a mechanism for enabling QC, and testing extends beyond QC to serve as the gate for validating performance results and taking drastic corrective actions. The principles of testing are simply what to test, when to test, how to test, how to score, and how to interpret scores [5]. These principles are integrated into specific types of tests and schedule-driven test events. Common test events are explained as follows.

- **Unit testing:** This is the testing of a single system component or software code segment immediately after development to validate that it has meet specifications. Physical components can be tested against design, anticipated stresses, and ranges of motion. Software codes can be tested by simulated runs and reviews of code quality.
- **Developmental testing:** This is the testing of the system while in development and as the produced units are being integrated. If there is an environment for incremental system integration testing, then development testing and integration testing can be combined. Otherwise, the development test will typically focus on internal system components integration and the integration of the system with external elements will be tested later. In both Agile and spiral software development, this testing is built into the sprints and spirals, and the results of these tests support the development process.

■ **Systems integration testing:** This is the testing of the system in an environment where integration with external legacy systems, data centers, and devices can be simulated. For physical systems, the test might include communication links, passing of sensor data, logistical processes, and command and control processes. For IT systems, the test typically includes network connectivity, functional connectivity with legacy systems, and data synchronization with systems and databases. The tests sometimes identify data transformation errors, incompatible APIs, and capacity alignment issues that delay network processes.

■ **Operational testing:** This test can sometimes be conducted in the system integration test environment. However, the focus is on the performance of the system under simulated operational conditions to include variations in operational loads, environmental stresses on operations, and system adaptiveness to special operational scenarios. For IT systems, automated testing tools can simulate the operations of thousands of simultaneous users and the compounded outcomes of thousands of run cycles. For physical systems, scenario-based testing can identify system-to-system interaction issues.

■ **Security testing:** This test focuses on the protection of data from corruption and theft as well as the maintaining of system operational integrity under threat of infiltration. For IT systems, automated application scanning and network vulnerability testing tools will identify the effectiveness of firewalls, encryption, identity management, access control, network monitoring, intrusion detection, and other security mechanisms. Physical data centers will further have guards, gates, and sensors that are a part of the total SSP. System security requirements are based on the purpose/criticality of the system and security levels established in FISMA. The security levels are achieved through hundreds of NIST-established security controls.

■ **Compliance testing:** This is testing to validate compliance with specific statutes and regulations. For example, federally developed or procured IT systems with externally facing user interfaces must have its software displays and other forms of user interaction be compliant with Section 508 of the Rehabilitation Act to support access by the disabled. Another example is that all systems containing or managing protected health information (PHI) must have data protection standards that comply with the Health Insurance Portability and Accountability Act (HIPAA). And, all systems containing or managing personally identifiable information (PII) must have data protection standards that comply with privacy laws. Statutes requiring development compliance are interpreted by either a lead agency, such as White House Office of Management and Budget, or all impacted agencies to establish new regulations or policies for implementation. These regulations and policies will have metrics for testing and compliance validation.

■ **Independent validation and verification (IV&V) testing:** For developed systems with many requirements or complex requirements, the government may elect to acquire an independent contractor to test and validate the performance of the produced system against requirements. For waterfall development of IT systems, this test is conducted after the completion of development and integration testing. The system is then provided to the independent contractor to start the government acceptance process. In Agile development, the IV&V contractor can be asked to participate in sprint testing events to represent the interests of the user community.

■ **User acceptance testing:** This is the gate testing where systems that have passed are allowed to proceed to deployment and sustainment. If an IT system has already passed IV&V testing and corrected identified issues, then UAT is largely a formality that focuses on the intangible aspects of the user experience that might need further refinement. Alternatively, IV&V testing is folded into UAT with the user community validating that their requirements have been satisfied.

Returning to the principles of testing, the implementation of each test event will require planning, preparation, tester procedures, data capture, and test data analytics. The selection of appropriate tests for a program and definition of how these tests interrelate is presented in the test master plan. Test planning ensures that there is adequate time for the test event in the overall program schedule. Test preparation ensures that the environments, tools, data used for testing, and system configurations are all set for the test event. Tester procedures include instructions for the conduct of the test event, scripts for operating the system, and guidance for collecting test results. Data capture starts with defining the test results data format and repository that must be prepared prior to testing, and ends with verifying that the data is of the quality anticipated based on testing procedures. A key format decision is how the scaling of data will match the natural capabilities of the testing approach. If the scale in data capture is too low in fidelity, details of the test are lost. If the scale is too high in fidelity, then cruder tests will yield many similar results. Finally, the test data must be analyzed to support the approval, correction, or rejection of the system. The most well-executed test event will fail if its data is misinterpreted. So after each test event, adequate time and resources must be devoted to understanding the results of the test.

C.3.4 Risk Management

In Appendix B, the methodology for assessing acquisition risks is explained as a function of probability of occurrence and level of potential impact. The same methodology can be used to assess program execution risks after contract award [6]. What is different are the specific risks identified and how those risks can be managed. During the source selection process, the separation between the government and the contractor creates a segmented risk management approach. The government identifies the risks, the contractor proposes risk mitigations, and the government evaluates the acceptability of proposed risk mitigations. After contract award, the identification and mitigation of risks should be a collaborative effort between the contractor and the government.

The collaboration mechanism between contractor and government on risk can be a registry where each risk connected with a task in the IMS is identified. As risks are connected with execution after contract award instead of just evaluation factors and subfactors, the mitigation of risks can be specific. Risks and issues can still be categorized as low, medium, and high for prioritizing corrective resources, but the focus of execution is to understand each risk well enough that (1) a corrective action can eliminate the risk, (2) a preventive action can reduce the likelihood of risk occurring, (3) a preparation can reduce the consequences of the risk, or (4) a decision can be made to accept the risk and recover from impact as required.

There is always a subjective element to risk assessment unless the program involves repeated common tasks where statistical data on failures can be gathered. Given that risks do not mean that adverse events will absolutely happen, the decision to accept risks lies with the art of management. The art of management is where we will note that the priorities in government oversight presented in this appendix is merely a reference frame for how contractors could respond to the government to achieve basic success. Each government organization could have very specific expectations of process and reporting that go beyond the fundamentals presented. Some government expectations may be extensions of areas presented in this appendix, and other government expectations may be reinterpretations of best practices presented in this appendix. Such is the prerogative of government authority. Regardless, it is the responsibility of contractors/solutions providers to meet and exceed government expectations.

References

1. Kerzner, H. 2013. *Project Management: A Systems Approach to Planning, Scheduling, and Controlling*, 11th ed. Hoboken, NJ: Wiley.
2. Stellman, A., and Greene, J. 2013. *Learning Agile: Understanding Scrum, XP, Lean, and Kanban*, 1st ed. Sebastopol, CA: O'Reilly Media.
3. Knaster, R., and Leffingwell, D. 2017. *SAFe 4.0 Distilled: Applying the Scaled Agile Framework for Lean Software and Systems Engineering*, 1st ed. Boston, MA: Addison-Wesley Professional.
4. Boehm, B. 1988. A spiral model of software development and enhancement. *IEEE Computer*, 21, 5 (May): 61–72.
5. Ammann, P., and Offutt, J. 2016. *Introduction to Software Testing*, 2nd ed. Cambridge, UK: Cambridge University Press.
6. Jordan, A. 2013. *Risk Management for Project Driven Organizations: A Strategic Guide to Portfolio, Program and PMO Success*. Fort Lauderdale, FL: J. Ross Publishing.

Appendix D: Acronyms List

Acquisition category (ACAT)

Acquisition Professional Development Program (APDP)

Advanced Concept Technology Demonstration (ACTD)

Analysis of alternatives (AoA)

Application program interfaces (APIs)

Artificial intelligence (AI)

Assessment and authorization (A&A)

Assistant Secretary of the Air Force for Acquisition (SAF/AQ)

Assistant Secretary of the Army for Acquisition, Logistics, and Technology (ASA[AL&T])

Assistant Secretary of the Navy for Research, Development, and Acquisition (ASN[RD&A])

Authority to operate (ATO)

Blanket purchasing agreement (BPA)

Business development (BD)

Business Transformation Agency (BTA)

Capabilities development document (CDD)

Capability Maturity Model Integration (CMMI)

Change control board (CCB)

Change requests (CRs)

Command/control/communications/computer/intelligence/surveillance/reconnaissance (C4ISR)

Commercial-off-the-shelf (COTS)

Component Acquisition Executive (CAE)

Composite Health Care System (CHCS)

Concepts of operations (CONOPS)

Configuration items (CIs)

Contractor Performance Assessment Reports Systems (CPARS)

Contracting officer (CO)

Contracting officer representative (COR)
Cost Analysis Improvement Group (CAIG)
Cost as an independent variable (CAIV)
Defense Acquisition Board (DAB)
Defense Acquisition Executive (DAE)
Defense Acquisition University (DAU)
Defense Acquisition Workforce Improvement Act (DAWIA)
Defense Integrated Military Human Resources System (DIMHRS)
Defense Support Program (DSP)
Defense Systems Acquisition Review Council (DSARC)
Department of Defense (DoD)
Development and operations (DevOps)
Earned value management (EVM)
Earned Value Management System (EVMS)
Electronic health record (EHR)
Evaluation notice (EN)
Federal Acquisition Regulations (FAR)
Federal Information Security Management Act (FISMA)
Federal Procurement Data System (FPDS)
Federally funded research and development center (FFRDC)
Final proposal revision (FPR)
Firm fixed price (FFP)
Five year defense plan (FYDP)
For Official Use Only (FOUO)
General Services Administration (GSA)
Global position system (GPS)
Government Accountability Office (GAO)
Governmentwide acquisition contracts (GWACS)
Healthcare Management System Modernization (DHMSM)
Health Insurance Portability and Accountability Act (HIPAA)
Heating, ventilation, and air conditioning (HVAC)
Human resources (HR)
Improvised explosive devices (IEDs)
Indefinite delivery indefinite quantity (IDIQ)
Independent cost estimate (ICE)
Independent government cost estimate (IGCE)
Independent validation and verification (IV&V)
Information Technology Infrastructure Library (ITIL)
Infrastructure as a service (IaaS)
Initial capabilities document (ICD)
Initial operational capability (IOC)
Integrated circuit (IC)
Integrated master schedule (IMS)

Integrated product team (IPT)
Intercontinental ballistic missile (ICBM)
International Organization for Standardization (ISO)
Internet protocol (IP)
Item for negotiation (IFN)
Joint Capabilities Integration Development System (JCIDS)
Joint Chiefs of Staff (JCS)
Joint Concept Technology Demonstrations (JCTD)
Joint Direct Attack Munition (JDAM)
Joint Requirement Oversight Council (JROC)
Joint Surveillance Target Attack Radar System (JSTARS)
Justification for a Major Systems New Start (JMSNS)
Key performance indicators (KPIs)
Level of effort (LOE)
Life cycle sustainment plan (LCSP)
Local area network (LAN)
Lowest price technically acceptable (LPTA)
Machine to machine (M2M)
Major automated information system (MAIS)
Micro-electromechanical systems (MEMS)
Milestone Decision Authority (MDA)
Mission Element Need Statement (MENS)
Multiple independently targetable reentry vehicle (MIRV)
Mutually assured destruction (MAD)
National Defense Authorization Act (NDAA)
National Institute of Standard and Technology (NIST)
National Security Agency (NSA)
Net-Enabled Command and Control (NECC)
Nondisclosure agreements (NDAs)
North American Free Trade Agreement (NAFTA)
Office of Management and Budget (OMB)
Office of Personnel Management (OPM)
Organization conflict of interest (OCI)
Other direct costs (ODCs)
Performance confidence assessment group (PCAG)
Performance work statement (PWS)
Personally identifiable information (PII)
Planning, programming, budget, and execution (PPBE)
Planning, programming, budgeting system (PPBS)
Platform as a service (PaaS)
Point of contact (POC)
Pre-planned product improvements (P3I)
Probability of win (P-Win)

Program executive officers (PEO)
Program management office (PMO)
Program manager (PM)
Program Objective Memorandum (POM)
Project lead (PL)
Protected health information (PHI)
Representational state transfer (RESTful)
Request for information (RFI)
Request for proposal (RFP)
Risk Management Framework (RMF)
Rough order magnitude (ROM)
Security Technical Implementation Guides (STIGs)
Service acquisition executives (SAE)
Service-disabled veteran-owned small business (SDVOSB)
Service manager (SM)
Small Business Administration (SBA)
Small Business Innovation Research (SBIR)
Software as a service (SaaS)
Source Selection Advisory Council (SSAC)
Source Selection Authority (SSA)
Source selection evaluation team (SSET)
Source selection plan (SSP)
Standard operating procedures (SOP)
Statement of objectives (SOO)
Statement of work (SOW)
Strategic Arms Limitation Talks (SALT)
Strategic Arms Reduction Treaty (START)
Strategic Defense Initiative (SDI)
Subject matter expert (SME)
System security plan (SSP)
Systems engineering plan (SEP)
Teaming agreement (TA)
Terminal High Altitude Area Defense (THAAD)
Terms and conditions (T&C)
Test-driven development (TDD)
Test evaluation master plan (TEMP)
Total quality management (TQM)
Under Secretary of Defense (Acquisition, Technology, and Logistics) USD (AT&L)
User interface (UI)
Wide area network (WAN)
World Trade Organization (WTO)
Work breakdown structure (WBS)

Index